Being British

The Search for the Values That Bind the Nation

Introduction by **Gordon Brown**

Edited by **Matthew d'Ancona**

All royalties go to **PiggyBankKids**

MAINSTREAM
PUBLISHING

EDINBURGH AND LONDON

This book is dedicated to
Zac, Teddy, Tino, Darcey and Frankie: true Brits
Matthew d'Ancona

First published in Great Britain in 2009 by
MAINSTREAM PUBLISHING COMPANY
(EDINBURGH) LTD
7 Albany Street
Edinburgh EH1 3UG

ISBN 9781845964146

Grateful acknowledgement is made for permission to reprint on pp. 59–60
an excerpt from Gwyn Prins and Robert Salisbury, 'Risk, Threat and Security:
the Case of the United Kingdom', *RUSI Journal*, Vol. 153, No. 1 (Feb 2008)

A catalogue record for this book is available
from the British Library

Typeset in Caslon and GillSans

Printed in Great Britain by
CPI Mackays of Chatham Ltd, Chatham, ME5 8TD

ACKNOWLEDGEMENTS

MY GREATEST DEBT IS TO THE CONTRIBUTORS, ALL OF WHOM gave generously of their time, without payment of any kind. The royalties from this volume will go to charity: Piggy Bank Kids for the Jennifer Brown Research Fund.

At Mainstream, Bill Campbell made the entire project possible and worked hard to see the volume into print: he and his colleagues Graeme Blaikie and Karyn Millar were much more patient than I deserved, even when, like Willard meeting Colonel Kurtz, they discovered all too often that there wasn't 'any method at all'. I thank them.

In Number 10, Stewart Wood and Konrad Caulkett were always helpful, while over at the Ministry of Justice, Michael Wills was generous with advice. Thanks, too, to Wilf Stevenson.

Ann Sindall was my research assistant and manager of the project, and carried out the task brilliantly. It is no exaggeration at all to say that this book would not have happened without her lionhearted work. I owe her a huge debt of gratitude.

A final thank you to Gordon Brown: the idea was his and – whether or not I have done it justice – it is still a good idea. I am grateful to him for asking me to take on this task in the first place.

Matthew d'Ancona

CONTENTS

NOTES ON CONTRIBUTORS

KENNETH BAKER (now a member of the House of Lords), as Education Secretary in the Thatcher years, introduced the National Curriculum and City Technology Colleges – forerunners of City Academies. He was also responsible for the privatisation of BT, Cable & Wireless and the water industry. Joint founder of the Cartoon Museum, he has published four books on the history of cartoons, six poetry anthologies and his memoirs.

DR MUHAMMAD ABDUL BARI, MBE, is currently the Secretary General of the Muslim Council of Britain and Chair of the East London Mosque. Dr Bari is a community activist and is the author of several articles and three books. A physicist and teacher, he is a Fellow of the Royal Society of Arts and an Honorary Fellow of Queen Mary, University of London.

PAUL BEW read Modern History at Cambridge, where he also took his PhD. He is currently an independent Crossbench peer and Professor of Irish Politics at Queens University Belfast. He is the author or co-author of over a dozen books on modern Irish history and politics, including, most recently, *Ireland: the Politics of Enmity 1789–2006*.

SIR IAN BLAIR was the 24th Commissioner of the Metropolitan Police based at Scotland Yard, from 2005 to 2008. He commanded the service during the London bombings of 2005. He now lectures extensively in the UK and abroad on police reform.

SIR VICTOR BLANK is chairman of Lloyds Banking Group. He has had a City career, starting in 1963, as a solicitor, as a merchant banker and as a company chairman. He has undertaken a number of government-related appointments, was the first external member of the Council of Oxford University and has been involved with various charities.

GORDON BROWN was elected MP for Dunfermline East in May 1983. He was Opposition spokesperson on Treasury and Economic Affairs (Shadow Chancellor) from 1992. With the election of the Labour government in May 1997, Gordon Brown became Chancellor of the Exchequer, and held the post for ten years, making him the longest-serving Chancellor for two hundred years. Following the resignation of Tony Blair, he became prime minister in June 2007. Gordon Brown is married to Sarah Macaulay and they have two sons.

PROFESSOR TANYA BYRON is a practising clinical psychologist with 20 years' experience. She presents programmes for the BBC on child behaviour, science and current affairs (including *Little Angels*, *Teen Angels* and *House of Tiny Tearaways*). She writes a weekly column for *The Times* and has published three books on child behaviour. Tanya is Chancellor of Edge Hill University and is married with two children.

GEORGE CAREY (Lord Carey of Clifton) was Archbishop of Canterbury from 1991 to 2002. In retirement, he chairs the United Church Schools Trust, an organisation that is in the forefront of creating City Academies. He is involved in interfaith dialogue around the world, working with the World Bank and World Economic Forum. He is Chancellor of the University of Gloucestershire and lectures in the USA.

J.C.D. CLARK is an historian of the British Isles, who has also written on the American and French revolutions and on recent geopolitical questions. His ancestors include English, Scots and Irish, and he currently teaches in the USA. He has edited a history of Britain, to be published in 2010.

MATTHEW D'ANCONA is the award-winning editor of *The Spectator* and writes political columns for the *Sunday Telegraph* and *GQ* (where he is also a contributing editor). He has published three novels to critical acclaim, including *Nothing to Fear*, a modern re-telling of the Bluebeard story, and he is a regular presenter on Radio 4's *Week in Westminster*. He is a member of the Steering Board of Lord Carter's *Digital Britain*. His next project will be a history of England, co-authored with John Cleese.

MARK EARLS is the author of *Herd: How to Change Mass Behaviour by Harnessing Our True Nature*. Mark talks to audiences around the world about our herd nature and works with a number of different organisations, from Unilever to the Gates Foundation. He has been described as 'Malcolm Gladwell on speed' and 'the marketing geek's geek'.

STEPHEN FRY is an actor, writer and director. He is the author of four bestselling novels, as well as the highly acclaimed autobiography *Moab is my Washpot* and a well-received guide to writing poetry, *The Ode Less Travelled*.

PROFESSOR CAROLINE GIPPS trained as a primary school teacher and psychometrician before entering a career in research. She has published widely on assessment, primary education and equity, and has an international reputation in educational assessment. She has been Vice-Chancellor of the University of Wolverhampton since October 2005.

MICHAEL GOVE is Shadow Secretary of State for Children, Schools and Families. He was elected to the House of Commons in 2005 as MP for Surrey Heath. He has written a biography of Michael Portillo and a book on Islamist terrorism, *Celsius 7/7*, published in 2006. Michael was founding chairman of Policy Exchange. He is currently a trustee of the Henry Jackson Society and the John Smith Memorial Trust, two charities that support democracy abroad.

JOHN GRAY is Emeritus Professor at the London School of Economics. He has been Professor of Politics at Oxford and Visiting Distinguished Professor at Harvard and Yale. His recent books include *Black Mass: Apocalyptic Religion and the Death of Utopia* and *Gray's Anatomy: Selected Writings*.

TIM HAMES is Head of Communications and Public Affairs at the British Private Equity and Venture Capital Association. He was chief leader writer and a columnist for *The Times* from 2001 to 2008. Before entering journalism, he was a lecturer in politics at Oxford University.

ALEX JAMES is the bass player in Blur. In 2007, he released his first book, *Bit of a Blur*. A regular columnist and writer, he now produces organic cheeses and lives on a farm in Oxfordshire.

DYLAN JONES is the award-winning editor of *GQ*, a syndicated columnist and an internationally bestselling author. His most recent book, *Cameron On Cameron*, is a series of interviews with the Conservative leader that took place over the space of 12 months. He has won seven British Society of Magazine Editors awards.

JOHN KAMPFNER was Editor of the *New Statesman* from 2005 to 2008. He was the British Society of Magazine Editors Current Affairs Editor of the Year in 2006. His books include the bestselling *Blair's Wars* and the forthcoming *Freedom for Sale*. In a long journalistic career, he has been Moscow and Berlin correspondent for the *Daily Telegraph*, and political correspondent and commentator for the *Financial Times* and the BBC. He is currently Chief Executive of Index on Censorship.

NASEEM KHAN's working life has covered journalism, broadcasting, policy development, research and arts administration, but with a central focus on diversity and citizenship (for which she received an OBE in 1999). Her benchmark report 'The Arts Britain Ignores' (1976) opened the ongoing debate on the current nature of British culture.

ANTHONY KING, a Canadian by birth, came to Britain as a Rhodes Scholar in 1956. He was a Fellow of Magdalen College, Oxford, before moving to Essex University during the 1960s. His most recent book is *The British Constitution*. He broadcasts frequently on politics and elections for the BBC and served on the original Committee on Standards in Public Life (the Nolan Committee).

CHARLES LEADBEATER is author of *We-think: Mass Innovation, Not Mass Production*; a Fellow of the National Endowment for Sciences, Technology and the Arts; and co-founder of Participle, the public-service design consultancy. His Demos pamphlet, *The Pro-Am Revolution*, was published in 2004.

SARFRAZ MANZOOR is a prominent writer, broadcaster and critic, whose journalism has appeared in *The Guardian*, *The Observer*, *The Spectator* and *Esquire*. He is also the author of an acclaimed childhood memoir, *Greetings From Bury Park*, which describes growing up in the 1980s as a working-class British Pakistani Muslim.

GEORGE MARTIN was knighted in 1996. For 50 years he has been writing music and producing records, including early comedy records with Peter Sellers, Spike Milligan, Bernard Cribbins, Rolf Harris, Flanders and Swann, *Beyond the Fringe*, Peter Cook and Dudley Moore, as well as working with Matt Monro, Shirley Bassey, Cilla Black and, most famously, the Beatles.

RAJA MIAH, MBE, has been working in poverty-stricken communities across different regions, ethnic groups and religions for 20 years. Long before the community-cohesion agenda took shape, Raja helped shape the PeaceMaker organisation, which has successfully been supporting communities to work together to overcome the challenges they face.

PIERS MORGAN, at 28, became the youngest-ever editor at the *News of The World* before moving on to the *Daily Mirror*, where he stayed until 2004. Winner of the American *Celebrity Apprentice*, he became a judge on the top-rated TV programmes *America's Got Talent* and *Britain's Got Talent*. He is currently working on travelogue programmes and a new chat show, *Piers Morgan's Life Stories*.

CARDINAL CORMAC MURPHY-O'CONNOR was ordained in 1956. He was Rector of the English College in Rome before becoming Bishop of Arundel and Brighton in 1977. He became Archbishop of Westminster in 2000 and was created a Cardinal in 2001.

DOUGLAS MURRAY is the Director of the Centre for Social Cohesion. A bestselling author and political commentator, his writings have appeared across the British and foreign press. A columnist for *Standpoint* magazine, he writes regularly for many other publications, including *The Spectator*, and appears regularly on the BBC and across the British and foreign broadcast media.

JOHN O'FARRELL is the author of such bestselling books as *An Utterly Impartial History of Britain* and *May Contain Nuts*. He is the founder and editor of Britain's leading satirical website, 'NewsBiscuit', and regularly appears on such TV programmes as *Grumpy Old Men* and *Have I Got News For You*.

TREVOR PHILLIPS, OBE, is the Chair of the Equality and Human Rights Commission. Formerly Chair of the Commission for Racial Equality, Chair of the London Assembly, a respected journalist and President of the National Union of Students, he is well known as a commentator on issues around equality and discrimination.

LIBBY PURVES is a writer and journalist, was formerly presenter of the Radio 4 *Today* programme and for the last 25 years has been the host of *Midweek*. She has been a *Times* columnist for 18 years, and is the author of 12 novels (most recently *Shadow Child*) as well as acclaimed non-fiction works on family life, sailing and radio.

IAN RANKIN is an award-winning author. Born in the Kingdom of Fife in 1960, he graduated from the University of Edinburgh in 1982. His first Rebus novel was published in 1987, and they have now been translated into 32 languages and are bestsellers on several continents. Ian is also the recipient of several honorary degrees. A contributor to BBC2's *Newsnight Review*, he also presented his own TV series, *Ian Rankin's Evil Thoughts*.

SIR JONATHAN SACKS has been the Chief Rabbi of the United Hebrew Congregations of the Commonwealth since 1991. He has earned international acclaim both as a scholar and spiritual leader. He was awarded a knighthood in 2005. The Chief Rabbi is the author of many books and has made numerous appearances on national radio and television. Born in 1948 in London, he has been married since 1970 and has three children.

JUNE SARPONG is one of the UK's most intelligent and dynamic young presenters, and has interviewed, among many others, Nelson Mandela, Prince Charles, Gordon Brown, Tony Blair and Bill Clinton. June is an ambassador for the Prince's Trust and also campaigns for Make Poverty History. She was awarded an MBE in 2007 for services to broadcasting and charity.

SHARON WALKER works in London as an educational researcher specialising in equality and diversity. She has a strong interest in gender issues, ethnicity and heritage, and has a Masters Research degree from the University of London. She has a background in primary school education and has also lived and worked in France.

ARCHBISHOP ROWAN WILLIAMS became Archbishop of Canterbury in 2002. He is acknowledged internationally as an outstanding teacher, poet and scholar with a range that encompasses theology, philosophy, spirituality and religious aesthetics. He has also written extensively on moral, ethical and social topics, and, since becoming Archbishop, has turned his attention increasingly to contemporary cultural and interfaith issues.

MICHAEL WILLS has been Minister of State for Constitutional Renewal at the Ministry of Justice from July 2007. Elected to Parliament as MP for North Swindon in 1997, he has held a number of ministerial posts. He founded the independent television production company Juniper in 1985. Michael is married with five children.

EDITOR'S PREFACE

MATTHEW D'ANCONA

THIS BOOK IS BASED ON AN ORIGINAL CUP OF TEA WITH Gordon Brown.

In the summer of 2007, the new prime minister told me that he had hoped to edit a series of essays on Britishness but that – what with one thing and another – he didn't have the time to pursue the project. Was I interested in editing the volume instead? I was delighted to accept the offer, which included full editorial independence. This book is best described, therefore, as inspired by Brown but not controlled by him. He was generous with ideas, but not once did he query my choice of authors, or object to the content that they delivered.

What this shows is that Brown's interest in this particular subject, though profoundly political, is also intellectually authentic. He was genuinely interested to see what those who disagreed with his own perspectives came up with. And he was willing to cede management of a project close to his heart to the editor of a right-of-centre magazine that – to put it mildly – did him no favours in the period during which we were compiling the book. This does him credit.

As editor of *The Spectator* and a political columnist in the *Sunday Telegraph* and *GQ*, I have often been critical of this prime minister. But I think he is right about the need for a debate on national identity. It is routinely claimed that his fascination with Britishness is opportunistic and skin-deep, a way of dealing with the fact that he is a Scottish-born MP with a Scottish constituency who is governing the whole of the United Kingdom. This, I can say with some confidence, is not true. Whether or not Brown arrives at the correct conclusions about British identity, institutions and values is for each reader to judge: but his passion for the subject is deep and serious.

My own interest – from a very different political perspective – reflects a long-standing belief that Britain's cultural diversity is a national strength and true to a long history of porousness and heterogeneity. But it is no less clear that British society in the early twenty-first century is subject to unprecedented stresses and strains. Population mobility, globalisation, technological revolution, cultural relativism, historical ignorance, the erosion of confidence in traditional institutions, the spread of religious fundamentalism, the impact of constitutional change: to this list could be added many other pressures, all conspiring towards a crisis of identity. Against such a tumultuous backdrop, the question 'what does it mean to be British?' is hard to answer. All the more reason for asking it. We may stumble in our inquiries. 'No matter,' to quote Samuel Beckett. 'Try again. Fail again. Fail better.'

This volume does not aspire or pretend to be comprehensive. It embraces many points of view, some diametrically opposed, all different in nuance and priority. But it does not reflect the opinions of every political party or interest group. The idea was to assemble a series of interesting reflections on the issue, not to launch a tick-box survey or conduct a focus group that would deliver a lowest common denominator slogan, acceptable to all. I wanted analysis, of course, but also memories, imaginative interventions and short, sharp bursts of thought like Professor Tanya Byron's and Piers Morgan's. There may be complaints that one perspective or other has been scandalously overlooked. ('Why no piece by an expat Freedonian?' 'What about philatelists?' etc.) So be it. This book is meant to launch a debate, not complete one. If you see a gap in the pages that follow, fill it: continue the conversation.

By design, there is less about the consequences of devolution and European integration than on other subjects. These forces are of huge importance, as Paul Bew recognises in his chapter on the Union. But they have been discussed constantly in other forums for many years – and rightly so. I hoped to explore other avenues.

I wanted, first of all, to delve into writers' personal experiences as much as to mine their intellectual conclusions. Alex James describes his own pilgrimage from metropolitan Britain to the ancestral wonders of its countryside; Dylan Jones explores the entanglement of class and Britishness and his own perceptions of the two. Sharon Walker asks rhetorically whether racial groups are different 'like a horse is different from a bird': a single image more thought-provoking than pages of academic analysis would be. The importance of myth and folklore (old and new) flows through the pages that follow: what Libby Purves calls 'a mishmash of more or less inaccurate but immensely nourishing daydreams'.

Myth competes with modernity in our national imagination, our collective inner landscape. Mark Earls argues that the Web and the social networks it has created have drained old hierarchies of their power to define the cultural parameters of our lives. Britishness is 'no longer something that can be crisply and clearly defined; no magic constellation of values, stories and information can capture it'. Charles Leadbeater describes modern national identity as a 'rising tide of pebbles', in contrast to the cultural monoliths of the past. Together, Earls and Leadbeater plot a course towards Britishness 2.0.

The conservative historian J.C.D. Clark argues, with characteristic brio, that the whole debate is a self-indulgence and that 'the current "crisis" of Britishness has been got up by the bourgeois intelligentsia'. Anthony King, author of the best book of recent times on the British constitution, agrees that 'there is no single, overarching problem of "Britishness" . . . Britishness has survived for more than three centuries substantially as a blur, on the whole an amicable blur. Sharpen it up and it might come to have a cutting edge, one that would cut two ways.'

John Gray, meanwhile, takes issue with those who would reduce Britishness to a blueprint. 'All these schemes involve refounding the British state on terms that are at odds with its history and present condition,' Gray writes. 'The British makeshift contains elements that are liberal . . . and socialist, Tory and Whig, cohering in a fashion that allows for many inconsistencies.' But Gray does concede the need to find 'a modus vivendi between the many varieties of belief and unbelief' – and notes, correctly, that this 'is not going to be easy'.

Trevor Phillips assents to that and warns further against placing our faith in an inventory of 'foundational values' that are 'Olympian and universal . . . values to which any liberal democratic society would subscribe'. We have to move off this terrain and on to the question of how we treat each other and our collective desire for 'higher standards of behaviour'. Britishness, he says, is 'malleable and modern', but 'it is not formless – its form is in our principled behaviour towards one another'. He foresees a day when the Equality and Human Rights Commission, which he chairs, 'will have to stand up and say, for example, that you cannot both uphold your desire to force your daughter to marry a man against her will and still claim allegiance to a British identity'.

On this basis, the core of the project is the recognition of certain non-negotiable norms in British social practice. But, says Michael Gove, the context in which that social practice arose has to be understood, too. The work has to begin in the classroom with the teaching of narrative history – 'a fuller understanding of what actually happened in Our Island Story' – and of great English literature. In Douglas Murray's eyes, this is a task of depressing enormity: 'In Britain, our dominant theme has become not just unrecognisable but also increasingly undiscernible.' We inhabit, he says, 'a culture that is jingoistic only in its self-denigration'.

For church leaders, the debate on Britishness presents both perils and opportunities. Perils because, prima facie, this appears to be an essentially secular undertaking; and opportunities because it need not be so, and, in practice, can take gentle inspiration from many ancient sources. The Archbishop of Canterbury suggests that the entanglement of the Church of England with the emerging modern state has helped to nourish and guarantee our treasured traditions of tolerance, legal moderation and coexistence.

Cardinal Cormac Murphy-O'Connor, meanwhile, questions the notion that 'values' are the heart of Britishness, preferring the more robust 'virtues' embedded in the nation's Judaeo-Christian heritage: 'a genuinely British multiculturalism will not be a secularising project that unhooks Britain from its Christian roots, but something best conducted from within Christian faith and life'.

As if to pre-empt those who claim that 'Britishness' is just a faddish abstraction fussed over by the chattering classes, many of the contributions constitute a call to action in one form or another. Dr Muhammad Abdul Bari, the Secretary General of the Muslim Council of Great Britain, invokes the inspiration of Barack Obama as a community organiser in Chicago, while Naseem Khan sees the regeneration of Arnold Circus in the East End as a microcosm in which identity, place and history become richly intertwined.

On a broader canvas, the Chief Rabbi, Sir Jonathan Sacks, declares unambiguously that 'we will have to engage, consciously and actively in society building . . . Covenantal societies are created when people come together in an act of collective self-determination . . . a national narrative, civic rituals and the enlisting of the many groups – religious, charitable, educational and community based – that make up the still dense texture of our civil society'. Look at national Holocaust Memorial Day, he says: 'If it can be done in

Britain for something that lies in the past and did not happen in Britain, then it can be done for the present and for Britishness itself.'

I find the Chief Rabbi's spirit of optimism infectious. There is indeed much that can be done – and it need not be a bleak enterprise. Far from it: the debate on twenty-first-century Britishness should be, first and foremost, a celebration, rather than a defensive operation. The confidence to adapt to new historic settings is one of the defining characteristics of the British personality.

This book should be seen as a preface to a much grander discussion: if it provokes, stimulates, entertains, infuriates and triggers conversations, it will have succeeded in its objective. 'I believe in starts,' says Joey 'The Lips' Fagan, in *The Commitments*. It's a movie set in Ireland. But what could be more British than making a start?

INTRODUCTION

GORDON BROWN

WHEN I WAS GROWING UP IN KIRKCALDY, THE IDEA OF needing to have a debate about Britishness would have struck me as peculiar. I didn't think any more about my Britishness than I did about being Scottish, or supporting Raith Rovers, or coming from a long line of Fife farmers. That was just the way things were. I saw no contradiction between my Scottish heritage and my fierce pride in Britain – and I still don't. Back then, there were comfortable certainties, and no conflicts, and few would have questioned that Britain was our home, our inheritance and our ideal.

The intervening decades have seen old assumptions changing, with more people now wondering whether and where they belong, and to what they owe their allegiance. And over these decades, my generation of Britons has seen many changes: the end of the long retreat from worldwide power that evoked from across the Atlantic the pointed comment that Britain had 'lost an empire and not yet found a role'; an era of resigned acceptance summed up in the phrase 'managed decline'; a change in the centuries-old pattern of immigration – from Europe, then from nations oceans away and once our colonies, now from Europe once more; the long confrontation of the Cold War followed by the dramatic break-up of the Soviet empire; a decline in traditional manufacturing offset by new services, and creative and entrepreneurial activities; and the rise of a new and increasingly influential Europe, towards which Britain's early attitudes had ranged from coolness to ambivalence. Most recently, the remarkable advance of globalisation – bringing new challenges and opportunities to a Britain well equipped by history, geography and instinct to take full part in it – has now been threatened by a still-unfolding global financial crisis and a resultant worldwide downturn in production, trade and confidence.

So I welcome this book on Britishness: for what it tells us about who we are, how we came to be as we are, where we are going and what is to be our role in an ever more rapidly changing world; and for what it adds to an important debate on the subject. And I believe this debate is well timed, because of its relevance to the recent financial crisis. When it struck, no one questioned the British state standing behind banks headquartered in Scotland, or discussed what a Wales-only response might be to the selling of sub-prime mortgages, or wondered how Northern Ireland might find its own solution to changing global conditions. Similarly, when terrorists struck London on 7 July 2005, it was not seen or felt to be an attack simply on London, or even England, but against Britain itself. Why? Because for generations Britain has been a country in which many different nationalities and cultures live together, confident that in times of trouble we share risks, rewards and resources.

Today we face new challenges and uncertainties: pressures arising from globalisation and a worldwide financial crisis, climate change, security threats unimaginable 50 years ago; and, of course, the changing role of the state and its relationship with our regions, with communities and individuals, and with Europe and the wider world. We can and will find ways to respond; and in the face of changes of such speed, scale and scope, I believe we will do better as a nation if we are clearer about what we share, about what unites us across race, religion, and the nations of the United Kingdom, and about the challenges we face together.

Britain today – with its unique centuries-long history of resilience, adaptability and outward-looking engagement with the world; its inventiveness and creativity; and its traditions of openness and internationalism, tolerance and respect for liberty – has much to be proud of and much to give: both to us, its citizens, and to the world beyond its borders.

Many other countries and peoples are having to adapt as their societies become more complex and identities within them multiply. But we should be clear that we in Britain can be proud of our record. We are a living testament to the idea that pride need not be secured only by separation, identity only by independence, self-confidence only by political isolation.

We have shown, over three centuries, that a common ground of Britishness, of British identity, can be found in the stories of the various communities and nationalities that inhabit these islands. We have shown, too, that a strong sense of shared patriotism can be built that relies not on race or on ancient and unchanging institutions, but rather on a foundation of values that can be shared by all of us, regardless of race, region or religion. So Britain's living example and therefore message to the world is that we don't protect identity by protectionism or secure self-confidence by turning inwards, but that we draw strength by embracing the wider world – as befits an island trading nation.

The essays that follow – reflecting a great range of perspectives, experience and expertise – together form a rich body of material: wide ranging, divergent and sometimes challenging. Academics, clergy, journalists, men and women from public life, and others less well known, have all contributed. Britons old, newish and very new – together representing the successive centuries of immigration that together have shaped our nation – make their views known.

I want to take this chance to share my own contribution – to place my own perspective on record as part of this energetic and urgent debate.

A number of themes recur through the book, and I am intrigued by the frequency with which tolerance appears, and the pride with which so many essayists place tolerance as the chief British virtue.

Archbishop Rowan Williams offers an interesting insight into its possible origins in the 'unsuccessful victories' that have punctuated our history, from the Roman invasion and the Norman Conquest and on to the Civil War: victories whose effects he describes as 'curiously muted'; with the victors and vanquished accommodating to the outcome within the confines of an island from which there is no ready exit; and the vanquished acquiring, sometimes remarkably soon, 'a capacity to infiltrate, inflect and change what thinks of itself as the dominant voice'. I find that heartening: a functional resilience in what might be the worst of circumstances, bringing about easily the least worst of the foreseeable outcomes.

That is a form of tolerance ultimately of high historical significance, but our widespread and habitual tolerance – even in its minimalist manifestation, as in that characteristically British day-to-day formulation, 'mustn't grumble' – is an everyday virtue all too easily overlooked or just taken for granted. This book reminds us of it. As Professor Caroline Gipps, the daughter of a Dutch mother and an English father, writes:

> Being British in the twenty-first century is a lot to do with
> being who you are and proud of it, being allowed to be a
> number of things without censure, but similarly not being
> intolerant or jingoistic towards others. Above all, it is being
> somebody who subscribes to a view of tolerance: tolerance
> in what people believe, tolerance in what people may say and
> tolerance in how we run our individual lives.

Some would argue that tolerance was the way that our nation on this small island could secure a way for very different faiths and traditions to live together. But whatever the roots of our tolerance, and despite our occasional and regrettable lapses from it, in the long run it serves, and has served, us well: in the myriad day-to-day interactions of our lives in Britain now; in the relative stability and continuity of our history and our political institutions; and in the progressive enrichment of our nation by the long succession of newcomers it has both attracted to these islands, and then helped to integrate into our society over the centuries.

So we should celebrate the intuitive empiricism and rationalism that has seen our nation eschew fanaticism and extremism, in all its many poisonous manifestations, for all of our modern history. It accounts for much of the bias shown in our constitutional history towards evolution rather than revolution: one that has allowed much change with remarkably little bloodshed. It is reflected, too, in the long absence of serious religious conflict, in Great Britain if not in Northern Ireland, and in our relatively easy absorption of centuries of successive immigrations. Our hard-headed common sense and deep suspicion of fundamentalism has been not only saving; it was, and is, enabling, too: in terms of leaving space for difference and scope for individual freedom and inventiveness – surely among the greatest benefits of our liberty – and thus allowing the emergence of a society and a state that in only a few centuries generated the intellectual ferment of the Scottish Enlightenment, the giant technological forward leap of the Industrial Revolution, and the British Empire – proverbially acquired 'in a fit of absence of mind', but ably administered by people from all parts of these islands – that by its reach and commercial vigour could almost be said to prefigure the global economy. It certainly gave the world its lingua franca.

But for me, tolerance is not a first-order virtue, but rather a foundation for the most important British value: liberty.

Liberty might be seen as a universal value, the same the world over, but liberty in its uniquely British incarnation, and the way it has been forged through our history and evolved over the centuries in a tradition of common law, is a recurrent theme of this book. British liberty is not the given of a constitutional settlement, but the outcome of a long contention about the distribution of power. But from the time of Magna Carta, to the civil wars and revolutions of the seventeenth century, through to the liberalism of Victorian Britain and the widening and deepening of democracy and fundamental rights throughout the last century, there has been a British tradition of liberty – what one writer has called our 'gift to the world'.

And our hard-won liberty goes beyond the individual sphere; it has a communal dimension that greatly enhances it. As Gertrude Himmelfarb has pointed out, the British tradition of liberty carries with it an expectation of duty and responsibility, combined with the individual protection that liberty affords.

That combination of duty and liberty, of rights and responsibilities, lives and breathes each day in our now deep-rooted British commitment to fairness. In the nineteenth century, people of good conscience embraced charity and paternalism; in the twentieth and twenty-first centuries, as democratic values rose and prevailed, there has developed here a much more expansive and inclusive commitment to fairness, no matter how challenging its demands.

More than any other national institution, our National Health Service is an expression of that concept of fairness. We cherish it now as much as ever because it was founded to serve the principle that, in a fair society, healthcare should not be a commodity to be bought by some, but a right to be enjoyed by all. Our NHS wasn't always there, and it is useful to remind ourselves why it was necessary, as I was when, in 2008, I listened to a speech given by Aneira Thomas, the very first baby born after the introduction of Aneurin Bevan's NHS. She said:

> I was always a curious child, and I'd be forever asking my mother questions about her childhood. One story was of her looking out of the parlour window and seeing her own father, my grandfather, being carried home from the coal mine by two men: he had broken his leg. A doctor was called, he asked for him to be laid down on the kitchen table and then asked the children to help by holding him down while he operated

on him without anaesthetic. My mother told me she could
still hear those screams today.

Aneira went on to say, 'There was no NHS then. Things have changed
enormously since Bevan's day. I'm certain that if he could see how the National
Health Service has progressed with the advancing of expertise, he would be
extremely proud.'

If Britishness is about our shared values, then the fair insurance we provide
in every part of the United Kingdom against ill-health, unemployment and
old age is surely the most inspiring manifestation of our togetherness.

And when I think of some of the times in my own life I have been proudest
to be British, I can see that they too are defined by fairness. Just recently I was
filled with pride, but not at all surprised, that the British people, even when
facing tough times, responded so generously to the Comic Relief appeal. A
record-breaking Red Nose Night showed Britain at its best: generous and
totally committed to the idea that where a child is born should not determine
how long it will live. Hard times may bring out the worst in some people
– but they've always brought the best out of the British.

A Britain defined by its sense of fair play and fairness is a theme that recurs
throughout this book. Few social offences evoke as much immediate total
disapproval as queue-jumping. As Trevor Phillips writes:

> Fairness sums up our belief in cooperation for the common
> good. It is made possible by a robust rule of law and stable
> institutions. It inhibits our naked self-interest while also
> giving us the space to be unique, different and as odd as we
> like. And that, in today's age of diversity, is crucial.

And in broader terms, Phillips sees Britishness – with its combination of
tolerance, fairness and responsibility towards each other – as a bulwark against
the two risks that might otherwise threaten a society increasingly characterised
by diversity: the first being fragmentation, the second a centrally enforced
coercive unity. Britishness, he writes, 'offers us an overarching common identity,
available to anyone who chooses to live here. Second, in and of itself it can
provide a framework by which we negotiate our diversity and accommodate
it. This is not easy. It takes tolerance, humility, ingenuity and patience.' But if
these can be mobilised, Britishness 'can give us codes of conduct, dignity and
respect to resolve – and, crucially, to avoid – disputes'. And, more positively, 'A

stronger sense of Britishness could draw us out of our shells a little more. At its best, Britishness is easily adopted by people of all backgrounds; it is malleable and modern, it is capacious and inclusive.'

In this book are stories of individuals and families who are part of that British inclusivity: stories I found fascinating – both moving and heartening. Naseem Khan, the child of a German mother and an Indian father, finds herself in London's East End, in Shoreditch (in itself a microcosmic history of immigration, successively populated by Huguenots, Jews and now people from Bangladesh), and describes a community project – the regeneration of a long-neglected public space – that gave the multi-ethnic primary school children who took part in it a sense of involvement and achievement together, in what comes across as a wonderful short course in modern Britishness for beginners. And she describes, too, how her British-born son – who has been at it a bit longer – feels British because he can 'go into a pub and banter with the barman'.

The stories and views that emerge in this book from post-war immigration from the former colonies paint a complex picture. June Sarpong writes:

> Britishness means so many things to me. First of all, it means being fortunate enough to have been born in a multicultural, tolerant Britain, a country that has given me, a child of African immigrants, so many opportunities.
>
> Secondly it means being a proud Londoner, yet feeling resolutely connected to the rest of the country (except for when it comes to football where I'm always cheering England all the way).

But there is hurt, puzzlement and even anger in Sharon Walker's account of how her parents had come from the West Indies and were met with overt racism, and how she herself senses the complexity still encountered in being black and British:

> I live in England. I just want to *be*, achieving the best that I can, defined by nobody (whether that be black or white), belonging where I live and have grown up, being aware of the many voices that have made me who I am and with the freedom to make this country my home.

To read her contribution is to be reminded of how much more still needs to be done to promote real fairness for all: a matter Trevor Phillips addresses in powerful detail in his contribution.

A third theme that several authors touch upon is that of identity and multiple identities in relation to the concept of Britishness. Most of us feel we are British and something else as well: British and Scottish – as I am – or British and English – or British and Welsh and Asian, too. Michael Wills's essay, both scholarly and practical, cites convincing polling evidence to this effect. Indeed, the list of contributors to this book demonstrates a full and vivifying range of 'Britishness-plus', and I believe that the wider acknowledgement of the importance of this concept is long overdue. It makes sense of both our diversity and what we have in common, and can do more than that. As Raja Miah notes, there is a real potential for alienation on the part of young British Muslims of South Asian descent – an alienation which leaves some vulnerable to the temptations of bigotry and extremism, and, in the worst instances, to participation in violence and even terrorism. But, as he points out:

> To overcome this as a society we need to accept and champion the concept of multiple identities. None of us is either one or the other, whatever these constructs may be . . . My response to all of the Muslim young people with whom I work is that you do not become less of a Muslim through developing a strong sense of identity and patriotism with the land of your birth.

Interestingly, both Charles Leadbeater and Mark Earls point out in these pages that a major recent technological development has greatly facilitated the expression of such multiple identities, and the depth and fulfilment that such expression can bring. How fitting that the World Wide Web – the invention of Britain's own Sir Tim Berners-Lee – offers such a ready and near-costless means of creating among us communication and connections with others who share our interests and with whom we share identities. They bring people together in all but presence, and can take shape around professional and leisure interests, religious or social commonalities, pressure groups and even old comrades' associations. They thrive and give pleasure, fulfil serious purposes, empower good causes, or simply match our innate gift and need for interaction: we could rightly think of them as a vigorously thriving twenty-first-century manifestation of those long-established and characteristic British entities: Burke's 'little platoons'. And these myriad new Web-based formations, in Charles Leadbeater's words, 'help create a greater sense of coherence among the people who inhabit these islands' – in other words, they can add to our sense of Britishness.

So can we be more precise about this elusive Britishness that we recognise when we see it? Maybe the answer lies in George Orwell's distinction between nationalism and patriotism: are the multiple communities we inhabit primarily nationalistic expressions of our communality, and is the Britishness that we all acknowledge and value – along with the economic and social ties that bind us – the other, patriotic, side of that coin? Is it in fact part of the British genius, to have built on what Linda Colley has argued is a tight/loose eighteenth-century construction, a coin – or 60 million coins – with two sides? On one side, our nurturing Scottish, Welsh, Irish and English identities and sensibilities, now, of course, added to by many others – mixed in with our religious, local, recreational, cultural and sporting identifications; on the other, carefully balanced and held in tension, the organisations and operations of a British state that, shorn of nationalistic baggage, can properly fulfil Orwell's patriotic aspect of the nation state. Thus we can comfortably support our local or regional or national teams, and equally comfortably feel patriotic about the great overarching public institutions that unite us, such as our NHS, our armed forces, the BBC and the monarchy, wherever we live.

Our various institutions and constitutional arrangements have served us well down the centuries, though perhaps for reasons that are not immediately obvious. Many are less ancient– 'the invention of tradition' is now well documented – than they seem to be, and also more malleable and more adaptable than is generally assumed, but they survive and serve us because as they change they continue to reflect our enduring values. So we are entitled to take an active and functional view of their flexibility, changing them further so as to serve us better. If we are to do this, while retaining our 'robust rule of law and stable institutions', as Trevor Phillips adjures, we need both to build on the successful constitutional changes introduced by this government since 1997, and to fully describe the covenant that the state makes with those who hold UK citizenship, across the whole range of rights and responsibilities involved.

There are external reasons, too, for taking our Britishness more seriously than we have in the past. Among the most striking historical developments of the last half century are the rise of the new Europe to the global influence

33

that a population of half a billion and major trading-bloc status commands, and the more recent vastly increasing influence and power of globalisation. But in every European country there is a very strong sense of patriotism: of people in Poland being Polish, and in France being French and in Britain being British, because we want to be rooted, to feel a sense of belonging, to feel that we are part of a community more tangible and immediate than the larger grouping. And while almost everyone recognises the opportunities that globalisation has brought, we see also the insecurities that have come with it. So in times of such unprecedented change and pace of change, there is much to be gained from a clearer sense of ourselves, our common values, behaviours and traditions, and – as we face together the risks and benefits of globalisation – a need for a stronger sense of common purpose, too: one that recognises our strengths and the need to build on them – our past achievements and our potential for the future.

Of course, none of this means that we need to think of ourselves any differently. We are what we are, and what our traditional values of openness, tolerance, respect for liberty, and all the other things we have taken for granted, have made of us. In changing circumstances, the task now, and the reason for having a debate about Britishness, is to be more explicit about all this, about the values and conventions that for far too long – though entirely in keeping with the typically British form of reticence known as understatement – have been almost exclusively implicit. And I believe that this book shows how we are discovering that what unites us is far greater than what separates us, that the values we share most are those that matter most, and that recognising them, and with them the rights and responsibilities that citizenship involves, will strengthen us as an open, diverse, adaptable, enabling and successful modern state.

So I am convinced that this book and this debate about Britishness are timely, that the continuing debate will be a liberating experience and that its outcome will offer us scope for real progress. With a clearer sense of who we are and of the values we share, we are far better equipped as a country to manage constitutional change, citizenship and security, and – with a clearer sense of our common national purpose – to address the challenges that Britain faces in a rapidly changing world.

This book reminds every reader just how much there is to celebrate about the busy, beautiful, rain-drenched islands in the Atlantic that together we call home. It is as good a reminder as we could ever have of all the things that inspire us about the country we love.

WORLDS WITHIN WORLDS

IAN RANKIN

AS A CHILD, I WAS GIVEN A NEW DIARY EVERY CHRISTMAS. I would open it and mark the inside front cover with my details:

> Ian Rankin
> 17 Craigmead Terrace
> Bowhill
> Cardenden
> Fife
> Scotland
> Great Britain
> United Kingdom
> Europe
> The World
> The Universe

To me they seemed concentric circles, with my house at the very centre. I was a child of the world, and of Europe, but more locally (and more meaningfully) belonged to the village of Bowhill, which was in the process of being swallowed up by the postal designation of Cardenden. I seem to remember the thrill of writing down that lengthy address. It connected me to the whole world – and beyond. Come Saturday, I would watch the football results on TV, willing the Fife teams to have won. When the national team played, I would shout for Scotland. If Great Britain were in competition at the Olympics, I'd be rooting for them. At the Ryder Cup, I'd be keeping fingers crossed for Europe against the USA. As a family, we only ever took one summer holiday outside the UK – to Malta, to visit my sister and her husband (he was stationed there as an RAF engineer). I didn't start to explore Europe until I'd left university, hitching around France and Italy with my girlfriend. If asked, I always explained that I was Scottish rather than English. 'British' didn't bother me, but 'English' did, mainly because it was just plain wrong. These days, when I head overseas on promotional trips, I'm often asked by interviewers about whether I'm British or Scottish. I explain that it is possible to be both. Most Scots don't have a problem with England or Englishness. What they object to is actually the ubiquity of London in the media, and if (like me) you travel widely in England, you'll find that the locals in Liverpool, Manchester, Birmingham, Bristol, Newcastle, Nottingham and Carlisle complain of the self-same thing. We Brits do like a good moan . . .

THE KIDS ARE UK

PROFESSOR TANYA BYRON

WHEN I CONSIDER WHAT IT IS TO BE BRITISH, I LOOK TO my children: Lily, aged thirteen, and Jack, aged ten, and their generation.

Despite what we mostly read about, our British young people make me proud. Listening to my children talk to their friends, I hear opinions forming around complex issues that I had no idea about at their age. They are positive and optimistic in a way that we are so often told that they aren't. They can show extraordinary empathy for their less fortunate peers (those of their generation who are often demonised and written off by society at large), and they express strong beliefs around equality, fairness and social justice.

They are British in the best sense of Britishness.

These young people are buried by a morass of negativity around their generation – societal views that are skewed in the direction of those that are the most destructive and dysfunctional. However, the British spirit is strong, and I see it alive and well in so many of my children's generation – young people who refuse to give up and give in. Minds that are optimistic about the future and hearts that are compassionate and strong.

They are British in the best sense of Britishness.

Being British is about being resilient – in Britain we are at our best when united in the face of common adversity. Our vast and complex history is littered with examples of times of incredible hardship where we have all pulled together and seen each other through.

The plucky sense of optimism. The ability to rally together. The sense of 'we shall overcome'.

I believe that this British spirit of resilience is alive and well in so many of the upcoming generation – we don't hear about it, but it's there. Indeed, my children and their peers are incredibly resilient in the face of so much disillusionment, and this makes me so very proud of them all. From this, I am also all the more optimistic about the future as they become older and are more involved in the onward shaping of Britain.

They are British in the best sense of Britishness.

Thank goodness for these unacknowledged and often overlooked young people; thank goodness for their Britishness in a world that predominantly focuses on all that is wrong; thank goodness for their optimism and for their dogged self-belief.

Indeed, in Britain we should all give thanks for these young people – our future – and for all that they represent in terms of the best of what it is to be British.

3

LIVING IN TWENTY-FIRST-CENTURY BRITAIN: A GENERATIONAL VIEW

PROFESSOR CAROLINE GIPPS

WHAT DOES BEING BRITISH MEAN IN THE TWENTY-FIRST century? I think one issue is that many British people do not actually think in terms of their nationality, and particularly not in a patriotic sense.

Asking the question of some visitors from China, they distilled their view of what is unusual about Britain, which is that we have many very beautifully maintained old buildings, but inside them the activity, the design, the structure is very modern. This suggests that actually Britain (and therefore being British, perhaps) is a country of contrast.

My younger friends point out the contradictions: we export some of the finest literature, music and art in the world and yet have a rampantly commercially driven society, in which every high street in the country looks the same. We talk about how tolerant we are as a nation (which deep down I believe we are), but many show resentment towards first- and second-generation immigrants. A nation in which we feel safe and are absolutely free to express ourselves as we wish, but one in which DNA is kept on record and there are CCTV cameras on every corner. We invented 'the beautiful game' and are also responsible for turning it into the most money-grabbing of commercial ventures. Another young friend believes that feeling British is not the key issue: he is a Londoner first and foremost, Canadian by birth, with Welsh interest by familiarity. He would define himself rather as a liberal, an atheist and so on.

The important thing about being British is that one is allowed to be all of these things, and not necessarily in contradiction, and that in itself is an extremely good thing; trying to define being British too narrowly means that people will be forced to fit into a definition – or not – which is even more difficult. For these young people, the really important thing about Britain is the tolerance, and for tolerance to survive, things must not be too carefully defined.

So what do I think about being British? Well, there is something critically important about tolerance, which is not quite the same as live and let live, because it is more active) I grew up in a small town where tolerance was not particularly obvious; there was a lot of gossip and judgement. I went to a small, religious, girls' school, in which tolerance of other ways of believing was not at all encouraged, and I became switched off their rather narrow, missionary view of Christianity: if you weren't their sort of Christian, you weren't a Christian at all. It effectively ended my engagement with organised religion. (And I have never regained a love of small towns.) So what else does it mean to be British? For my mother, who came from Holland just before the Second World War, and who married an Englishman during the war (in uniform, a very good thing), the important thing about Britain was the type of man that it produced: 'Always marry an Englishman: they have much better manners.' I'm sure she was right, but I feel that is also something to do with tolerance, because the essence of good manners is that you are conscious of the feelings of other people, and this, deep down, is part of being tolerant. The more you wish to impose your views (and yourself) on other people, the less you are recognising them, their views and who they are.

(So being British in the twenty-first century is a lot to do with being who you are and proud of it, being allowed to be a number of things without censure, but similarly not being intolerant or jingoistic towards others. Above all, it is being somebody who subscribes to a view of tolerance: tolerance in what people believe, tolerance in what people may say and tolerance in how we run our individual lives.

THIS LITTLE WORLD

GEORGE MARTIN

I AM NOT SURE WHO WE BRITISH FOLK ARE ANY MORE. I KNOW who we used to be, but so much has changed since I was a boy. Perhaps I have answered my own question.

We British are a mongrel race; we always have been, and now it is more evident than ever. Even before William invaded our shores in 1066 we were a motley crew, with Normans and Danes and Saxons and Scots all intermingling (and fighting each other for their share of the land) so that a typical Briton then could equally be a dark Celt or a blond, or even boast a mane of fiery ginger hair. Does it matter? Well, I think it does. Our very diversity explains much of our character, coupled with a maverick streak that asserts itself from time to time.

As a child I did not really give much thought to being born British. Of course, at school we would look at the map of the world and we would see vast areas coloured red, which signified our great empire, and we all felt rather proud and special. And we were made to believe that we were special; never did we think that our nation had ever been unjust. Our wars were always in honourable defence of the realm; it went without saying. It took me a little while to realise that all was not quite as it seemed.

How could it be possible for such a tiny island to be so completely dominant in the world, to rule over hundreds of millions of people? With perhaps little more than 5 million people crammed into a group of islands off the coast of mainland Europe, we were able to preserve our integrity and develop a unique kind of life. As a nation of seafaring people we were able to use our sea power and military prowess to conquer, and then we could leave the rest to our enterprising traders. Like the Vikings, and all those who had invaded our shores so many times during the first millennium, we would sail off to faraway countries to pillage and plunder and bring back the spoils. Sir Francis Drake and Sir Walter Raleigh were, under the patronage of their monarch, Queen Elizabeth I, little better behaved than fearsome pirates like Blackbeard and Captain Kidd, who terrorised the Caribbean. But our adventurers had established naval supremacy, and in Elizabethan times the British had become the finest seafaring nation in the world, much to the annoyance of our European neighbours, France, Holland and Spain. Islands and territories in the West were fought over time and again, with countries coming under the domination of one or the other European kingdom, but Britain seemed constantly to have the advantage. In our wars against the dictator Napoleon we fought gallantly, sometimes winning but never quite able to administer the *coup de grâce*. Fortunately we had the brilliant Lord Nelson, who in the Battle of Trafalgar finally established Britain as the supreme ruler of the oceans, and that power on the high seas gave us clout in trade and access to markets that other nations were denied.

I suppose the peak of the great British Empire was during the nineteenth century, which was an unprecedented period of growth for the creative Britons who led the Industrial Revolution. So many inventions came from their fertile brains, all designed to make the manufacture of goods easier and cheaper. The spinning-jenny revolutionised the cotton industry, the raw material in the looms coming from the colonies in the West Indies. The invention of the steam engine by James Watt led to the development of the railway network by George Stephenson, and their work completely changed transport throughout the entire world. Not only did it bring people all over Britain into contact with each other, but the system was also effectively copied in our overseas territories. The American Wild West, for example, was eventually tamed less by the Winchester rifle than by the progression of the railroad from east to west, and today the railway system in India remains a lifeline for its people. Coal was the oil of the day, mined to power the machines in our factories, giving hard labour to thousands, while Henry Bessemer invented a new process for making steel of the highest quality, the envy of other nations. In medicine, enormous strides were made by Joseph Lister, Edward Jenner and Alexander Fleming.

I am now much older and wiser than I was as a schoolboy, and I realise that this amazing growth did not come easily and the human cost was high. The main proportion of our population was very poor, little more than serfs in their time, and had to work extremely hard to make anything like a decent wage. Conditions in the mills and factories in the heartland of England were dreadful, and many of the workers were little better off than slaves. In the beginning I used to be annoyed by those who tried to make us feel ashamed of that Victorian regime. After all, the great British Empire did a lot of good, did it not? We administered justice and introduced good laws to the uneducated people in our colonies, and in exchange we received precious minerals and raw materials that they did not need anyway. I thought we had earned a reputation for fairness in our administration of those overseas territories, but we suffered the inevitable charges of cruel arrogance and subjugation, and others saw us as contemptuous people who always thought they were superior, always in the right. Not to put too fine a point on it, we were disliked pretty well everywhere. Not without cause, apparently, were we regarded as a haughty, callous race, trampling over smaller nations in the cause of trade. I had clung to the belief that we did bring justice and fair play to our colonies and we had achieved a great deal of good in the world. Now, however, I realise that many of my forebears were a greedy lot, happy to exploit the work of their poorer brethren who lived in squalor. But those were cruel times, and was not every nation equally guilty of similar misdeeds?

Today we see other countries filling the gaps with empires of their own, committing injustices in just the same way as we did hundreds of years ago, and mostly in the name of democracy. In truth, we gave most of our Victorian empire back to the people of the Colonies reluctantly, apart from the odd ones who volunteered to stay with us and, incidentally, are today being subsidised by the tax regime in our homeland. I am not complaining; life moves around and in the end we get what we deserve. Ironically it seems that we have been in a reverse situation, with thousands flooding across our borders in the hope of living here.

I was brought up as a Catholic, and I attended a school run by Jesuit priests. They, like my parents, instilled in me the virtues of truth and kindness and decency. One of the things that was firmly impressed upon me was the thought that I should never ask anyone to do something that I would not do myself. It is not a bad idea, and it was certainly followed by some of our better nobles in mediaeval times. A king such as Richard the Lionheart would fight on the battlefield alongside his men, often in hand-to-hand combat, inspiring them to great victories. One cannot forget Agincourt, where an outnumbered

British force led by Henry V defeated a mighty French army by the superior firepower of its archers (aided, possibly, by the thick, trampled mud of France, which hindered the attacking enemy cavalry), and I am prepared to believe that King Henry made sure that he shared the hardships of his men.

Drake calmly scuppered the 'invincible' Spanish Armada in the English Channel and preserved the integrity of our island for his queen, and centuries later Nelson gave us an amazing victory at Trafalgar against another heavily armed Spanish foe, securing our domination of the seas for many years to come. Wellington, with a raggle-taggle mob of infantrymen and cavalry managed to pull off a momentous win at Waterloo, outwitting Emperor Napoleon and stopping him from crushing us as he intended, thus giving a lesson to all would-be dictators everywhere. Unfortunately, another dictator in the last century ignored that lesson and plunged the world into a dreadful war, which I experienced for myself.

What great warriors we had as our forebears! Those archers at Agincourt, our sailors at Trafalgar and our gallant men at Waterloo were all the stuff of legend, but one can get carried away with admiration for those in battle. It bore a heavy price. My parents had seen for themselves the ghastly effects of war. My mother had been a nurse, tending the casualties in the British Army during the First World War, and she had been traumatised by the death of her brother, killed by a German sniper, just after two more brothers were seriously wounded. Sometimes my uncles would tell me of the misery and some of the horrors of the Western Front, which frightened the life out of me and made me determined to try to make peace with others, even those I disliked. The Great War ended just eight years before I was born, and the world was soon in the depths of a great economic depression. Sounds familiar? With two young children to raise, my parents had a really hard time, and my father found himself unemployed for nearly two years in the 1930s. He was unable to obtain work in his trade as a skilled carpenter, and I remember seeing him in London on the corner of Cheapside in the depths of a cold winter, practically freezing to death, selling newspapers in order to collect the princely wage of one pound ten shillings each week. There was no dole, no state help at all. My mother scrubbed floors to get money for food, although being a child I was not fully aware of the deep hardship they had to suffer. Through it all I basked in their loving care, ignorant of our plight.

The First World War had left the people of Britain in a state of shock, and as a consequence my parents dreaded the sabre-rattling that slowly led to the precipice of the Second World War. In 1939 they prayed that it would not last long enough for their children to be called up to fight. In the '40s I was in my early teens and headstrong, and although I could not show it, I was secretly thrilled to witness the Battle of Britain taking place above my head in Kent, where we then lived. I would watch the Spitfires and Hurricanes ducking and diving, leaving white trails against the blue of the sky, and after I had joined the Air Training Corps I often used to visit Biggin Hill to talk to those pilots I had seen above. I heard many stories of valour, always told with a nonchalant disregard for drama, but after the miracle of Dunkirk we knew we were all fighting for our lives and freedom. I decided that when my time came I would join the flying branch of the Royal Navy, the Fleet Air Arm.

I had heard of the amazing victory that a handful of men in ancient biplanes had achieved when, taking off from an aircraft carrier in the Mediterranean, they flew many miles above the sea, through the night, to attack the Italian fleet safely harboured in Taranto. Despite fierce opposition they virtually destroyed the fleet, changing the balance of power in the eastern Mediterranean. This did not go unnoticed by the military leaders in Japan, who copied the idea when they attacked Pearl Harbor on that 'Day of Infamy', as Roosevelt put it.

I heard of another action in which eighteen ordinary airmen led by Lieutenant Commander Esmonde flew in just six antiquated Swordfish biplanes against the might of the German navy and air force in an effort to stop the warships *Scharnhorst* and *Gneisenau* from reaching a safe haven in Germany. These ships were making a desperate dash to join their sisters in Hamburg, where they were to form a marauding squadron that would decimate our Atlantic convoys. Esmonde had been promised fighter protection, but he saw none: not one Spitfire or Hurricane to shield him and his crews. Nevertheless, he pressed on with his attack under murderous fire from all sides. It proved to be a useless gesture. All his planes were inevitably shot out of the sky and only five airmen survived. Esmonde was one of those who perished, and he received a posthumous Victoria Cross. Later, when I flew with the Fleet Air Arm, I got close to that small part of the war when I met one of the surviving heroes of that action, Donald Bunce. He was my instructor for a while before I got my wings, and I discovered that during that Channel Dash he actually managed to shoot down a Focke-Wulf 190 with his single Lewis Gun from his open cockpit just before his plane was downed. One cannot but be humbled by such calculated courage.

I was very lucky. I went to a state school but managed to get a scholarship to St Ignatius College in north London, and all the time I was growing up in the best environment – a loving family. Once the war started we all moved south to Bromley in Kent, and I found a place in the local grammar school, but my father had found employment in Shoreditch, east London, and consequently had to travel 16 miles morning and evening for his work. He cycled. Yes, all through the Blitz he cycled, dodging bombs and avoiding the craters that appeared in his path. My dear sister joined the Women's Royal Air Force, and I was not too keen on hanging around to be conscripted. If I had done so, I would in all probability have become a foot soldier in the army, and, remembering the tales of my uncles, I decided that I would rather fly. Unknown to my parents, I walked into a recruiting office and volunteered to serve as air-crew in the Fleet Air Arm. I was 17 years of age. My mother in particular was aghast. She broke down and wept, so convinced was she that I would be killed in action. I promised her faithfully (and rather irrationally) that I would live, but it was of little comfort.

Once my sister had left for the WRAF and I left for my time in the Fleet Air Arm, my parents felt our absence keenly, worrying for us both while they endured the horrors of the Blitz and, later on, the flying bombs and rockets that fell on them from the skies. I heard of their trials in letters I received while I was in comparative comfort serving abroad. They were incredible people, honest and brave, and, I thought, typically British. Nowadays, of course, such folk can be targets of satire, mocked for the stiff upper lip that is their trademark. But who is to mock this happy breed today? Only those who can have no idea of what it is like to serve their country in foreign lands. We do seem to take for granted the bravery and skill of our fighting men, expecting them to die for their country while being paid in peanuts. If we have to have a fighting force at all, they should be given pay at least as good as they would earn as civilians. I am proud to be a friend and supporter of them. I am proud to be British.

There, I have said it. I am proud to be British and glad that I was born on this tiny, crowded island. Why? Because we have been tempered by our trials and emerged as a compassionate and caring race. We have opened our doors to refugees from all parts of the world and given them sanctuary. We, who in 1940 stood alone against the mightiest armies in the world, kept our belief that we would survive and did so against all odds, showing the resilience that is one of our chief characteristics. We paid for the war by borrowing against the future, and we found ourselves in a state of virtual bankruptcy for many years afterwards. We finally paid off our wartime monetary debt to America just a couple of years ago. No wonder that we are hard up!

What other nation can equal our great achievers over the past millennium? One can immediately call to mind a very incomplete list of names of great writers – Chaucer, Donne, Shakespeare, Milton, Wordsworth, Dickens and Austen. Musicians like Elgar, Vaughan Williams, Delius, Walton, Holst and Britten. And think of our scientists and engineers – Faraday, Newton, Wren, Watt, Stephenson, Brunel, Logie Baird: creators all, leading us to the present jet age of invention and discovery. Few people realise the World Wide Web was created by an unassuming Briton – Sir Tim Berners-Lee. They all have enriched our lives immeasurably. The same holds good today. We are still punching above our weight, giving the world entertainment of a high artistic quality with our films, their actors and their directors. In popular music, and here I must try to remain unbiased, it is obvious that we have spread our music far and wide, giving immense joy and pleasure to the world. There never has been a musical group as ubiquitous as the Beatles, for I believe there is now nowhere on earth where their music is not known.

We are a creative nation, and our future depends on our maintaining that status. All of this would mean little without a generous spirit, which I believe Britain has. In a time when the world is undergoing great stress we need to exercise the finest of our characteristics. We must continue to show our generosity to those who are worse off than we are, and to extend the hand of friendship to all other peoples. We should only go to war to protect our homeland. It returns us to basics and can be summed up by what my parents gave me in my childhood, with words that have been immortalised by great songwriters I have known. John and Paul sang 'All You Need Is Love' and, even more succinctly, Hal David, partner of Burt Bacharach, reflected what I feel most strongly in the title of his famous song 'What The World Needs Now Is Love'. Indeed.

5

QUITE A PERSONAL ACCOUNT OF THE ENGLISH COUNTRYSIDE

ALEX JAMES

CHRIS GASKELL RUNS THE ROYAL AGRICULTURAL COLLEGE. Could he come over, he said, with a group of kids from urban environments who'd shown an interest in becoming farmers?

Wide-eyed and whispering, clasping their packed lunches, they poured out of the college minibus and assembled obediently, timidly, in the yard in the sunshine. They looked really cool: hoodies in new wellies. I would have willingly bought vegetables from them there and then.

I started to explain about the history of the farm. Just as I was getting to the Inclosure Act of 1801, the exciting bit, I spotted Fred in the distance and beckoned him to come over. Here was a bona fide expert, a man of the soil, of the field, an award-winning husband of nature to enlighten them, right on cue. I introduced him to everybody and asked him to say a few words about his sheep.

'Well, them ewe lambs just 'bout last 'em. Got them tups up in Yard 'spose. Ooh, aren't them buggers, though! Eh . . .? Goh!' Just then Ray managed to fire up the circular saw. It had been playing up all morning. We'd had a good old fiddle with it, but I'd more or less given up on the thing. Now it was clearly back in business and Ray was waving it around for joy with a blissful toothless grin on his face, drowning out Fred's authentic rustic oratory.

'Maybe we'll go crayfishing?' I shouted over the din, grabbing the nets and heading for the river. 'Bit of farm business diversification. It's a free crop. It's a nice walk. There are sheep on the way. They're fairly self-explanatory, really, sheep, you'll see.'

The top field had just been cropped for hay, and was looking spectacularly good. Suddenly it was high summer, one of those bright days that makes you remember why billionaires have always lived on farms, why pop stars buy them to live happily ever after, why it might be better mucking about making bonfires and gazing like Fred does than staring at a computer screen and wondering whether to have a sandwich or sushi. It's a tough sell at the moment, agriculture, but the butterflies and dragonflies were skipping on the hedgerows, everything was out. It was busy. It was beautiful, wherever you were coming from.

'Is dat your tree?'

'Yep, I guess so.'

'No way man. How can you laak, own a tree? Is it? Das so cool! Laak, how much is it? Dis place.'

'Well, you can rent the fields for 25 quid an acre a year, at least Fred does. I throw the trees in.'

I'd been looking forward to seeing the river. I don't get down there often. It was flowing steadily and purposefully towards London. We built the nets as we munched sandwiches in the long grass by the waterside, brushing away the buzzers and bombers. The kids were enthusiastic, inquisitive and completely and involuntarily engaged with it all, suddenly. They asked Professor Gaskell endless questions that led to more questions, and he sprinkled his expertise over them delicately, like seasoning for the sandwiches.

We caught four crayfish. Not a huge success, but I think the fields won a few hearts that day.

I guess it started for me about 15 years ago. I was tearing around Manhattan in the middle of the night with the keyboard player from Blondie and a lady with huge bosoms. It was just another day at the office in rock and roll. We'd all met about an hour before and now we were going somewhere in his car, very fast. He was enjoying the empty streets, squeaking the tyres, driving with purpose and glee.

'How come you've got a such a crap car, Jimmy?' I said. I had to ask. I'd have thought he'd have a helicopter.

'Look at me,' he said with a huge grin on his face, 'look at me when I say this. Don't do what I do, do what I say. Buy land. Buy buildings. They don't go away.'

I don't know why I ignored all the professional advice and took my cue from a man who'd sold a hundred million records and yet was driving a backfiring banger, but when we first looked at buying this farm his words came back to me like the blessing of a holy man and we spent all our money on it, on land and buildings.

What is a field anyway? It's a blank canvas, really, anything you want it to be. It's an ink-blot that reflects the beholder.

I knew I could trust Jimmy. The price of land has suddenly gone up. It stands to reason; a chunk of land is a slice of the ultimate pie.

It's actually quite hard to make money out of owning land. It takes time. That's actually been the good thing about it. Spending time is more important than spending money. Living here in the heart of rural England has given me something to do, something that absorbs me completely, and after 20 years of life in the rock and roll fast lane I was going to take some absorbing when I came back down to earth. We've been pretty skint since we arrived here. I work harder than I ever have done on my new vocation. There are always at least three emergencies, two traumas and a leak in progress, and usually a chicken unaccounted for. I am always worried about something, but existential angst left me the day we got the keys.

You've got to live a little before you die. I think that was Jimmy's main message. Although he never said it, it was implicit in the late-night Manhattan safari, and in his smile.

I fell in love with England twice: the first time was when I left it. I spent my 20s living out of a suitcase. The second was when I saw it from the air, and it was from the air that I first spotted the Cotswolds. As far as I can tell, the countryside is all very nice. If you're thinking about it, it probably doesn't matter which bit you pick. From above, the Cotswolds is identifiable by a particular shade of green that doesn't appear anywhere else. On the deck, it's harder to say what's what. You can sometimes only tell you're in the Cotswolds because there are more people called Giles than usual.

The urge to fly has left me now. After 15 years of endless loops of world tours passing through hotel rooms, ballrooms and bedrooms, I'm at anchor, at rest in Rural Britain.

'Rural Britain' doesn't really mean anything. Some of my neighbours live in castles and some live in caravans. Some want for nothing and some have no teeth. Life in the Cotswolds is enhanced by that variety. The countryside is the playground of the fantastically rich. Exotic creatures that live in secret under big stones: normally only visible when on the move. Too many helicopters to count pass overhead each morning. It's astonishing. There has always been wealth to stagger and stretch one's eyes in this neck of the woods, and my rock and roll dollars can't compete with the might of dynastic splendour or hedge-fund wealth. Sometimes it seems there are more famous people and billionaires here in the Cotswolds than there are in Monte Carlo. The entire area sits high on a plateau of human achievement wrought by go-getting, hard-nosed pastoral-dream builders, its manicured perfection the toil of high-density ancient dynasties and arriviste nobility, but every neighbourhood has its lairds and ladies. I'm sure it's no different in Morocco or Mozambique.

I forget that moving to the country was such a gamble. When we left London five years ago, I really thought my life might be over. My band was disintegrating. I shed a skin of boozy mates and girlfriends and got married. I had no job, no mates and absolutely no experience of farms or the countryside. I lived in a Covent Garden flat with a small balcony. Buying a knackered farm appeared a reckless move to everyone who knew me – and to me when I thought about it. I suppose getting married was the start of something new. It's the bit at the end of the book that goes 'and they all lived happily ever after'. All happy endings implied some kind of garden, when I thought about it.

The English countryside, which is without doubt the prettiest in the world, is a vast, dilapidated stately home. Fields in Europe and North America are different: huge things, great for colossal machines, but not for people. England's green and pleasant land is totally impractical for agricultural purposes and hugely expensive to run, but the whole thing is a kind of Grade I listed national monument and a wonderful place to live.

I keep getting arrested, not on top of pyramids in Mexico or halfway down the Caledonian Road, like the old days, but by details. Maybe it's because I'm listening to so much Beethoven at the moment that everything seems interesting. Sometime last Thursday, after repeated cramming of his First Symphony at high volume, the entire shebang of the English countryside suddenly transformed in my mind into a monster-budget video commissioned specifically to accompany his music. Since then I've been wandering around inside this perfect film hearing imaginary violins and oboes, beguiled, sometimes to a standstill, by the excellence and variety of the colour green or the exactness of sunshine on yew. I'd rather like to be left alone for long enough to go peacefully insane, but people will keep wandering up and asking questions. And then the beautiful Beethoven bubble bursts.

All my favourite things about the country come unannounced: stoats and weasels, low-flying jets, poppies, puffballs, moonlight. A clear, cloudless night that coincides with a heavy moon is rare enough to always take me by surprise.

It's one of those things that will certainly keep happening, but whenever it does I'm never prepared for it, like the first really cold snap of winter or the first flush of spring.

Moonlight is something that doesn't properly exist in cities. Even in towns it doesn't really. It's too delicate for domestication, as subtle and precarious as ancient history, but just as absolute: an unexpected inestimable perk of a life unconnected to mains sewage or gas. I took a big step back from the edge into the middle when I got married, the middle of nowhere, but then out comes the moon and reminds me that we're right out here on our own being just as delightfully stupid as ever.

I love never having to throw anything away, being able to build mountains (subject to planning), and chickens, but weather is about the biggest difference between town and country. All significant weather conditions are a misery in the city. You don't really get the whole picture. You just get a slice. It's like not being able to see the telly when you can hear it. It's annoying. Out here there are horizons in all directions, and big sky. It all makes perfect sense in glorious Technicolor and surround sound. It's a slow-motion roller-coaster ride, the passing of the seasons.

When you've got the right gear on, winter is a picnic. Growing up in Bournemouth, the sea was always as beautiful in February as it was in August, but there was something forlorn about deserted ice-cream kiosks and shivering surf dudes. Here, everything springs to life in February. It still feels like being on holiday. Formerly, February made me think 'grey, drizzly and cold'. It is cold, usually, although some calm, bright mornings you can have your coffee in the sun outside in your pants. A completely grey day, a Yarborough deal, is quite impossible, though. There are always black bits and silver streaks. When the wind is howling and the rain is beating against the windows, I don't even need to put the telly on in the evenings. I spend more time watching the fire than watching the telly. It makes staying in so much more appealing, when it's foul out. It's nicer to have a reason to stay in than a reason to go out, as I get older.

Friends dashed up from London for the afternoon. It was gusty, grey and cold and raining a little bit. I could see they thought they'd made a big mistake. The idea of spending a whole afternoon at someone's house is a terrifying thought in a city. I lit a fire. We spent the afternoon poking it. They didn't want to leave. As they were getting into the car, the sun did one of its appearing tricks and lit up the whole valley a brilliant orange. It was just getting good.

I suppose I might easily have stayed in Covent Garden for ever, having bubble baths instead of spending Sunday afternoons in a field in the rain with my head up a drain, but no one needs or enjoys his bath quite as much as the man who has spent the afternoon at the other end of one.

Of course, what I understood, at the time, as a great romantic leap was in fact just another ageing rock gentleman conforming to stereotype. All rockers go out to pasture on farms. Dreams of happily ever after never usually make any suggestions of work to be done, but we all need something to do. It's the most important thing. As soon as I have something to do, I can happily do nothing again. A nice house with mains plumbing and a cellar that didn't have things living in it probably would have suffocated us quietly. After five years we'd be dreaming about running away, sailing around the world or moving to France, like all profoundly bored people do. Five years of panic and confusion in dust, debris and muck and I finally feel like I'm getting on top of it. There's nothing actually finished as yet, and a lot of things haven't even been started. The five-year plan we drew up five years ago is due to get underway next month. The dream is still way on the horizon, the end of a rainbow we'll never get to, but where else to set the compass?

It's taken a few years for us to get to know each other, the countryside and I, but now I'm most at ease in the pastoral situation. It's a great big palace of art. Saturday morning I drove through hobbity hills and dragony dales in streaming golden sunshine that made telegraph poles look glamorous and concrete look like magic stuff. When I arrived home, a hot-air balloon was floating past, very low and large. When a hot-air balloon goes past that close, there is something inside all men that wants to run after it. I ran over the fields chasing as it gently climbed over the trees and slipped away in silent slow motion. There was hardly any breeze, and it all suggested victory for the serene and the immaculate. My perspective flipped; I'd been on top of the world all day, but I had a sudden sense that I was standing at the bottom of the sky.

I remember the trees were just coming into blossom and there were gypsies camping on the roadside at the top of the drive when we first laid eyes on the farm five years ago; we bought it on our honeymoon a month later. It's hard to remember exactly why we rose to it, or precisely what we wanted from it, now. I know it was irresistible, ultimately, a romantic stroke, probably the most romantic thing we could have done, to leave our old lives behind and build a new one together in what I took for the middle of nowhere. It has become the centre of the universe; and, ironically, the upshot of that starry-eyed plunge was a million practicalities, and our dream has only been kept afloat by both of us pulling our heads out of the clouds, parking the aeroplane and taking care of business.

Not so long ago, people couldn't get away fast enough. They fled these shores to live where the sun shines hotter, but I feel like this is where I belong.

I've been richer, more relaxed, more on top of things, definitely, but I've never been less bored. After years tearing around the world in a rock and roll band, I never imagined life would get more interesting as it went on. I was expecting an anticlimax. Maybe ten years ago if you'd told me Blur would be down the drain, I'd never have thought I'd find drains so satisfying.

Living on a farm is a lot like piloting a vast ship. Sometimes I'm overwhelmed by the scale of it, cowed by how far it is from the tip of the mast to the tiny wheel that steers it. I always keep one eye on the horizon, but the vast, relentless momentum of the thing lends exquisite charm to the occasional moments of perfect stillness in the foreground. I feel like I'm in exactly the right place, and I'm happy sailing this ship round the sun. Every year the gypsies return with the blossom. I'm staying put for the time being.

6

IN DEFENCE OF OUR
SHARED VALUES

DR MUHAMMAD ABDUL BARI

FOR THE PAST FEW YEARS IN NOVEMBER, I HAVE STOOD shoulder to shoulder as part of this great nation to honour all those who have given their lives for this country. The thought that is poignant in my mind is that this is perhaps a unique expression of what 'Britishness' is all about. Remembrance Sunday is one of the days when our people, young and old, irrespective of race, gender or creed, come together officially to remember one of the more sombre periods of our history.

We recognise and give tribute to the heroism and bravery of our warriors past and present, particularly in those just wars of national survival. Amongst the countless First and Second World War memorials are emblazoned Muslim names, which represent the tens of thousands of Muslims who have stood as part of this great nation, who fought bravely and who fell defending this country in corners near and far all around the world. The poignancy of this should not be lost on any of us, especially Muslims who have now made Britain their home. Recently, an exhibition at City Hall in London entitled 'We Were There' provided many examples of Muslim sacrifice, highlighting how over 1 million men from the ethnic minorities served in the Great War, with a very large number drawn from Muslim villages of the Punjab. In the Second World War the Indian Army alone provided 2.5 million men. Muslims have been with Britain in good times and in bad, contributing to its welfare, standing and defence, and protecting the values of justice and freedom that make it the country it is today.

For me, Britishness is at once cognisant of this reality of the past, painful though it may have been, and optimistic and confident in the future. This is a formal recognition of our achievements as a country; but our national life also has a vibrant, organic nature, and our collective moments of joy reflect this, often undertaken with unbounded and ad hoc festivity. We celebrate sporting achievement and pride in those who have fairly and squarely obtained merit. Lewis Hamilton's recent triumph as the youngest Formula One champion was celebrated for his youth, and it was a euphoria that was proudly colour-blind to his race. It was a marker of acknowledgement of where we have come from and a signal to a confident and flourishing future that we wish to embrace.

This essay will look to this very confidence in the future – which we can reach with the help of our collective experience and will. But to do so, we must unburden ourselves of the shackles of ignorance, fear and loathing. As we explore notions of what it means to be British, our nation is experiencing epoch-making transformations that will affect generations to come. The deepening financial crisis may well reorder the relationship between state and citizen, and how citizens relate to each other. The current predicament presents an opportunity for all of us.

The rampant consumerism that was a precursor to our current woes can give way to an enlightened re-evaluation of our collective priorities: where we restate our notions of community and common purpose against the backdrop of a British society deeply affected by globalisation and the historical legacy of empire that forms a part of our unwritten cultural DNA.

To underscore the notion that we are not an island, our discussion of Britishness takes place against the towering achievement of the United States, a nation to whom we can claim some proud provenance. That country has demonstrated the art of the possible by electing a black man with Muslim heritage as its head of state. It highlights the potential that a nation vibrant in its multiculturalism can prevail over the painful process that was endured to reach a place where we are told that American society is now post-racial and has learned about accommodating difference. It remains to be seen whether that is the case and whether the old world can emulate the progressiveness of the new. It remains to be seen whether here in Britain a Briton from the minority community can confidently defy Barack Obama when he said in the 2004 Democratic National Convention speech, 'that in no other country on earth, is my story even possible'.

Conversely, our current difficulties could in fact result in the fracturing of our society. With economic and global crises tightening their grip, fear may start to take hold on sections of our community that will be naturally worried for their livelihoods, safety and well-being. History has shown a frightening tendency for communities to face inwards in times of difficulty and highlight difference through ignorance of each other. With resources to invest in communities becoming scarce, we will need to make heightened efforts on the quest to understand and empathise with each other. It should be of great concern to all right-minded people that fear-mongering demagogues will exploit our difficult circumstances to play to our base anxieties. If the experiences of Remembrance Sunday, the post-racial world, and the sense of unified national joy mean anything to us as a nation, then we must emphatically reject the malignant cancer of hatred and social division.

There were two days in July 2005 that serve us well as a metaphor for the crossroads that we find ourselves at as a nation. On 6 July, Britain's capital city was announced as the host for the 2012 Olympic Games. The decision gave way to immense euphoria, a sense of pride and a warm feeling that London was a world-class city, and highlighted its welcoming attitude to newcomers. Britain was open for business, confident in its identity and ready to welcome the world. But less than twenty-four hours later, on 7 July, the joy and pride were shattered as four British citizens wreaked havoc on the streets of London, to the shock of the nation. Even more horrifying for British Muslims was that this atrocity was carried out wrongly in the name of Muslims. Since then, we have accelerated our discussion on what it means to be British, but that conversation takes place through the fear of 7 July rather than through the confidence of the preceding day.

Since 11 September 2001, and even more so since 7 July 2005, the very idea of what it means to be British has been disputed more than ever before. With disputation comes a constant quest for it to be defined. The casualties of this discourse are the natural and inherent assumptions that bind peoples of these isles together – British multiculturalism. This became the scapegoat for the events of 7 July, and it was misrepresented and maligned for facilitating the conditions that allowed the bombers of 7/7 to develop their hatred toward fellow Britons. In February 2008, the security experts Gwyn Prins and Robert Salisbury affirmed this notion in their RUSI (Royal United Services Institute) report 'Risk, Threat and Security: the Case of the United Kingdom' by stating that a 'misplaced deference to multiculturalism, which failed to lay down the line to immigrants, has contributed to a lack of national self-confidence and a fragmenting society that has been exploited by Islamist terrorists'. Recent discussions on Britishness have therefore been overshadowed, and perhaps prompted, by the assumption that the men who killed and maimed people on the streets of London in 2005 were the product of a failed consensus, which allowed communities to lead separate lives. They come, so the narrative goes, from a community that was allowed to maintain and foster its own set of values that was at variance to the deeply held but unwritten notions and values that exist in Britain. The assumptions on which this argument rests are shaky and insidious to say the least, diminishing the very humanity of the communities that live peaceably as part of the British nation.

There is indeed a pressing need for a national conversation about our identity. But we will do well to avoid framing this around security imperatives. To position this discourse on the simplistic and flawed assumptions that there are certain minorities who refuse to integrate and are therefore a threat to societal harmony is a step backwards and will initiate a downward spiral of fear. Instead, we must muster up the confidence, pride and dignity that are inherent in Britishness in order to embrace the future, instead of entering it with fear, prejudice and a reduction in humanity. We are undertaking a flawed analysis if we simply, and clumsily, link Muslims to security and make this the extent of our inquiry.

A discourse on Britishness must move beyond the rhetoric that encompasses Muslims only in terms of national survival. Rather, we must focus ourselves on confidence and a sense of national purpose, which are incredibly important. One need only observe the sense of jubilation that engulfed our country when London won its bid to host the Olympic Games in 2012. That confidence took a knock the day after, when murderers struck London, but Londoners showed their resilience by defying the bombers and seeking common cause, standing up to those who wished to take out their resulting anger on British Muslims. This came from the confidence about who we are, the sense that Britain is an inclusive nation and the resolve that Britons will not allow terrorists or far-right extremists to win the day.

Both 6 and 7 July 2005 are emblematic of our national identity. Both events demonstrated our own confidence in ourselves and our values. For many, this display of defiance and common resolve in the face of calamity is a bold testament to the modern values of multicultural Britain today. It exudes the modern confidence of British society, and the confidence in a future that accepts the idea that difference can enhance British identity. It is a confidence that is at variance with the same group of assembled security experts who – despite their years of valuable experience – understand this misplaced confidence through the prism of the past, through an age where a 'lesser race' knew their place and who readily submitted to masters who 'laid down the line'. It is the humble contention of this author that such notions do not envisage a Britain of equal citizens.

Unfortunately, the misplaced bully-boy confidence of the past is slowly gaining resonance amongst some sections of our media. Our traditional 'silly season' has been replaced by silly stories, which are both ludicrous and fabricated, of mad mullahs, of Muslims wanting to ban Christmas or Muslims demanding the Talibanisation of Britain. However, as Peter Oborne and James Jones so effectively demonstrate in their pamphlet *Muslims Under Siege: Alienating Vulnerable Communities*, often such stories are made up or stretched beyond the purported facts. Their conclusions are damning, but they offer all of us hope and optimism in the 'British way':

> We should all feel a little bit ashamed about the way we treat
> Muslims in the media, in our politics, and on our streets.
> They are our fellow citizens, yet often we barely acknowledge
> them. We misrepresent and in certain cases persecute them.
> We do not treat Muslims with the tolerance, decency and
> fairness that we so often like to boast is the British way. We
> urgently need to change our public culture.

Multiculturalism may well have its critics, but if we are to have any discourse at all, it must be rational and anchored to citable evidence. If we operate under the current assumptions so strongly set by our opinion makers, then the British way will suffer.

Despite this call for a compassionate discourse on our notions of Britishness, the fear many may have of British Muslims and the concern that certain deeply held Muslim beliefs are incompatible with British values and ideals are not lost on this author. As Muslims, we have unreservedly spoken out against this perversion of our faith. Terrorism is against religion and outside religion, despite those who claim otherwise. Muslims everywhere have tried to repudiate these assertions and worked hard to dissuade from violence those who choose to go down this futile path. Our best defence is found within the traditions of our faith and the higher principles of justice and humanity embedded in it.

Beyond this, the issue highlights a wider problem pertaining to the massive dislocation many young Britons feel. Young people from the white working class feel the same dislocation experienced by fellow Britons who happen to be black, Muslim or Jewish. Gun crime, domestic abuse and youth violence are other blights on our collective conscience that need our attention.

We are witnessing a changed, post-devolution Britain: a Britain where the Internet facilitates connections across borders but also gives way to fragmentation in local neighbourhoods. Separation, the watchword attached so simplistically and negatively to a diverse British Muslim community by misguided bishops, applies equally to other sections of the population. There are certainly many worthwhile initiatives undertaken across the land that aim to tackle these issues. Many of us in society set up projects to save our own children from social difficulties. But we often fail to appreciate that if our neighbours' children are not included in this endeavour, soon they will influence our own children as well. We swim or sink together. However, this sense of community togetherness must not be born only from a message of self-preservation but also because it is the right thing to do: to reach out regardless of the outcome or who the people are.

Many realise this, and we see light and hope at the end of the tunnel when we learn of communities coming together to tackle the social issues that affect them. Take the Citizen Organising Foundation as a case in point. This burgeoning organisation aims to create a network of competent, informed and organised citizens who act responsibly in the public life of their communities and are able to influence, for the common good, decisions which impact on their communities. During its short existence, this institution has campaigned for a living wage for our most vulnerable workers, sought to welcome those who have made Britain their home as fully fledged British citizens and sought to harness the power of local communities to tackle crime and disorder.

They are the focal point for an increasingly diverse alliance of congregations, community groups and labour organisations. Mosques have joined churches and synagogues to effect meaningful change across all sections of society. Those who help initiate change in such institutions are called 'community organisers' and draw inspiration from the United States, where such initiatives were born. The most famous community organiser was one Barack Obama, whose work in Chicago was instructive in his subsequent belief that great things can be achieved through collective action. Not only do the words and actions of Mr Obama the community organiser present our young people with a role model; they also underline the necessity for active citizenship. This demonstrates to all of us that people of all faiths and none should use the agency and requirement that exists within their own creed to seek the common good and the betterment of the whole of society.

Along with active citizenship, there is a need for active encounters. In the Muslim holy book, the Qur'an, God tells us 'O mankind, We have created you male and female, and appointed you races and tribes, so that you may know one another. Surely the noblest among you in the sight of God is the most God-conscious of you. God is All-knowing, All-aware' (Al-Hujurat, v. 14). How wrong we are to interpret and employ our 'otherness' to create division and discord while the primary purpose of this 'otherness' is simply to enhance awareness and understanding. It is also, like so many such exhortations in the Qur'an, a call to know and understand one another. These words are a call to all of us to go out and meet each other, share with each other and learn from one another. It is a clear repudiation of the idea that we must lead separate lives.

As I mentioned earlier, in spite of the knowledge revolution that is the Internet, we are in fact undergoing a compartmentalisation of knowledge that refuses to empathise and learn from others. Instead, the age of new media is in real danger of cementing ignorance of the other. The media was once small and focused, serving up knowledge and information to an audience under a prescription of comparative homogeneity. Knowledge sharing with the aim of informing, educating and entertaining was pioneered by the BBC, which held the hand of the British nation in bringing together a disparate empire and then of a British nation learning to live without vast territories overseas. The focus that the BBC gave to the media meant it was able to tell the new British story to one single audience united at first by the wireless and then through television. Welshmen laughed and learned at once with Scotsmen and Englishmen, and they all discovered the world around them as newcomers came their way. The BBC was a collective space that allowed us to know one another; we must now carve out a new public space where we can all be part of a national conversation without the shadow of prejudice, ignorance or misinformation cast over us.

As someone working in the field of education, I feel more can be done through our schooling system to remove ignorance and foster an active, collaborative citizenship. I believe it is a great pity that history is dropped by so many young people in secondary education in England, Wales and Northern Ireland when they progress from Key Stage 3 to Key Stage 4. (I believe almost 70 per cent of pupils discontinue the subject.) So we have many young people whose insights into the past are drawn mainly from television. There is so much that could be done if history were made a relevant and popular subject again, and strengthened with content of interest to the typically diverse school classroom in, for example, London or Birmingham. At the same time, we must go beyond the virtual and look to foster the public spaces that facilitate active encounters between the diverse peoples of Britain. Beyond school and the workplace, we need to cultivate regular opportunities for British people to meet and interact.

There is certainly a need to reappraise Britishness and determine a confident future and identity for all of us. The whole essence of being British is that our notion of national identity, like our constitution, is organic, understated and unassuming. We are bound together by our elegance and our sense of fair play, and this is what has been our constant animating force.

This is a discussion that takes place not because of Muslims or other minorities, but it should include Muslims and others as equal and valued stakeholders in that conversation. The Muslim faith community, for example, is evolving and learning to live with pluralism both within the community and in wider British society. Outside the hajj, the annual Islamic pilgrimage, the British Muslim community is perhaps one of the most diverse faith groups not only in Britain but also in the world. Bound together by that faith, but set apart because of a different experience of that faith, this paradox presents an opportunity where we can discover cosmopolitan values that will equip us for an uncertain globalised world. Muslims can contribute to the future progress of Britain by deriving values from their faith. That contribution has pedigree, and the sacrifice of British Muslims endures to this day with the continued participation of Muslim men and women in our armed forces, and our emergency and public services. Muslims have been part of Britain's success story and have helped contribute to the vitality of multicultural Britain.

BEING BRITISH AND
BECOMING BRITISH

NASEEM KHAN

W HEN MY HUSBAND WANTED TO ANNOY ME, HE USED TO deride the notion that birth determined identity. 'If you were born in a matchbox,' he'd say, 'would that make you a match?'

But paradoxically, a matchbox – something small, immediate and everyday – might be no bad place to start reflecting on Britishness. For it is at the micro level that our first identities are shaped. It is here that we acquire our first ideas about civic engagement – to vote or not to vote, to believe in its efficacy or not, or to believe in the benevolence or disinterest of government, and to acquire identification with being or not being British It is also currently an area at which several government initiatives are being targeted, with the praiseworthy aim (albeit insufficiently implemented) of activating, strengthening and empowering communities. And lastly, it is at the local level that the issues of diversity make themselves felt in a distinctive, sharp and unmistakeable way.

Living as I now do in London's East End, I see signs of them around me almost every day. During Ramadan, I wake around dawn and see pinpoints of lights going on in dark tower blocks where local Muslims are up and preparing for the meal and prayers before the day's fast. Out later in the day, I pass the St George's flag that a neighbour has mounted prominently on the roof of his house. And sitting on a graffiti-scrawled bench in a park that was created by Victorian philanthropists for the delectation and refreshment of

East Enders, I wonder about the relevance nowadays of that old heritage.

In such a fractured society, how realistic is it to look for a shared view of Britain and Britishness? In recent years, it has become common practice for those of us of non-British origin to talk about 'multiple identities', listing a number of allegiances that we claim we can hold in tandem. British-Asian, Asian, European, black British, white, Western, not to mention gender roles and familial ones.

Given that the mainstream portrayal of Britishness is so vague and unapproachable – mired in lofty ideals and grand institutions – it is hardly surprising that so many of us have grasped at this superficially attractive bloom. Information technology and its urge to make global communities of interest rather than those of locality and birth has made it seem even more a pattern for our times. But it could be up for questioning. For many years, I blithely espoused rootlessness and internationalism, but recent experiences have led me to rethink. Could it be too easy, I started to wonder – too much a case of wanting to have it all? Can identity really be simply an amalgam of elements, like a hopefully packed suitcase straining at the seams?

There is a way that 'multiple identities' tend to obviate or excuse choice, and even to encourage a moral skittishness. My Muslim background, for instance, had told me that female docility was good; my Western upbringing tells me that it is to be avoided. My multiple identity allows me to haver and prevaricate.

The emergence of the concept is easily explained: it is, in part, a device that helps maintain a necessary state of equilibrium. Particularly when one comes from families where values and value judgements are diverse, some accommodation has to be found. In my own case, I grew up with at least three versions of what being British meant, each of them mutually exclusive and each of them fiercely determined to push its own case. My parents might have been emigrating to two separate countries, so diverse were their views of Britain. To my father, coming from the chaos of pre-independence India, it was a haven of law and order, sobriety and predictability. To my mother, coming from the uniformity of Hitler's Germany, it was a place where individualism, eccentricity and social mobility could flourish. And when I was sent to an English public boarding school, Britishness presented itself to me in yet another guise. Roedean in the 1950s was a fiercely conservative milieu, full of girls who talked eagerly of pony clubs, Young Farmers' dances, dogs and debs (plus a very small, beleaguered group of Jewish and Parsee girls). Its ethos was Home Counties, its horizons were narrow and its politics were true dyed-in-the-wool blue. In my first term, I gathered near a noticeboard where the results of the general election were being posted. 'I don't suppose anyone here has parents who would ever vote Labour,' came a clear cut-glass voice. I knew – even at 11 – that this was not the time to announce that my parents did, that my grandfather was a staunch union activist and my father had campaigned for Indian independence. It was not that these areas were taboo but that they belonged to a less settled world, so foreign to my schoolmates as to be incomprehensible.

Ambiguity is a useful tool. It guarantees survival and, far more admirably, can lead a person to question: to not accept things as natural, inevitable and God-given. The position of being – as commentators such as Homi Bhabha have put it – 'in-between' has its virtues. It is a terrain in which nothing can be taken for granted and where there is no ancestral hiding place.

But it also denies a human need that is as established as the need for food, warmth and shelter. Community is vital to us: belonging matters. But belonging to what? The conventional view of Britishness, with its reliance on heritage, excludes those of us whose forebears were at the sharp end of imperial adventures. And the current emphasis on physical integration and its assumed correlation with emotional integration seems too simplistic, based more on alarm than on practicalities. The history of immigration has always shown that like goes to like. When African Asians were being expelled in the late 1960s and early '70s, Leicester took out advertisements in East African papers advising people not to come to that city, saying there were quite enough Asians there already. Predictably, this announcement proved to be an inducement rather than a deterrent. Leicester incidentally thrived with the input and is now set to be Britain's first city with a non-white majority.

Ghettoes get a bad press, but they are not intrinsically harmful. They provide support, infrastructure, ease of communication and security: the food you like, the clothes you want and the religion you favour, and this is as true in Cheltenham as it is in Southall. The problem lies not so much in the existence of ghettoes as in the difficulty of getting out of them. For, in actual fact, we all pick our ghettoes – places where we feel comfortable – but not all of us are confined to them.

And might the concept of multiple identities be said to be yet another ghetto: comfortable, but nevertheless an isolation? It runs the danger of turning its back on the sharp places where traditions collide, and rather than focusing on creating new identities, contents itself with maintaining a slew of old ones. It also fails to give adequate credence to the changes that have taken place, with the reinvention, along the way, of a form of Britishness. The history of immigration in this country has been nothing but a continuing tale of negotiation, confused and troubled though it has often been. Change has come about – my own parents, from the marginalised status they took for granted, would not be able to recognise society today. Masked by outward signs of visible difference, the manifestations of change are rarely noticed, for osmosis is at work and changes in attitudes take place quietly over time. Assumptions and perspectives become ingested silently, and a sense of 'Britishness' comes in similarly small and subtle ways – body language and concepts of personal space, for instance. Trevor Phillips once recounted how he was regularly tagged as British when he walked down a West African street, despite being black. It was because, it was explained to him, that he walked so quickly. 'Britishness' comes out in learned inhibitions – an acceptance, say, of the British disinclination to enthuse or hug. It comes with the indefinable sense of being back home that so many people of every type report on returning from abroad: hard to pin down, but unmistakeable in its presence. Language, rhythm, quality of light, interactions: who can say? I asked my 20-something son once what made him feel British. 'Well,' he said slowly, after reflection, 'it's when I can go into a pub and banter with the barman . . .' Being part of a country brings an awareness of what is appropriate in what sort of situation. You know without being told how far you can go, what the rules of engagement are, when to back off. They are small navigation marks that prevent wreckage on the hidden rocks of convention.

Back in the 1980s, as Asian comedy was taking off, a sketch of two streetwise youths mischievously made the point about unconscious absorption. They were in conversation, and one of them was curious about all the jewellery and copious religious symbols that his friend sported. 'What's this one then?' he asked, fingering a yin-yang symbol. 'Get your hands off,' his friend retorted. 'That's my ethnic heritage, innit?' And the crucifix? 'Oh, that?' he replied in an easier flow, 'That shows that Jesus Christ died for our sins on the cross and then he rose again on the third day, innit . . .'

That quality of knee-jerk Britishness – the easy parrot knowledge of Bible stories learned in primary school or of friendly banter in a pub – is fine so far as it goes. But it has more to say about familiarity than it does about deep in-the-bone belonging. It is not something that would ever appear in a canon of Britishness, or be taught in citizenship courses. Coming to feel British – or to become British rather than simply to be British – in a more profound way requires another process altogether. It requires a tool that is, I believe, all too rarely used.

An academic essay on Indian diasporic literature might not seem as if it would throw much light on the matter, but Professor Jasbir Jain's analysis pinpoints an area not commonly found in dissertations on migration. 'The New Parochialism: Homeland in the Writing of the Indian Diaspora' tracks the development of integration not through social statistics but through references to creative fiction written by migrated Indians. Jain argues that the way in which writers feel able to present their mother country to the country in which they have settled reveals states of belonging or unease. It is a litmus test, she suggests, of the community's own deepest attitudes. The timeline she traces goes from exotic representation of India – complete with footnotes and glossary to explain unfamiliar words – to a more freewheeling realm of fantasy and magic realism. Later, she says, writers come to focus on areas of cultural conflict and finally come to rest in a negotiated 'third space' that is neither Indian nor the traditional identity of their new country. The difference between the first and final steps neatly echoes Paul Gilroy's distinction between diversity being 'where you are at' rather than 'where you are from'.

The approach is intriguing in itself, but more to the point is the power that Jain gives to the imagination as a transformative force. Writers, in this formulation, act not only as mouthpieces for wider states of mind but also create the language that articulates those states. And it is imagination that is the missing element in the debate over Britishness and citizenship. Imagination is what lifts the issue from a sterile collection of abstractions, that can marry the grand design of Britishness with local understanding and make it real. And in that process, the disparate multiple identities find themselves taken on and fused.

These are grand words in themselves, but enough examples exist in the real world to demonstrate their validity. Inevitably it is in the arts that, first and foremost, the most obvious ones are to be found. I can think of no better instance than the large-scale event staged by the Akademi (once the Academy of Indian Dance) on the terraces and exterior of London's Southbank Centre in the summer of 2000. Indian classical dance has been present in Britain for almost as long as migration, but generally has been covert and contained within the home community. When I sought out a class myself, in the 1960s, I found myself wandering around the discreet backstreets of Chelsea looking for the unmarked house where the great dancer Ram Gopal had set up his school (a brave endeavour that was before its time and doomed to failure). It took all of those 40 years to cross the river to the South Bank, and an even greater quantum leap in thinking, scale and prominence. For where Ram's school had been uncertain and private, the Akademi event was confident and public. Called 'Coming of Age', it marked 21 years of the Akademi's life and brought together multitudes of dancers. They took over and colonised the open-air spaces, and crowds milled around the various stages taking in what was nothing but a who's who of Indian dance in all the varied styles that have anchored themselves in Britain – from Indian classical to hip-hop, from folk to Bollywood. Every corner seemed full of it. Turn one way and you'd catch sight of a group gravely performing a classical item on a flat roof of the complex, turn another and you'd see a limousine advancing along the river-walk to disgorge a crowd of bright hip-hop dancers. At the very top of the building itself, director Keith Khan had sited a single male dancer moving slowly in the classic series of liquid poses associated with Siva, the Hindu god of dance. The area hummed with vitality. Khan had seized all opportunities offered by the site and scrawled 'diverse Britain' vividly and firmly across it.

'Coming of Age' did not only make that point to the ten thousand who experienced it over two August evenings; it also constituted an act of ownership. None of the dancers who took part – from toddlers to octogenarians – are likely to look at this iconic site again without a sense of connection. And its location, at the very heart of London's cultural scene, established the dance as central to Britain and accessible to all. It was a far cry from a small studio in Chelsea or marginal community centres in the suburbs. Locally based, using the full gamut of Western stage technology, set up to speak to all types, ages and races, it was indeed a sort of coming of age.

It would be easy to list quite a number of other conversations in which artists have used their whole emotional and experiential range and – rather in the manner of using a kitchen – 'cooked' it to create a new expression of a state of being. It is – as the well-known choreographer Shobana Jeyasingh once described her own work – 'British, because I live here'. The formation of a different cultural language denotes the presence of a new attitude towards Britishness, and how to express it. Many artists of all types are now working at this fault line of identity and quarrying it. But I want to turn to another event that struck me in a different way, because it indicated how a sense of belonging can be shaped at a local level.

When I moved to the East End, I had not given much attention to the idea of community. I found myself in an intriguing and unexpected situation. My area was once a byword for East End working-class community – cohesive, supportive and family focused – and recorded by Michael Young and Peter Willmott in their *Family and Kinship in East London*. Its history had been a fine one: a haven first for Huguenot refugees and then Jews fleeing persecution. In recent times, Bangladeshi Muslims have come to form the next wave of arrivals on an estate that had been built in the 1890s by the brand-new London County Council as its very first foray into social housing.

But by the time I arrived, the area was giving every sign of having lost its heart, and the core of the old Boundary Estate showed that more than anything. Right at its centre, on Arnold Circus, the LCC architects had placed a little hill with gardens on two circular tiers, along with a delicate little bandstand. It was expected that the original inhabitants would promenade, socialise and listen to the band. And so they did. But as time went by, the bands retreated, the vegetation went wild and the bandstand got vandalised. Arnold Circus sat at the centre of the crumbling estate, shunned by the Bangladeshi families who made their way (as did everyone, except for the rumoured gangs and drug-dealers) round the hill – never up it and over it.

Two worlds were overlaid, on top of one another. In the background lay the old and very beautiful Boundary Estate, created by historic vision and idealism. A key moment in the development of British local democracy, it had come to seem little more than a backdrop to contemporary life and to an increasingly impoverished community. And to the Bangladeshi children at the primary school just next door to Arnold Circus, it was terra incognita.

Could the historic site be reclaimed and re-established in the popular imagination? In 2007, I became involved in a programme that sought to see if it could. The venture promised little at the start, for the gulf seemed too great. A number of children volunteered that it would be better to pull Arnold Circus down and build houses. Few of them were involved with growing anything, and when they went out on school trips were very squeamish about the natural world and its mud, beetles, worms and country mess. These were urban children, used to bricks and mortar, crowded flats and the asphalt of the courtyards amongst the buildings of the Boundary Estate. The tall, dark trees of Arnold Circus gardens and the tangled bushes and the creatures that inhabited them held no allure. Its history meant nothing.

For a whole year, the children focused on the Circus. They were brought up, class by class, to plant bulbs and flowers on it. They worked with a local community group and made bird-boxes for the site. They drew. They wandered around with clipboards and found things they wanted to write about – a small grave where someone had buried their much-loved pet rat, the evidence of a fox, the fact that the creatures that fell out of the trees when they banged them were so diverse and individual. They looked at them under microscopes and wondered at the variety of life up on the Circus. They heard about olden days in the earlier slums known as the Old Nichol and the significance of the new Boundary, and they found out about the waves of immigration – Huguenot, Jewish and their own Bangladeshi one – that had formed and shaped this area.

The survey taken at the end showed a decided shift in attitude, and one that subsequently spread slowly through the school. The children had engaged with it via their imagination and had themselves become part of its ongoing history. They had, said staff members, 'adopted' it. Children would drag their mothers up there to show them what they had planted. They were no longer so determined to kill every bug that crossed their path, teachers reported. 'Look, miss,' they had called proudly when they ushered a butterfly out of the classroom window, 'we're not killing it!' Views changed: 'It used to be all dark,' explained a nine-year-old girl, 'but now it feels like home.'

The example is an extended one, but to the point. The connection between community and identity had been obscure in Hampstead – the area was perhaps too secure for its inhabitants to question it. But in east London, with its shifting populations, it was possible to see it in action and as a dynamic force. People can – when the right conditions are created – come to own an area, and they need to do so. The act of writing oneself into a public space (as the dancers did on the South Bank) has a very particular potency. It is powerful and moving, especially when your roots are not there, and it is a road into identifying with that elusive state of 'Britishness'. And yet, in this particular case, it was so simple. All it required was focus, attention and time.

Between living in an area and living fully in an area lies a crucial world of difference. Citizenship has no real meaning without the latter – and maybe more than citizenship, claimed the recent review of the primary schools' curriculum. Professor Robin Alexander and his team were forthright in criticising the way that creativity has been pushed out in favour of a narrow focus on literacy and numeracy. It led, they considered, to inadequately educated and 'impoverished' children. The Arnold Circus example, in its small and contained exercise, proved the review's point. It showed that people – given the tools – make their own form of Britishness. The process has to be active, creative and forward-looking, and it has to come from people themselves. It responds to positive frameworks: it thrives where there are structures in place that enable creative expression and wider sharing. (This is why the government's initiatives around community engagement are lacking several vital cogs.) It starts at ground level – the local is its heartland – and grows outwards. In the process, it uses everything – our varying perspectives, histories, diversities – to hand. And its upshot is a healthy form of investment that is close to pride, but far better grounded.

Is it being British, or becoming British? Both coexist, the one passively acquired, the other actively shaped. I prefer the latter, because it carries a sense of critical self-awareness and openness to change. It is a perspective that has been particularly developed by those of us who have had to make our Britishness rather than inherit it. But as populations become more diverse – as they inevitably will, given our economic need for immigration – it carries lessons that could generate a newer and more flexible and relevant brand of Britishness.

8

DREAMING THE LAND

LIBBY PURVES

LET US BEGIN MANY, MANY MILES AWAY AND 30 YEARS AGO. When China was first tentatively opening to the West (but a decade before the Tiananmen Square massacre), it let in the Radio 4 *Today* programme, to make the first live broadcast from Beijing. As the presenter, I spent the preceding fortnight travelling round with the producer Steve Rose, the heavy old tape recorders of the day and a brace of interpreters called Shing Si-Ling and Mr Wong.

At first, in every conversation, they spouted cautious slogans, generally about the Four Modernizations and the need for Community Criticism. But as days went by, and they saw that we were interested in the good things about China as well as the dubious ones, we became friends; to the point that, as we left for the airport, Steve made Shing laugh immoderately with his parting gag: 'Now look, we'll be back in ten years. And if you've only got three of those Four Modernizations finished, I'll want to know why.'

There were farms and feasts, factories and palaces to visit, and dissidents and ministers to interview. But the moment which stays with me most vividly, and taught me a lesson which resonates to this day, happened when we went to walk on the Great Wall, rising and plunging in its dragon-scales along the sharp-peaked northern mountains. It was the clearest of days, and Shing and I walked a little apart from the others, talking about the immense journey that lay ahead for China: a journey of modernization and – he admitted, in that lonely place – political change. He grew quiet for a few minutes as we puffed up to a peak, and at the top he stopped. When I caught up, I saw tears of emotion shining in his eyes as he looked into the green and grey distances, at the odd symmetrical peaks and the rise and fall of the Wall.

He smiled and said softly, 'A journey of a thousand miles starts with a single step. If we fail to reach the Great Wall, we are no heroes.' I recognized Chairman Mao's line. And I knew, of course, about the lies and twistings and propaganda, the deaths and dissimulations and the semi-legendary quality of the Long March. But at the same time I saw Shing's eyes shining. This was no fanatic: a pragmatic, earnest, well-read and socially aware man with a strong streak of human kindness. But the words lifted him out of himself, into a higher dream, a Platonic archetype of a China that maybe never was but which might yet be striven for. And thoughts of crazy wonderful old William Blake came to me: 'I shall not cease from mental fight, / Nor shall my sword sleep in my hand.'

I realized that if you are ever to get close to a country, you have to accept and understand the daydreams it has about itself: the idea (to pick up the Judaeo-Christian image) that everyone needs, of what would constitute the Jerusalem in your green and pleasant land. The daydreams may sometimes be dated; worse, they may be adopted and fostered by charlatan leaders for evil ends: like Hitler's Aryan dream. They may be qualities that the nation itself has rarely lived up to. But the very persistence of these national daydreams, their ability to hook onto their people's inward desires and linger in a million hearts, makes them something vital to understand and respect.

So what are ours? Some of them are obvious, even hackneyed, and part of their charm is that Britons are a little embarrassed about them, a little ironic. A high point of the Golden Jubilee year was standing on the Mall looking up at the tiny form of the Queen on the balcony, and roaring out 'Land of Hope and Glory' with 2 million others. The pleasure was doubled, rather than halved, when I looked around at the grins of others and realized that even as we hit 'wider still and wider', none of us really wanted India or the Caribbean back. Not even a bit.

But the tunes, the dreams, are part of us, whether imperial or gentle, hierarchical or democratic or an impossible mixture of both. (TV's *Upstairs, Downstairs* pulled off a brilliant double many years ago by feeding both the sentimental attachment Britain has to lords and ladies and upright Scottish butlers, and the leftie instinct to side with downtrodden parlour-maids and betrayed maidens.) Pastoral and metropolitan, heroic and comedic dreams can all live together in this mazy mush of feeling.

So I felt the same sadness as many others when Mark Damazer axed the Radio 4 early morning theme tune in favour of what he rashly called a 'pacy news bulletin'. As a small-boat sailor, I had often heard this distillation of daydreams while creeping out of harbours into grey threatening dawns and been buoyed up by Fritz Spiegl's composition. A medley of national tunes put together by an Austrian who came here at thirteen and loved us as only a refugee can, it was a five-minute master-class in national identity daydreams. It began with 'Rule, Britannia', rendered with more playfulness than pomp, then eased into the 'Londonderry Air', expressing the mournfulness of the Irish fringe. Then 'Annie Laurie' as counterpoint from the other side of the Celtic sea; whereon drums kicked in for the drunken sailor who links the islands together and hurls their trade and power out across the globe. He in turn was mischievously interwoven with Henry VIII's courtly 'Greensleeves', then 'Men of Harlech' marched through, and the betrayed rustic maiden of 'Early One Morning' got her moment. Add a quick trumpet voluntary, 'Scotland the Brave' and a final burst of 'Britannia' (who I always think of as ruling her waves from the back of a big old penny piece) and that was the finale. It cleared the morning air. I have heard that tune at sea, in a frozen lambing yard at dawn, on grey motorways; I have fed babies in the weary dawn hours and murmured half-jokingly 'See, brat? You're British. Islands, rocks, sailors, trumpets, kings and queens, milkmaids, rolling history. Whatever's in the news, Britain can take it.'

But the tune was axed, and conspiracy theorists put it down (wrongly, I think) to modish BBC leftishness and post-imperial embarrassment. I remember thinking that actually, I wouldn't have minded if some more modern Britishnesses had been woven in – a bit of reggae, perhaps, a dash of bhangra, a wisp of the Euro-conscious 'Ode to Joy', a hip-hop moment and a football anthem. Because national daydreams grow and change, feeding off each other and twining into multicoloured richness. And their insubstantial nature means that many of them can coexist quite comfortably in the same head.

Cultural consumption gives both an illustration and a clue. There is no reason that somebody who enjoys the pastoral-nautical-royal-sentimental emotions of the old UK theme may not also have an affection for the raucous tradition of the Mersey beat, the sweet-natured absurdities of glam rock, or the urban energy of hip-hop. One can enjoy Hampton Court and

Tate Modern with equal pleasure (and an equal dose of scepticism about their significance). Many of the young crowd at the London Hippodrome, whooping with joy at the Anglo-Spanish comedy strip act from Croydon, Ursula Martinez, and the Freddie Mercury juggling tribute act entitled 'Mario, Queen of the Circus', will be found a month or two later among the standing groundlings at Shakespeare's Globe. They may on the way have taken in a night or two at a hip-hop club and an old Tony Hancock repeat on the telly. Go to Oxford and you find that the city's identity and flavour is as much bound up with lost causes, intellectual Marxists, morris dancing at dawn, Lord Nuffield's car industry and trades union scholars at Ruskin College as it is with rich yahoos at the Bullingdon Club and earnest theologians at St Benet's hall. The nation may bafflingly adore Posh and Becks and *Celebrity Big Brother*, but when polled on its favourite poem, it always seems to go for Kipling's 'If'.

The somewhat vapid, but entertaining, early New Labour obsession with BritArt, pop, multiculti festivals and painfully self-conscious modernity was just another facet of this confusing interwoven diversity. It was only a problem because particularly at the millennium they bossily wanted to outlaw every older daydream, banning military bands and history from the Dome and insisting against all reason that we are 'a young country'. Even so, determined campaigners managed to sneak a copy of the Tyndale Bible into the Dome display. And the Frenchman M. Gerbeau, brought in to manage the place, was utterly bewildered at the absence of shiny-helmeted Horse Guards. He thought they were *magnifique* and *historique*. He could not see the problem in mixing them with the Damien-Hirstery of today. Any more than the English language has a problem with mixing up its ancient Saxon, Norman and Celtic roots with borrowings from every other tongue on the globe.

So who are we, where are we? Everywhere and nowhere, baby, as Scott English (an American) wrote in the '60s. We have adopted his song 'Hi Ho Silver Lining' as we adopt everything we fancy: many a pub crowd and Wolverhampton Wanderers stand will now happily roar it, beer in fist, Saturday after Saturday in this mixed-up, ironic land. Everywhere and nowhere, running down a hillside, feeling unexpectedly groovy: that's us.

Sing and shine. Britishness is – like every national identity – a mishmash of more or less inaccurate but immensely nourishing daydreams. Some are shared by Britain's immigrants (if you want a real Kipling fan, try an educated Pole; if you seek a proper old-fashioned matriarch out of Dickens, she'll be Jamaican). New communities that won't join in are, indeed, a problem to themselves; but their problem is only that they are trapped in their own narrower cultural daydreams of the Gulf or the subcontinent. Whenever they lighten up and throw their own dreams into the mad, rich mix, they (and we) do just fine. Hi ho! Dream on, Britain.

BRITISHNESS AND THE
MIDDLE CLASS

DYLAN JONES

L AST YEAR, IN FEBRUARY 2008, THE RADIO 4 *WOMAN'S HOUR* presenter Jane Garvey said her programme was too middle class, as though this were an inherently bad thing. She didn't endear herself to her listeners by saying her programme focused too much on cooking and women's problems and should be more upbeat to attract younger listeners, but the main thrust of her interview with *The Guardian*, or at least the thing she said that resonated the most, was the middle classness of it:

> I would also like to have . . . less middle-class ladies talking about cookery. Although there is nothing wrong with cookery . . . I think there is a massively middle-class bent to every programme on Radio 4. Find me a programme that isn't like that.

There are few things that could be more British than the middle class, but they are an endangered species. Don't believe me? Just look around you. And ask people if they're happy being labelled that way. The middle classes are the new minority.

Many years ago, as the 1970s swiftly turned into the 1980s, I was briefly a member of a post-punk group called the Timing Association, an overly intense art-school five-piece whose songs weren't quite as clever as Orange

Juice and not quite as loud as the Buzzcocks. Having released a single – 'It's Magic', and you won't be surprised to learn that it wasn't, not in the slightest, not at all – we began having 'creative differences', arguing on a daily basis about everything from the singer's hair (the rest of us thought it was too short) to the lead guitarist's trousers (too wide, made of denim, wrong provenance). The only thing we could agree on was our name: it was rubbish.

But what did for us, the thing that caused us to split up before our 'groundbreaking eponymous first album' (our first single was our last single) was class. One night after a torturous rehearsal in the middle of Leyton in north London (the band next door were called the Armitage Shanks Band), our singer, Colin (you can tell we weren't going to be big), abruptly walked out, throwing his metaphorical toys out of the pram as he did.

'What's wrong?' I asked as he pushed open the heavy studio door.

'I can't work with him [the lead guitarist] any more,' he said, looking for all the world like a man who had just been asked if he had ever slept with his sister.

'Why not?' I countered, feeling a little like Bette Davis in some 1930s melodrama.

'Why not?' he screamed, in his broken Midlands drawl. 'He's middle class, that's why not. And I can't play in a band with someone who's middle class.'

I was only 19 at the time, and I'd rarely heard that most fundamental of British diseases articulated with such clarity. The ability to claim a working-class background was all the rage at the time, as this was one of the defining tenets of punk rock, one that most of us involved felt duty-bound to lie about. The divisions between the middle class and the working class (who had only just stopped being labelled 'lower class') were never more pronounced – at least not for my generation – and musicians and journalists alike would bang on for ages in the music press about 'authenticity' and how any kind of privileged background (i.e. not being brought up in a council flat in Hackney) was mutually exclusive to 'cool', 'credibility' and acceptability.

For the Timing Association the clock had stopped, although we almost felt at the vanguard of something when we heard that a short while later the Specials – who had just had an enormous hit with 'Ghost Town' – had essentially split up for the same reason, their singer Terry Hall complaining that it was difficult for him to work in a band that contained middle-class musicians.

Back in the days of punk, as soon as a band were discovered to be middle class and – worse – intent on disguising the fact, the critics started sharpening their pencils and oiling their Remingtons. There were precious few who escaped this forensic attention, and even fewer who were let off. Joe Strummer was one, strangely. The son of a diplomat (not the son of a bank robber), educated at public school, when he joined the punk fraternity he totally changed the way he spoke, adopting an almost subterranean mockney drawl that only the Sex Pistols' John Lydon had the gumption ever to question. (Interviewer: 'Do you really hate Joe Strummer?' John Lydon: 'Of course not. Joe's a very nice bloke. He's just ashamed of his own class roots.') Mick Jagger, on the other hand, the most famous mockney of them all, didn't care what people thought of him, and his appropriation of someone else's voice was always thought of as either cute or faintly ridiculous; and because he wasn't aligned to any movement – or at least no movement celebrating the overthrow of a cultural orthodoxy by a largely proletarian underclass – he was welcomed as a harmless cartoon. Of course, the '60s were completely about class empowerment, but there was no 'year zero' like there was in the '70s, and you didn't have to disguise where you came from. And in Jagger's case, the voice didn't really kick in until later.

Class was important when we were young, and it was openly referred to in our house. My parents were part of a generation who had escaped the working class through sheer hard work, by devoting themselves to bettering their positions and embracing the social mobility of the 1950s and 1960s. They were under the impression that being aspirational was a thoroughly decent thing, almost a *raison d'être*, although they knew the path to prosperity wasn't smooth. 'Everyone will hate you when you grow up because you're middle class,' my mother told me encouragingly when I was about 14. 'The upper classes will hate you because they'll think you're encroaching upon them; the working class will hate you because you're trying to leave them behind; and the middle class will hate you because they see themselves in you, and don't want to be reminded of where they came from. And they all came from the same place.'

But that was long ago, before the death of our manufacturing industry and the birth of the leisure class, before Thatcherism made class a by-product of economic reform. If you were part of the economic miracle you found your way into a gated community, and if you weren't you ended up on a sink estate. The working class became the underclass as everyone else supposedly became middle class, seduced by the thought of a job in 'light industrial', a semi in a Home Counties new town and a spanking new burgundy Mondeo. Of course, the middle classes are different to what they used to be, but they aren't fundamentally different. As Penny Wark said in *The Times* in 2008:

> What distinguishes the contemporary middle classes is that they have established new ways of identifying themselves. The affluent are middle class because they have the money, the educated are middle class irrespective of whether they have money, and we live among people like ourselves because that way we belong.

It's instinctive as much as anything else, but why are we afraid of saying so? New Labour even tried to convince us we were living in a classless society, a meritocracy with no glass ceilings and no class barriers. 'We're all middle class now,' the former deputy prime minister John Prescott famously said in 1997, although you'd be hard pushed to find anyone to admit to it these days. Under classifications produced by the Office for National Statistics, more than half the population is embraced by the new middle class. Over 50 per cent now fit the long-standing (and traditionally middle-class) National Readership Survey social grades A, B and C1 (those who work in professional, managerial and other white-collar jobs) for the first time in British history. The proportion working in manual jobs, what we used to call the working class, has fallen from 75 per cent a century ago, via 36 per cent in 1987, to 12 per cent today.

But try getting anyone to own up to it. We just don't want to know. Being middle class has become anathema to the modern ideal, to the very idea of being modern. And where once the middle classes were inviolate, now they are besieged at every turn.

A 2008 report from the National Centre for Social Research proved that far from enjoying the fruits of upward social mobility, most people aspire to the bottom of the barrel, or at least enjoy giving the perception that they do. A staggering 57 per cent of Britons believe themselves to be working class, ignoring the fact that only a relatively small percentage are actually employed in traditionally poorly paid, low-prestige jobs. Middle-class angst has manifested itself as a socio-economic diaspora, a nation of mockneys in Great Estuarial Britain. At the time, the *Daily Telegraph* did a vox pop of public figures, asking them which social class they considered themselves to belong to, and it was shocking how many middle-class notables found it impossible to admit to their ranking. Everyone had some sort of excuse, some clever way of denying their birthright: 'professional class', 'bohemian class', 'classless', 'the class of educated people', 'upper working class' or 'business class', as though they'd simply been asked to choose how they'd like to fly. The new moneyed middle class – those who have risen through the ranks – still think of themselves as well-to-do working class, while the traditional middle class find themselves incapable of owning up to what they are: 'Well, I suppose you could call us middle class, although we're not really like that at all.' Like what? Such is the stigma of being middle class in the twenty-first century. Bizarrely, at an age when I might reasonably be expected to join the Establishment, I fear I am in danger of becoming a minority.

Even David Cameron has a problem with the classification. When I interviewed him last year and asked him whether he was middle class or upper class, he said, a little disingenuously, 'I don't really buy these labels.' When I pushed, he said, 'Gun to my head, I suppose I'd describe myself as well off. I don't buy these class things because they're all going. What do these labels mean any more?' Of course he would never want to admit to being upper class (which he most certainly is), but if he hates being called upper class so much, what on earth is wrong with being called middle class?

These days, being middle class is as socially acceptable as herpes. In fact, I hear that in certain circles the latter is positively an advantage: 'Those with a sexually transmitted disease signifying a wayward and therefore socio-economically fashionable past, to the left. Those of you determined not to employ a glottal stop or aspire to drive a white van, to the right.'

And boy do they mean 'the right'. Politically, the middle classes are nowadays demonised as unacceptably right wing, upholders of the sort of family values no longer aspired to by the new meritocratic working class or the politically correct metropolitan commentariat. Where once the worst thing you could accuse the middle class of was aspiring to a petit bourgeois lifestyle, these days they are assumed to be politically venal rather than politically apathetic. When Paul Dacre, the editor-in-chief of the *Daily Mail* – the bastion of old-fashioned middle-class values – spoke out against the tyranny of the British media's liberal agenda, he was criticised by every left-wing journalist with access to a column. And what did Dacre espouse? Oh, simply madcap ideas like community, clamping down on crime, curtailing immigration, monitoring the welfare state and celebrating marriage. 'Now, more than ever, we need our middle classes,' he said. 'What possible explanation can there be [for fewer claiming to be middle class these days]? Well, one immediately springs to mind. It is that under New Labour, the liberal chatterers who constitute so much of the media and established political class openly sneer at the middle classes.'

Not only that, but we – the middle class, for I am one of the few people to readily admit my class – are now also penalised for being the engine of prosperity, and for being educated and aspirant. School-leavers are penalised by a university admission policy that encourages ethnicity above qualifications, we have been told that in future we could be taxed for having pleasant homes with attractive views, and road pricing – should it ever come in – will fall especially heavily on the middle classes. Though many middle-class inhabitants can't afford the property or the big-ticket items they may have aspired to a generation ago (their class being visible more in smaller consumer choices, particularly those concerning culture), their values and their aspirations for their children, and their obsessive devotion to educating them, is not only what sets them apart; it's also what defines them. And yet they are castigated for this – even by other members of their class. Even the middle classes hate each other sometimes. According to *The Times*, 'The middle classes drink too much. They're in debt. They worry about their health. They agonise over their children's education and are prepared to tell porkies to get their kids into a good school.'

Culturally, 'middle class' is now the ultimate pejorative, and belonging to the middle class – or at least admitting to being middle class – is fast becoming as socially unacceptable as voting Tory still is to the Islington Media Mafia. In 1995, when she gave her infamous MacTaggart Lecture at the Edinburgh International Television Festival, Janet Street-Porter challenged the 'male, middle-class, middle-aged' orthodoxy of TV executives as though the poor sods were rapists or muggers. In his BBC Four film *The New Middle Classes*, broadcast in 2007, Tim Lott said that, 'The children of Thatcher and Blair don't want to be middle class, they just want more stuff. I call them the moregeoisie.' When critics accuse the middle class of being 'smug', it's implicit that they obviously don't think they're middle class themselves. But, I ask myself, what exactly do they think they are?

Ironically – and how laden that word is with sarcasm – being labelled middle class assumes that you have for some reason 'had it easy', as though it is only the working class who can pull themselves up by their bootlaces (or are allowed to), ignoring the middle classes' obsession with self-fulfilment, with betterment, with the work ethic. Forget not that the middle class – or at least what we think of as the middle class these days – are simply the offspring of the working class who made good, who had the opportunity, the luck and the determination to 'get on'. Despising the middle class is not snobbery; it's a refusal to acknowledge a thirst for success, as though wanting to be middle class was somehow a demonstration of anti-socialist values.

This has nothing to do with the dignity of labour, has little to do with any identification with the working class of yore. No, for the new culturally downwardly mobile generation, culture and individuality are more important than heritage or family. 'Nowadays, most of those who claim to be working class had middle-class parents,' says the psychologist Oliver James. 'They aspire to working classness because of its associations with authenticity – and to conceal the proverbial silver spoon in their mouth.'

Where once the difference between the middle and the working class was a determination by the former to use the word 'loo' instead of 'toilet', nowadays the differences revolve around the latter's determination to wear outlandish designer clothes and talk like Damon Albarn.

But if everyone treats the middle class as the epitome of unacceptable bourgeois values, then the middle class will themselves soon become the new minority. Which means that in a few years you're no doubt going to see gangs of feral youths lounging around on street corners comparing their comprehension homework, showing off their freshly ironed chinos and arguing about the correct way to pronounce 'heterogeneous'.

It looks like Huey Lewis was right: sometimes it is hip to be square.

10

BARRIERS TO BELONGING: OVERCOMING THE CHALLENGES TO DEVELOPING A BRITISH IDENTITY AMONGST BRITISH MUSLIMS

RAJA MIAH

FOR NEARLY 20 YEARS I HAVE SPENT TIME WORKING ALONGSIDE young people from Britain's Muslim communities in a variety of community development roles. The vast majority of Britain's Muslim community are of South Asian descent, predominantly Pakistani or Bangladeshi, and tend to have a higher probability of appearing near the bottom of government tables that record poverty and underachievement; hence young people from these communities have always been the target of the latest government community interventions.

During both my time working alongside young people from these very communities and drawing upon my own life experiences, I have developed a comprehensive understanding of the many challenges faced by these young people. As with all groups of young people from ethnic minority communities, one of the key challenges they face revolves around their sense of belonging. While the majority of these are born in this country, some of whom are now third- and, indeed, fourth-generation UK-born, there still remains the challenge amongst them of both where their loyalty lies and as to whether the wider 'white' communities actually do accept them as truly belonging here.

Indeed, this notion of being British, continuously debated in the public arena, is of particular relevance to young people from the Muslim communities, particularly in light of recent events such as the 7 July bombings, where British-born ethnic minority young men identified so much with an alternative identity that they were willing to indiscriminately attack their fellow British citizens. Such recent events have placed particular importance upon this debate, and the historical approach to developing a sense of belonging that gradually overcomes prejudices and perceptions over a period of time no longer seems the most appropriate way in which to respond. With the potential of such disasters being repeated, there is an acknowledgement amongst many who work in this field that there is a need to be more proactive in supporting British-born Muslim young people in developing a strong sense of identity with Britain through which they can become resilient towards those who attempt to undermine their loyalty and sense of belonging, sometimes with very dangerous consequences.

By simply examining recent historical events and the political climate that we currently live in, it is all too easy to see why we must successfully increase the sense of belonging to our nation felt by young Muslims. The 7 July bombings and the subsequent government attempts to prevent the exposure to, and growth of, extremist ideology amongst young people from Muslim backgrounds have placed an added emphasis on a challenge that has been bubbling away in the background for as long as I can remember. Prior to the emergence of British-born terrorists attacking their own country, developing a sense of identity was seen by many to be a natural process strengthening over time. Unfortunately, recent events have shifted the focus where it is possible to sense the emergence of battle lines being drawn, where those of us who are seeking to strengthen British identity amongst Muslim young people are competing against an almost invisible alliance of individuals, organisations and schools of thought that see a British identity as, at best, insignificant and of no relevance to the lives, ideals, values and, of course, loyalties of British Muslims.

In my time living and working within these communities, I have come across very few people who would describe themselves as exclusively British. At best it would be followed by the word Muslim (to become British Muslim) or with the attachment of their ethnicity (British Asian, British Bangladeshi or British Pakistani, for instance). Now while the reference to ethnicity is not something exclusive to these communities (I know of many people who would describe themselves as Black British, for example), describing themselves through faith is something that we tend not to see other minority groups do. It is clear that this faith-based description is also a recent occurrence. The parents and grandparents of the young people whom I work alongside still tend to describe themselves through ethnicity rather than faith. You may have already begun to wonder why I make this distinction and why it is important. Let me try to explain.

When people from these communities describe themselves through their ethnicity, it is easier for them to develop a sense of attachment and, indeed, identity with Britain. There is the immediate link of the British Empire and the Commonwealth, where, most significantly, Britain has historically successfully integrated numerous ethnic groups into the British identity. Developing a sense of identity here is pretty much straightforward. We can examine the history books, find the untold or little-heard-of stories and demonstrate both to people from the minority ethnic background and those that already feel a strong sense of belonging how this particular minority group has contributed to the development of our nation. It has always been easy to demonstrate this through the contributions during times of war (times that always enhance a sense of patriotism felt by all concerned). This very technique has been used to develop a sense of belonging of all of the major immigrant communities in the twentieth century – the wartime Eastern Europeans, the post-war African Caribbeans and, indeed, South Asians. My own father stepped off a boat to live in Britain after serving in the Second World War, and when I learned of this as a young adult my sense of belonging immediately increased.

Where there is a common sense of history it is always easier to develop a sense of belonging. British ethnic communities' loyalty to Britain, though not always clearly evident on the surface (as clearly demonstrated by the infamous Tebbit 'cricket test'), is nevertheless real and means that such individuals and communities will never seek to cause harm to the nation in which they live. In fact, the thought would not even enter their minds. Clearly the situation is not always the same when we see young people from these very same communities describe themselves as British Muslim.

The greatest challenge facing Muslim communities today is how to develop and increase the sense of belonging to Britain amongst Muslim youth. There is a risk, whether people choose to acknowledge it or not, that if young people from these communities do not have a strong sense of identity with being British then they are more vulnerable to being exploited by those with extremist ideologies and intent.

This challenge, of developing a sense of belonging amongst a group that describe themselves through faith rather than ethnicity, is different from those that we have previously encountered in recent times. There is a certain sense of irony that these young people's parents and, in some cases, grandparents, who came here as adults despite facing far greater challenges of acceptance and, indeed, injustice and prejudice, consider themselves to be more British than their British-born children, who live in a society far more accepting than that of their parents' generation.

To begin to respond to this challenge, first of all we must identify why this situation exists and then develop specific interventions to respond to it. I have identified key challenges that need to be successfully responded to in order to develop a stronger sense of belonging amongst young British Muslims. Most significantly, the challenges that I have identified primarily lie within attitudes and behaviours from the Muslim communities rather than the usual but, indeed, still relevant and therefore well-discussed external challenges of poverty, prejudice, inequality and discrimination. It is my opinion that more needs to be done from within these communities alongside the valuable work that has taken and is taking place to tackle injustices from outside them, and in recent times, as a society we have spent considerable time and effort addressing these issues and challenges. Much progress has been made, but the situation has stalled in recent times. I think it is now time to refocus where we place our efforts. To maximise the progress already made, we now need to respond to the challenges within Muslim communities that are working against us in supporting young people from these communities in developing a stronger sense of belonging.

A BARRIER OF PERCEPTION

Young people who should have a strong sense of belonging with Britain often do not have as strong a sense as I would like to see. Far too often, conversations I have and witness go down the usual line of 'I'm British *but . . .'*

Their perception is that by being British, Muslim young people have to give up something of what they value within their identity. I often question where they get this impression from, for as far as I am concerned I have never seen a group give something up to become British; rather they bring the best of their traditions and enhance and enrich the Britishness that is valued across the world.

My conversations with these young people always identify a key barrier that inhibits them from identifying with Britain, developing a sense of loyalty and, indeed, patriotism towards this country. First and foremost, it is a belief that you are either one or the other. This myth has done more to prevent developing a sense of belonging than all of the other challenges combined. To overcome this as a society we need to accept and champion the concept of multiple identities. None of us is either one or the other, whatever these constructs may be. For instance, we are neither exclusively English nor exclusively British, neither Scottish nor British and, indeed, neither Welsh nor British. Depending upon the circumstances, we tend to identify with one identity more than another that we may have, but the emphasis is on the 'more', not 'instead of'. We have successfully achieved this, to varying levels, when identifying ourselves through ethnicity, but as yet we appear to be facing difficulties when attempting to do this through faith. My response to all of the Muslim young people with whom I work is that you do not become less of a Muslim through developing a strong sense of identity and patriotism with the land of your birth.

So where is the pressure coming from that results in this feeling that they have to choose one over the other? Of course, the manner in which the popular media has facilitated the multicultural debate over recent years has not helped. Far too often the only voices that are heard in this domain are those calling for young people from Muslim communities to become more British, without an appreciation of the barriers and exclusions they face that push them away from embracing a British identity. These voices are usually countered by individuals within the Muslim communities that openly criticise those with a strong sense of belonging, loyalty and patriotism as 'selling out'. In this climate, it is far easier for young people to conform to the pressures from within their communities than it is to seek to align themselves with what is often considered to be the bigoted views of outsiders.

There is a clear need to increase the profile and understanding of multiple identities both amongst those outside and within Muslim communities. Only through helping to create a climate where Muslim young people feel that they do not have to choose one identity at the expense of another will we begin to successfully counter the voices of the bigots and extremists from across all of our communities; voices which, in my opinion, do not want young Muslims to develop and improve their sense of belonging with our nation.

A BARRIER OF HISTORY

Secondly (and potentially controversially), when I have these very conversations, I often find that my desire to support Muslim young people in developing a strong sense of belonging with Britain is met with resistance from many of my peers who work alongside me. These adults do not consider themselves to be 'British', thus increasing the challenge when supporting Muslim young people. Of course adults have developed their ability to disguise or, indeed, legitimise their opinions; often they will talk of the exploitation of the empire or their experiences of racism and use this to show how they do not really belong here. This characteristic is not exclusive to Muslim adults working with young people; to a certain extent I have seen the very same traits when I've worked within traditional African Caribbean communities.

In most cases I am an outsider, brought in to deliver a specific programme or activity. In this context, my views of Britishness and belonging are nearly always ridiculed. These adults have the respect of their young people, with whom they have spent years developing these relationships – often these adults live in the very same communities as the young people. In such situations it is almost impossible to champion a sense of belonging amongst the younger generation.

I recently read of plans for testing Muslim imams to ensure that their teachings do not run counter to the values of our society. I cannot help but speculate how many Muslim youth workers, teachers, community leaders and, indeed, elected members would fare in such tests.

Of course, the experiences of these adults and their subsequent views have validity. I just cannot help thinking that their position makes it even more difficult to support young people from their communities, especially when in many cases the young people will never have encountered the prejudices and discrimination that the adults speak of, and would not feel any historical sense of injustice if not for one-sided accounts of the actions of the empire.

I often wonder why we fail to address this. The easiest way would be to train these adults, ensuring that they were up to a certain standard before letting them loose anywhere near young people. Of course, training takes place, but clearly the baggage that these adults carry with them is not addressed during whatever professional training they receive.

Additionally, the more of these young people that are positively supported by adults from different ethnic and religious backgrounds, the better the benefits for their sense of belonging will be. Forming positive relationships with adults who are different in faith and ethnicity will help build solidarity across communities as the young people experience the shared humanity across different groups and strengthen their ties with wider society. Additionally, they will come to realise and, indeed, value the fact that the outside world is not full of 'non-Muslims' who see them as the enemy. Unfortunately, in my experience the vast majority of community services for young people from these communities are delivered by adults who share their ethnic and religious identities. While there has been much talk of overcoming segregation within our communities post the 2001 disturbances in the northern mill towns, very little has changed in this area. Step into any town or city in the country and one will find that black people deliver community services to black people, Muslims to Muslims and so on. While this continues in the manner I describe, it will be almost impossible to strengthen the sense of belonging of young people from Muslim communities.

A BARRIER THROUGH WEAKENING SECULARISM

This situation is not helped by the greater emphasis on faith. I see a growing number of faith-based organisations delivering more and more initiatives to young people. This almost always results in South Asian Muslim (mainly Pakistani or Bangladeshi) adults delivering services to young people from the same background. Where the young people do not have the benefit of being supported by adults from different communities (something they would have been more likely to encounter in a traditional secular delivery context), it is far easier for them to feel that they do not belong and that there is no place for them in modern-day Britain. The combination of the negative media attention on their apparent lack of patriotism, the pressure from their very communities not to 'sell out' and the reinforcement of negative opinions from adults working with them create a situation where it is almost impossible to develop a strong sense of belonging.

A simple and effective response to this challenge would be to ensure that these adults are better trained and to ensure that within these communities we continue to provide interventions with a secular perspective. In the government's attempts to positively respond to the extremist threat, an unintended and damaging outcome has been the reinforcement of exclusive mono-ethnic and, indeed, mono-faith contact, often facilitated by those with little or no loyalty, patriotism, or sense of belonging to Britain. On the surface, many of these individuals and groups are well versed in making the right noises in public, but their practice within their communities with Muslim young people is not helping develop their sense of belonging. As far as I am concerned, developing a sense of belonging is critical to ensuring that these young people are resilient to extremists' attempts to exploit them. In my field of work, an appreciation of equality and diversity is a compulsory component for all professionals; unfortunately, the emphasis has been exclusively on how minority groups' needs are met rather than dealing with the prejudices held by professionals from these minority groups.

THE BARRIER OF EQUALITY

The final challenge is the potential expansion of Muslim faith schools. With the growth of a faith-based identity amongst Muslim young people, I have witnessed an increasing demand for Muslim faith schools. Historically few in number, these institutions have been increasing year on year, and while in the past they have been privately funded, there is now a growing call for these schools to become state supported. Calls for such Muslim schools tend to be loudest in communities that suffer high levels of segregation, under-achievement and, indeed, poverty. In such communities there is a growing sense of feeling that the mainstream has failed and that an alternative needs to be tested. Of course, the growing politicisation of the British Muslim community has led to a situation in which a range of alternatives is not systematically examined; rather, it is easier for the community to interpret the failure of a Western approach as meaning that a Muslim approach is the obvious alternative.

I am disappointed that the government has not taken a stronger position here. As these calls increase, far too simplistic arguments champion the cause of state-funded Muslim schools: the Christians have got theirs; we should be allowed to have ours. These arguments have no historical grounding: once examined, it would be found that Christian faith schools pre-date state schools because the Church was delivering education long before the state became involved.

Even when you put aside the historical context, I struggle to see how single Muslim schools will enhance a young person's sense of belonging. If anything, it will further segregate them from mainstream society and remove any opportunity that they would have had to positively interact and build relationships with people from outside their immediate community. Nor do I for one minute believe the myth that these schools will also attract non-Muslim young people, based upon the current levels of diversity within Muslim schools. I would also ask my non-Muslim readers, would you honestly send your child to be educated in a Muslim school? I doubt very much that many of you would.

Of course, as with all of the other barriers identified so far, an alternative intervention is also needed. After all, we cannot simply continue where we see too many instances of the state failing young people from Muslim communities in their education. One of our core values of being British is our continuous strive for equality. As with all of the other challenges, there is a simple solution here. For a number of years I have been championing the concept of multi-faith schools. Being a secular Muslim (as indeed are the majority of Muslims living in the United Kingdom), I see the similarities in values and teachings promoted across all of the major faiths. There is no reason why we cannot create multi-faith institutions that accommodate all of these faiths. I came very close to helping create such an institution only for it to be blocked by a local authority at the final stages. Both the Church of England and leading Muslim figures were positive towards the concept, as both groups understood my premise that if we do not create space for Muslims within the mainstream then they will seek to create their own separate provision. Separate provision increases the barriers to belonging.

Unfortunately, the local authority disagreed with my views and is now in the unenviable position of having to decide upon a number of planning applications for independent Muslim faith schools. Of course, once the first is granted permission then we will see these schools expanding according to ethnicity demographics. Anyone who lives within a Muslim community will inform you that their Muslim community is distinguished not just by school of thought (similar to different branches of the Christian Church) but also, most significantly, by ethnicity. So if the Pakistanis have one, it is only right that the Bangladeshis have one. Over time, we'll no doubt see the same approach being used by the growing Somali Muslim community.

What chance will the young people who end up in these mono-ethnic and mono-faith schools have of developing a sense of belonging in a modern multicultural and multi-faith Britain?

A BALANCED RESPONSE

I have spent almost all of my time exploring what I consider to be some of the key barriers from within Muslim communities and how to successfully respond to these. Of course, alongside these internal barriers exist the challenges within mainstream society that push away Muslim young people or make it more difficult for them to feel accepted. The challenges of racism, prejudice and poverty, while being nowhere near as acute and acceptable as in previous generations, still exist in our society. But my peers have discussed these challenges in detail elsewhere. I have concentrated on seeking to identify and explain the often hidden challenges from within Muslim communities that need to be successfully responded to alongside the external factors. When combined, these result in a sense of alienation rather than belonging, a feeling of conflicting allegiances rather than complementary values and an increase in division rather than the embrace of diversity.

I genuinely believe that if these internal challenges are accepted and addressed within the space of one generation, we will see a marked improvement in the sense of belonging, loyalty and patriotism of young people from our Muslim communities. It is essential that we respond to this challenge now and accept and are willing to deal with these contentious barriers rather than continue to debate and discuss abstract concepts of belonging.

In the current climate where young people from our very own Muslim communities feel that they are more on the outside than ever before, in a climate where those with extremist ideologies seek to exploit their sense of exclusion and victimisation, it is more important than ever to face up to and respond to the key challenges from within the communities themselves that work against developing a sense of belonging. For far too long the minority opinion amongst young British Muslims has been a sense of pride, patriotism and belonging. We must act to transform this, and in order to do so we must respond to the challenges within our communities as well as those outside.

BEYOND THE 'CRICKET TEST'

SIR VICTOR BLANK

BANN STREET IN STOCKPORT, I AM INTRIGUED TO DISCOVER, is now home to something called the Metropolitan Borough Council Ethnic Diversity Service – one of dozens of such bodies across the country caught up in the great and growing debate over 'multiculturalism' and just what it means, in the early twenty-first century, to be 'British'.

But this small cul-de-sac just off King Street, in the shadow of the town's famous railway viaduct, has for me older and much more personal echoes.

My father's parents lived there.

Like thousands of other Jews from Russia's Pale of Settlement in the Ukraine, they walked off a boat in Manchester at the turn of the last century with few possessions and no English – only the hope of a better life, free from persecution. My grandfather worked from dawn to dusk in a local textile sweatshop. He, his wife and their four children settled in Bann Street. They lived in a row of two-up, two-down houses, with outside loos. Though the houses have long since been demolished, I can vividly remember my father pointing them out to me when I was a boy. It is an image that quite literally remains with me to this day. Long ago, I managed to purchase a beautifully evocative portrait of Bann Street by the local artist Alan Lowndes. Over the years, through each new challenge in my professional life, it has retained pride of place on my office wall. My grandparents' first foothold in this country remains at the core of our family's, and my own, story of what Britishness is all about.

My grandfather moved on to become not merely a sweatshop worker but a tailor. His son, my father, built a family trade into a family business – a gentlemen's outfitters shop in Stockport's town centre. I had the immense good fortune not only to benefit from their sacrifices and hard work but also to come of age at a time of new openness, new opportunity and new self-confidence in our island nation. Having attended a local Church of England primary school, I gained a scholarship to our local grammar school and then went on to Oxford University. There I not only studied but also eagerly imbibed English history.

When I arrived for my first day as a trainee at the City of London offices of the august law firm of Clifford-Turner – now Clifford Chance – I suppose I was conscious, but also wonderfully unworried, about being one of the very, very few Jews there. It seems astonishing to me now. Clifford Chance has since begun hosting Chanukah parties for its Jewish friends, clients, partners and staff, an annual tradition much welcomed by the guests and steadily adopted by many of the firm's competitors. Yet I was told that at the partners' meeting that invited me to join their number at the absurdly young age of 26, in the late 1960s, one of this group of white, pinstriped, middle-aged Englishmen turned to another and said: 'Does it matter to us that he's Jewish?' The answer, unhesitatingly, was no, and they moved on. Some years later, I also moved on, to work not only in law but also in newspaper publishing, retail and business services, and now at the head of one of Britain's major clearing banks.

All of which is less important for what it says about me – no brighter or more gifted, no more ambitious or insightful, than countless of my other countrymen and women – than what it says about Britain. Asked to define 'Britishness', politicians and pundits inevitably use words like 'tolerance' and 'openness', 'freedom' and 'opportunity'. To a sceptical twenty-first-century ear, they sound like empty clichés. Not to me. For they are precisely the things that have allowed me to become all that I am.

Those qualities survive in contemporary Britain. When, a few months back, I suddenly found myself on the front pages for my role as chairman of Lloyds TSB, a profile appeared alongside one of the many newspaper stories. Victor Blank, it said, 'is the epitome of the serial chairman, and one of the City's most respected businessmen', an alumnus of Oxford and Clifford-Turner, a legal 'expert' on mergers and acquisitions.

Nowhere did it say that I am Jewish. That, to me, reflected one of the abiding strengths of contemporary Britain. By this, I do not mean that this country has given me the freedom somehow to hide my Jewishness. My faith and traditions remain something that I celebrate (in addition to chairing a great British bank, I am also chairman of UJS Hillel, the umbrella organisation for Jewish students on university campuses across the country, as well as being involved in a range of other communal activities). The point is that my Jewishness is one part of a wider, and seamlessly interlocking, identity – quite properly, for the profile writer, irrelevant to my role in a banking merger. I am a Jew. I am also, deeply and proudly, British.

If Britain is not 'broken', and I see too much that is vital and vibrant to believe that it is, Britishness seems to me to be in much less rude health. The bomb attacks of 2005 on the London transport system, by terrorists born and bred in Britain, was – to borrow a further cliché from the headline writers – a terrible and terrifying 'wake-up call'. On one level, of course, this raises issues of national security. Yet on a much deeper level, it calls into question the model of Britishness – a model that I and countless others have lived and benefited from – rooted in multiple identities held together by a shared and common sense of what and who we are, what we believe and hold dear, and how we should act.

In 1990, Norman Tebbit posed his famous 'cricket test' for Britishness. It was not only a singularly fatuous contribution to a debate that, now even more than two decades ago, cries out for nuance and not soundbites. It was particularly pernicious because it singled out a particular British community already under assault from far-right demagoguery. 'A large proportion of Britain's Asian population fail to pass the cricket test,' he declared in a *Los Angeles Times* interview. 'Which side do they cheer for?'

I was appalled by Tebbit raising the age-old spectre of 'dual loyalty' as some litmus test for citizenship. As a lifelong cricket-lover – who still counts as one of his fondest teenage memories having witnessed Jim Laker claim nineteen wickets against the Aussies at Old Trafford – I had not the slightest problem in understanding how some of my fellow citizens with Asian roots might well cheer a visiting Pakistani XI to distraction without in the least calling into doubt their Britishness.

But at least one kernel in Tebbit's ill-judged remark does go to the very heart of defining, and sustaining, a cohesive and contemporary sense of Britishness. 'Loyalty' is a mere symptom. But some overreaching sense of 'belonging', much more difficult to define, is indispensable.

All Britons, not just the children or grandchildren of immigrants like me, have multiple identities. Part of what makes us British, and part of what we cherish in Britain, is indeed tied up in now cliché-clothed values like freedom and opportunity and tolerance. Far more important is the tapestry of experiences that weaves the whole thing together. My own sense of Britishness is inseparable from the thrill of having watched Laker's record wicket haul, gloried in the Beatles, guffawed over *Fawlty Towers* – and, in less flippant mode, having listened to scratchy BBC recordings of Churchill's wartime oratory, or read Shakespeare.

Each of us will have very different memories, different experiences. But it is the overlap of these shared experiences that provides the most powerful sense of a common Britain – a single sense, different for each individual, of home. If there is that sense of home, of belonging and, in the broadest sense, of a shared culture, 'loyalty' becomes an automatic afterthought, deeply and instinctively felt. Who you cheer for at a test match conveys, and matters, far less.

For our politicians and policy-makers, nurturing and safeguarding that national sense of belonging is, of course, more difficult than devising loyalty tests.

It must begin, for all of us, with a sense of national assertiveness, cultural self-confidence and perhaps simple pride – attitudes that have gone out of fashion in modern-day Britain. A year or so ago, I happened to be having lunch with several Jewish-community friends. Each, like me, was fortunate enough to have risen from immigrant roots to the upper reaches of his profession. The conversation turned to an item in the morning papers about a local council that had banned the siting of a Christmas tree in the town centre for fear of alienating other faiths. We found the decision ridiculous – and worrying.

Each of us had grown up with – and delighted in – our town-centre Christmas decorations, broadcast services from St Paul's or Westminster Abbey, and Santas at the local department stores. None of this threatened our own faith or identity in the least. It did not prevent us from lighting our Chanukah candles, any more than my own C-of-E education had turned me into a Christian. The crucial point, we all agreed, was that Christianity was part of the very fabric of the country we called home, of our country. Some local councils in recent years have commendably moved to make space for other faith communities, for instance by sanctioning the public display of a Chanukah menorah or public celebrations of Diwali – but thankfully alongside, not in place of, the familiar Christmas trees and festive street-lighting. It may be that it is easier for Britons who began as outsiders, who happily operate at once inside and beyond the 'majority culture', to value it

– and to react with both puzzlement and concern to see it being undervalued or abandoned.

A great Jewish thinker, named Marx, once said that he didn't care to be part of a club that would have him as a member. Part of the contemporary challenge for Britain's national cohesion and identity is surely to recognise that the opposite is also true: that we cannot encourage and inculcate a sense of shared belonging if we become increasingly unsure of, or apologetic for, what belonging to Britain means.

The scrapping of a Christmas tree in a town centre may seem a relatively trivial part of that equation. But the broader issue – a need to value, and assert, the 'majority culture' of which each of us is a part – is anything but trivial. The Church of England is this country's official faith. English – the medium not only of Shakespeare and Marlowe but also of Monica Ali and Salman Rushdie – is our official language. Magna Carta, parliamentary democracy, freedom of expression and the rule of law are our political architecture. And yes, cricket – the arena of excellence not only for Ian Botham but also for Mark Ramprakash – is part of our cultural idiom.

To define Britishness merely as a matter of 'loyalty', risks acting only when it is too late – in a one-dimensional response to an outrage like the bombing of the London Underground, for example, rather than seeking to heed that warning, learn its lessons and find an inevitably more complex, nuanced and long-term reply.

Part of the answer, it is true, must be direct and muscular. My own family background, my political instincts, and my training and experience as a lawyer – all of these would, in other times, have driven me to the barricades at any suggestion of restraining our country's civil liberties. Now, I confess, I feel the need for a more balanced assessment. I believe that Britain, like any nation, has both a right and a duty to defend its law-abiding majority from the terrorism of a few. In extraordinary times, that may well mean extraordinary measures – greater security-force vigilance and restraints on the freedoms of potentially dangerous suspects – as long as such action remains subject to the strictest legal oversight.

And I have great difficulty in understanding the objections to introducing a national ID system of the sort that exists in many other countries with far less reason for concern than ours – assuming again that safeguards against its abuse, or simple incompetence, can be put in place. If it helps to protect us, why should the vast law-abiding majority have any concerns?

In the longer run, the emphasis must be less on the narrow and immediate issues of loyalty and security than on our country's broader fabric of belonging. As the grandchild of a family who arrived in Britain speaking only Russian and Yiddish, I would not for a minute suggest an end to the huge efforts made at both national and local level to provide access to services in languages ranging from Serbo-Croat to Swahili. Still less would I advocate a wholesale clampdown on the acceptance and welcoming of immigrants – a tradition that not only allowed my ancestors to build a freer and better life, but that is also a part of what I so value in Britain and Britishness. Worse still would be any move to abandon our readiness to provide a haven for genuine seekers of asylum on our shores.

It is time to shift the balance – to invest many fewer millions of pounds in translating official documents than in encouraging, enabling and ultimately requiring citizens to learn English. The recently introduced 'citizenship tests' for new Britons is, similarly, a step in the right direction. But one recent inductee, in relating a truly surreal postscript to his town-hall ceremony, suggests the need for a much more profound change – in our schools, our political discourse, our cultural and public life – to the way we define Britishness.

As my friend filed in for his citizenship rite, the local clerk politely handed him the lyrics to 'God Save the Queen', only to assure him with a pat on the shoulder: 'Don't worry. You don't have to sing if you don't want to.'

It was, I suppose, a reflection of the diffidence, the sense of apology, the reluctance to engage in any public display of national affection beyond the football terraces, that is also part of our national character. But while I recognise that it is unfashionable to cite the example of our cousins across the Atlantic with anything short of a sneer, an American-style sense of shared national narrative would go a long way towards reinforcing the cement of 'belonging' on which a sustainable definition of Britishness will depend.

Singing 'God Save the Queen' does not preclude republican sentiments any more than voicing pride in our armed forces need forestall debate on the rights and wrongs of the Iraq war, or prevent us from speaking out over our shameful failure to act more assertively to confront outrages like the situation in Darfur or Robert Mugabe's assault on his own people in Zimbabwe. Celebrating the achievements of the British Empire in our state schools need not blind students to the injustices sometimes committed in its name. Teaching Shakespeare and Rushdie, Darwin and Hobbes, Thatcher and Blair, need not trample on anyone's religious beliefs or political sensibilities. On the contrary, they should all be part of not only conveying but also asserting and celebrating a heritage without which any shared sense of Britishness would be left emptier and more tenuous.

So, too, should extracurricular forays into the broader cultural landscape that can in the end help to provide the cement of 'belonging' to a shared notion of Britain – to our museums, to Buckingham Palace and the Cabinet war rooms, to the fashionably disparaged Proms, and even, dare I suggest, to Lords or Old Trafford for a Test match.

The Americans are, perhaps, fortunate in having a much shorter and less complicated history than our own. But what they do have is a coherent national narrative, unabashedly told, proudly passed on, jointly cherished – even when, like all countries and all governments, their actions may occasionally fail to live up to it.

That, above all, is what will begin to provide an antidote to the unravelling of a shared sense of Britishness. It will not come easily, nor quickly. It cannot be boiled down to a single speech or a single policy initiative. But in the absence of a reassertion of national heritage and identity, and a willingness to champion and defend it, our increasingly fuzzy notion of Britishness risks leaving a void. It is a void likely to be filled by fatuous 'cricket tests', if not by far harder hatred and division from the extreme Right – or worse, sooner or later, by the more assertive 'narrative' that led a group of our fellow Britons with knapsacks full of explosives onto the London Underground.

Those attacks were indeed a wake-up call. Perhaps inevitably, our first response has essentially been defensive. We have shored up security, increased vigilance, infiltrated, rounded up and, where possible, prosecuted known terrorist cells. The paramount aim, quite properly, has been to do everything possible to prevent such an assault on innocent Britons from happening again.

The longer-term imperative, however, must be to use our looser armoury of schools, sport, other cultural institutions and public discourse assertively to promote a shared sense of Britishness to which all individuals and communities, of whatever faith or background, feel a shared sense of belonging. 'Multiculturalism' can and should remain a part of this picture, enriching it greatly. But its coherence, its survival, must depend on the broad brushstrokes of our 'majority culture' – its language and literature, its history and traditions, its legal architecture and institutions. To celebrate and champion them, rather than apologise or simply take them for granted, will seem to some oddly un-British. We Brits, they will say, don't do national narrative. We let it take care of itself. We don't do national pride. It's undignified, cheesy.

The fact is, we can no longer afford not to.

12

WHAT PLACE FOR ME IN THIS GREEN AND PLEASANT LAND?

SHARON WALKER

WHEN YOU ARE ASKED TO WRITE IN RESPONSE TO THE TITLE *Being British*, it is hard to know where to begin. 'Ha ha!' some may say. 'That's a sign, since, if you have to think about what it means to be British, then you're not really British!' Granted, they may be right, but I do not think that it is as straightforward as that.

Do I call myself British? I do most of the time, although I am not completely comfortable with the term. That is not because I dislike Britain but rather because I wonder if Britain truly likes me; whether I can ever truly be identified not as an imposter or a bringer of unwanted change but as an individual brought here by the complex storms of history, to be born, to be raised and to live.

The word 'British' holds so many meanings for me that it is difficult to let them all tumble out here between these pages. I see visions from my childhood of Union Jacks held as a symbol of hate, and I hear a government speaking about cohesion, belonging and a common British identity. When I think of the word, I have the impression of an indefinable solid fence encircling a pasture called 'British', a pasture that I can walk in without ever being able to move to the centre even though I entered through the gate.

I also find myself asking whether we are seeking to create something new when we talk about a British identity for the twenty-first century? If so, what links are there with the past, with the Britain of Byron, Constable,

Keats and Austen? Can a national identity be formed through a top-down approach or do these things just grow organically? And if they are left to grow organically, would I ever be fully included?

Perhaps being British used to be a tangible and understood entity in the days of *On the Buses* or *George and Mildred*, two popular British sitcoms that formed a part of my family's entertainment in the late 1960s and early '70s; and for me, as a child, they contributed to my forming ideas and impressions of Britain that ran parallel to being raised amongst people from various West Indian cultures. In these programmes, everybody looked the same, ate Sunday dinner at the same time and called each other by familiar expressions like 'love', 'cock' or 'ducky'. At least, that is my perception of a once-upon-a-time Britain as I experienced it growing up in the East End of London. But were people really the same, all sharing a common experience and perfectly understanding what it meant to be British? Or is this a myth masterfully retold through our televisions and old photographs framed within books with titles such as 'The Way We Were'? A myth, it is implied, that was shattered by the arrival of people like me, en masse, in the 1950s and '60s; an arrival that destroyed the green and pleasant land perused by Tess of the d'Urbervilles and recreated in BBC costume dramas like *Cranford* (which, I hasten to add, I watch with a delight that could be no more intense if the shade of my skin were lighter!).

I was born in 1969 in the shadow of placards with carefully painted words 'Keep Britain White' and white people marching in the streets to let my parents and others who had come from the Caribbean to work know that they were not wanted here, and that they should return from whence they had come – even though they had been invited. Admittedly, it was not the kind of invitation that you extend to your best friend; more the kind that you give to someone who you need to paint your kitchen before the wallpaper completely peels off. You could do it yourself, but you cannot be bothered, so you are happy for them to do it as long as they do not drink from your cups! Never mind that they may be qualified to do more than paint. You do not care, you even ask them to write their name when they turn up to interview for the job, just to check that they can write. 'Can you write your name, madam?' (Silence from the proud woman whom I called mother. I think that she was too surprised to reply, let alone pick up the pen!)

I grew up against a background of difference, of them and us. Maybe that is OK. Maybe it is OK to have a whisper somewhere in the recesses of your mind that you do not really belong, that you are in Britain but not of it. That is, perhaps, the natural consequence of somebody who has a history of immigration into this United Kingdom. I do not think that it is true, though, since this country has been built on waves of immigration spanning centuries. All of the people are not the same, as I had come to believe in my childhood. And yet somehow the majority of those who arrived in the past seemed able to carve a national identity that became so strong that it was transported across the world on the wind of empire and made stronger through a collective voice that screamed out 'I was here first!' They were perhaps able to achieve this because, as one theory goes, they came from what could be described as very similar people groups. I do not think that I could be categorised as belonging to those particular very similar groups, therefore making me outside the realms of fully belonging.

I suppose that the overarching thought that comes out of all of this is: how is one expected to understand oneself as being a full member of this society when, in the building blocks that make up identity, there is a collection of bricks on which the words 'different' and 'not belonging' have been carefully inscribed? Perhaps I am different? I mean fundamentally different from the white people who populate this land, like a horse is different from a bird. That reminds me of an interesting analogy that somebody once told me to explain why black and white people cannot form loving couples, have sex or have children together: they said it would be like a bird trying to make love to a horse. Um . . . ? It could not have been put better by an advocate of the Eugenics Movement!

In all seriousness, I do not think that it is a question of belonging to this country, but rather a question of to whom the country belongs. *Selah.*

For me, that is where the crux of the question lies, because if the aim is for us all to belong, does it remain that some belong more than others? If so, who are they? Can we all ever belong in the same way? Is that the aim? If not, do we need to allow people, all people, to talk about what the concept or the reality of belonging to Britain means to them and how it influences the way that they see, understand and talk about their neighbours – and even those whose words sometimes offend.

Perhaps put another way, can a country be said to belong to people? If so, is that because they have built layers of habitation there that bear witness to them throughout centuries and millennia? Again, I am using the word 'they' as if it refers to one group of people who are always the same and never changing, never being added to or influenced by those who come from elsewhere. If it is about time and centuries, I have often wondered who America belongs to and who Australia belongs to. There is something there that I cannot quite put my finger on: stories of belonging, of heritage and history that are told in certain ways which ultimately result in shattering the concept of longevity.

As I am writing, I can imagine that there are those reading this who may think that my desire is to be accepted into the bosom of the white man, that is, into England, at the loss of my true identity of being black. We need to stop talking like that. I live in England. I understand fully the wind of history that brought me here. I understand that people like me, whose achievements have been poorly recognised as a result of being bundled together and interpreted through the term 'black', have been in Britain for many centuries: serving as soldiers in the Roman army to defend Hadrian's Wall, leading the London Chartist movement in the mid-nineteenth century,[1] publishing works of prose in the eighteenth century[2] and playing as musicians in the court of Queen Elizabeth I. I am proud of them, and of my ancestors who struggled miserably against the cruelty of this country throughout an extended period of history, and of my parents, who forged a path here and set me on it, laying down a firm foundation for my feet. I know all of this and I live in England. The contradictions of my past and present as I stand on the soil of this land are potentially crippling, but I live in England.

I just want to *be*, achieving the best that I can, defined by nobody (whether that be black or white), belonging where I live and have grown up, being aware of the many voices that have made me who I am, and with the freedom to make this country my home.

1. William Cuffay, the descendant of an enslaved African taken to St Kitts, was born in 1788 and grew up in Chatham, Kent. He became involved in the universal struggle for suffrage and was voted president of the London Chartists in 1842.

2. Ignatius Sancho was born on a slave ship in 1729. Following the death of his parents, he was brought to England, where he grew up and taught himself to read and write, although the general opinion was that such capacity was beyond the reach of Negroes. In spite of barriers, Ignatius went on to compose music, and write poetry and plays, having his works of prose successfully published posthumously.

THE BRITISH

STEPHEN FRY

IF YOU ASK AN AMERICAN WHAT IT MEANS TO BE AMERICAN, he or she will probably find it very easy to answer: Opportunity, Liberty, Enterprise, Plurality, the Constitution, Justice, Democracy – all the Capital Letter words will come out. It is harder for the British. Perhaps 70 years ago we could still talk of fair play, phlegm and fortitude. But now? Well, I am pondering this question in the depths of a fiercely cold winter after a miserable summer and in the midst of the worst economic downturn in a generation. A fine time to ask a Briton what he thinks of anything.

Humour has to come high on the list. You will think this special pleading, perhaps. But banter, self-mockery and laughter at ill-luck surely do constitute one of our strongest and most defining qualities. I have travelled enough to see how rare it is and how beneficent its effects. Its downside (and every British characteristic has a thumping downside) is a tendency to laugh at what we don't understand, shrilly to mock the unfamiliar, the alien and the new. Our tolerance is similarly counterweighted with a moral apathy that takes laissez-faire to extremes. The empiricism that is perhaps the single quality that marked us out and allowed an empire and an industrial revolution to propel us to the status of world power is the virtue in which I would express the most pride and belief. Curiosity, allied with practicality and sane scepticism, opens the door to invention, innovation and progress. The very qualities we most need and which are now in danger of being least fed.

14

BRITAIN: A LAND OF OPPORTUNITY

JUNE SARPONG

BRITISHNESS MEANS SO MANY THINGS TO ME. FIRST OF ALL, IT means being fortunate enough to have been born in a multicultural, tolerant Britain, a country that has given me, a child of African immigrants, so many opportunities.

Secondly it means being a proud Londoner, yet feeling resolutely connected to the rest of the country (except for when it comes to football, where I'm always cheering England all the way).

It also means having a dry sense of humour that makes us stand out from the rest of the world. There's something poignant about how our cynicism makes us both strong and vulnerable.

We are so lucky to be citizens of this great country, and with the onslaught of globalisation and increasing conformity between nations, Britishness will mean defining a new role for ourselves in a rapidly changing world.

15

A MINI VERSION OF
THE HAPSBURG EMPIRE

JOHN GRAY

THERE IS A CERTAIN INCOMPREHENSION IN ANY ATTEMPT TO define Britishness. The assumption is that being British means having a national identity, in the way Americans and the French do, while – in familiar British fashion – taking it less seriously. In this view Britain suffers from not having the clearly defined sense of nationality of other countries, particularly the United States. It would be more cohesive and effective if it acquired a similarly robust sense of itself – an up-to-date patriotism that would give Britons the kind of strong identity enjoyed by citizens of other countries. What is needed, according to this familiar refrain, is a reformulation of what it means to be British that preserves the best elements of the past, modernised on the model of the most successful nation states.

The trouble with this view is that Britain is not a nation state, and Britishness is not (other than in a recent legal sense) a national identity. Britain is not a revolutionary regime founded on a set of supposedly universal principles, like the United States or France. Nor does being British mean belonging in a particular ethnic lineage, as being German meant until just a few years ago. Britain is more like a mini version of the Hapsburg Empire, a multinational state joined together by the contingencies of history, which include the device of monarchy. Of course, this is a thoroughly old-fashioned set-up, which is bound to look highly unsatisfactory when assessed by the standards of *bien pensants* in all parties. What could be more obviously in need of radical reform than a state grounded on a succession of accidents?

As I see it, however, the advantage of Britishness is that it is not a nationality, and at the same time does not rest on any universal principles. It is true that the contemporary British state has many features that are inconvenient and embarrassing. The monarchy has evolved into a postmodern soap opera; the future of the Anglican Church is in doubt; the union with Scotland is in some difficulty. More serious than any of these, the machinery of state has ceased to be 'fit for purpose'. The days when Britain could be admired for its efficient governance are gone. Nothing in the era of Atlee, when government was supposedly a bloated monstrosity, compares with the chronic failure that is now the British state's normal condition. The recurrent loss of sensitive data and the lack of reliable statistics, together with dysfunctional organisations such as the Child Support Agency, are not anomalies. They are symptoms of a systemic blight.

No one any longer believes the British state functions well, but its current malfunctions are mostly the result of treating institutions as instruments used by the government of the day. The British used to see themselves as pragmatic and commonsensical in their grasp of what it takes to make institutions work. Whatever truth this self-image may once have expressed, it is now an empty conceit. Not many countries have been as faddish as Britain in recent years, when a crackpot rationalism has been the ruling public philosophy. If any institution does not deliver whatever goals government has set, it must be 're-engineered' – a process that, given the ephemeral nature of these goals, is unending. The effect has been a hollowing out of ethos, now so far gone that it can hardly be reversed. The consequence is that nothing any longer works.

The same rationalistic mentality animates those who wish to sweep away the makeshift of Britishness. With all of its drawbacks, the British state has the overriding virtue that it is not founded on blood, soil or faith. In their different ways, the United States and France are both doctrinal regimes. To be a citizen of these countries is a matter of belief; it means subscribing to some sort of civil or political religion – in other words a creed, at once highly contentious and claiming to be rationally self-evident. In contrast, despite the recent introduction of an American-style citizenship ceremony, no declaration of faith is required in order to be British. At the same time, though no one could claim Britain is free of racism, being British does not mean belonging to an ethnic group. In its Lilliputian way, the British state is a cosmopolitan regime – a state to which one can be loyal without having to belong to any particular tribe or hold to any faith.

Cosmopolitan regimes have the invaluable feature that they allow identity to be largely elective, and also plural. People can be Scottish, Welsh or English, Asian or Afro-Caribbean, and at the same time Christian, Muslim or Jewish, Hindu or Confucian, evangelical atheists or reticent agnostics. They can define themselves by any set of beliefs they like, switching or mixing their identities at will, or – perhaps most importantly – not troubling themselves about their identity at all, if they so choose.

Ironically, the modern ideal of cosmopolitanism seems to be best realised in pre-modern regimes – monarchies, or relics of empire. The few genuinely cosmopolitan regimes in the world are nearly all of them antique survivals. Britain, Spain and Canada are not only multicultural countries that contain many distinct communities; they are also multinational states, in which different nationalities coexist, interact and freely commingle.

Pre-1914 Vienna was not without its blemishes, which included a political tradition of anti-Semitism. It was nevertheless far more civilised than the patchwork of nation states that emerged in interwar Europe after Woodrow Wilson completed the destruction of the Hapsburg Empire. The vicious attacks on internal and external enemies that followed in many of them were not reversions to the Dark Ages, as is commonly believed. Rather, they were the result of applying a modern progressive ideology.

Whether they were democratic or dictatorial, these states claimed to embody the identity of a people, which – liberated from the mediaeval shackles of empire – demanded to be self-governing. As Joseph Roth, one of the greatest twentieth-century European writers and an elegant elegist of the Austro-Hungarian monarchy, wrote in 1938: 'It had been discovered in the course of the nineteenth century that every individual had to be a member of a particular race or nation, if he wanted to be a fully rounded bourgeois individual.' The mass migrations that racked central and Eastern Europe between the wars came from chasing this dream of progress. Hapsburg cosmopolitanism was destroyed by nationalism, and like Nazism and Islamism, nationalism is a modern movement.

Much of the last century was ruled by a type of identity politics in which people were killed for no other reason than that they belonged, or were seen by others as belonging, in a particular group. Attributing an identity to someone has rarely been auspicious for the person concerned; quite often it has proved to be fatal. In the early twentieth century, pseudoscience was used to categorise people as belonging to racial groups, a practice that opened the way to history's greatest crime. But imposing a collective identity on individual human beings did not start, or end, with Nazism. Even liberal or civic nation states have tended to define people by reference to a single or primary identity, which may not accord with the more eclectic way they see themselves. Communism suppressed ethnic enmities, but they re-emerged with renewed vigour after its collapse. The European Union also attempted to transcend nationalism, and has succeeded in preserving peace. But it has failed to secure the loyalty of its citizens, and it is unclear whether the EU in its present form will survive the current financial crisis.

The problem with cosmopolitan regimes is that they are not easily combined with democratic government. A functioning democracy has seldom existed above the level of the nation state. The democratic deficit that is often observed in European institutions is in no way abnormal, and neither is it remediable. It follows from the supranational character of the EU. It is only in *anciens régimes* such as Britain that supranational government has been reconciled with democratic accountability.

If Britishness has a future it is not in a new-model Britain that has been rebuilt as a modern nation state. Conservatives have waxed deliriously about the 'British Dream', when one of the redeeming features of living in Britain is that it has no dream. Labour has also tried to import an American variety of flag-waving patriotism. The Left would like to remake Britain with a constitution that embodies flavour-of-the-month egalitarianism – the liberal legalism of John Rawls or Ronald Dworkin, say. Many on the Right want something not altogether dissimilar, though without the egalitarian commitment – a type of limited state, with the activities of government circumscribed by constitutional rules.

All these schemes involve refounding the British state on terms that are at odds with its history and present condition. The British makeshift contains elements that are liberal (in all the varieties of that elastic term) and socialist, Tory and Whig, cohering in a fashion that allows for many inconsistencies. Freud's wise observation that it is only in logic that contradictions are forbidden applies to the British political tradition, which has renewed itself through compromise between incompatible values. It may be possible to say something about these values, though I am not sure what purpose is served by doing so. But 'British values' – fairness and tolerance, for example – are not principles of the sort that figure in American-style constitutionalism. They are abstractions from a way of life that existed before anyone bothered to theorise or codify it.

The challenges that face this way of life at the present time are of several kinds. There is the rise of nationalism, particularly in Scotland; the reassertion of religion in the public arena; and the inability of the British settlement devised by Thatcher to deal with large-scale economic dislocation. Of these, Scottish nationalism may be the least important. It will be a pity if the Union fails, but hardly a disaster. The forms of common life invoked by cultural nationalists – Scottish or English – always have something kitschy and faintly oppressive about them. These ancient ways are for the most part very recent inventions. National cultures are not given us by nature or history. They are constructions set in place by the use of power, which always involve the assimilation of minorities, forcibly or otherwise. But in present circumstances one should not make too much of these fears. Post-independence Scotland, if it comes to pass, is not going to be a *völkisch* state, where minorities are oppressed in the name of an imaginary 'organic' culture. Most likely it will be liberal and pluralistic, and not much different from what it is today.

Dealing with religion may prove more difficult. The non-committal Anglicanism that once served to restrain the excesses of faith is plainly no longer sustainable. Religious allegiance has become the basis of a new kind of identity politics, which could turn out to be no less dangerous than earlier versions. The solution cannot be in attempting to purge public institutions of any vestige of faith. The elimination of all traces of religion from the public realm – supposing that to be possible – would simply replace one kind of faith by another, exchanging the rich inheritance of Christianity and Judaism for the banal formulae of liberal humanism. Nor would this protect us from fundamentalism. We know from American experience that a secular constitution in no way ensures secular politics. The separation of Church and state has not prevented fundamentalists from having more leverage on the political process than in any other advanced country.

A better way for Britain would be to expand the establishment of religion so that it is no longer confined to a single version of Christianity. The rudiments of such a solution are already present in state funding for faith schools – Christian, Jewish, Muslim and Hindu. A pluralistic establishment of religion is not without its own problems, however. What counts as a religion? What becomes of the many people who belong to none? Again, the readiness of some religionists to curb free expression is disquieting. Unlimited freedom of expression is not part of the British tradition; but the practice of toleration is central, and if anything that is deemed offensive to religion can be censored there is no freedom at all. Finding a modus vivendi between the many varieties of belief and unbelief is not going to be easy. At least in Britain we start with a regime that does not demand a confession of faith as a condition of citizenship.

The passing of the Thatcherite settlement may seem to be only marginally relevant to the character of Britishness. Yet it is bound to have a far-reaching impact on Britain's public culture. All three parties have converged on a consensus on the role of the state at just the moment in history when that consensus has definitively ceased to be viable. Whatever the upshot of the global financial crisis – and no one can reasonably claim to know – it has already triggered a large expansion of government. The orthodoxy that emerged from the Thatcher era – incidentally, an orthodoxy to which Thatcher never subscribed – required that government be restrained in its economic activities by independent institutions applying a body of rules. The Bank of England's role in controlling inflation is the obvious example. That orthodoxy has been blown away by events, and the political classes have been left gawping and mumbling.

The view of Britain that was installed in the Thatcher period was of a country where government existed to promote opportunity and facilitate risk-taking. It may never have corresponded very closely with facts, but this view was pervasive enough to become an integral part of the New Labour project. This image of Britain is one of the casualties of the financial crisis. As a result, politicians lack a narrative that is capable of interpreting events that are happening to us every day.

In effect, being British at the present time means not knowing what sort of country one lives in. For many, this may be a disorientating condition. Yet the last thing we need is the conversion of Britishness into an ideology. When it is hardened into doctrine, multiculturalism is an absurdity. As a description of reality it can hardly be faulted. The most valuable legacy of empire is the diverse country Britain has become. Being British does not demand that one surrenders one's past or beliefs, only that one accepts the shared practice of peaceful coexistence. Britishness is not a creed, religious or secular, but a way of life in which people with different views of things have learnt to rub along. It is true that the future of the British makeshift is not assured. Still, it has muddled through before and may do so again.

16

REDISCOVERING OUR CORE CULTURE

DOUGLAS MURRAY

IN THE INTRODUCTION TO HIS *CRITIQUE OF PURE REASON*, KANT gives us the image of 'the light dove, cleaving the air in her free flight'. He suggests a temptation. Noting the resistance of the air, the bird 'might imagine that its flight would be still easier in empty space'.

For more than four decades Britain has faced the temptation of Kant's dove. Successive generations of political and cultural leaders have mistaken what was holding us up for what was holding us back. They appear to have believed that if we threw off our past, revoked that past or denied that past then we would soar unencumbered. It hardly needs stating that the period of iconoclasm from which we might only now be emerging has, far from assisting our rise, brought us spiralling downwards.

The fact that we even feel compelled to have a debate on Britishness speaks of that failure. Strong identities do not have to discuss themselves or endlessly attempt explanations and definitions of what they are. They get on with it. The reason why Britishness is being discussed at all is because of the tacit recognition that as a society we have come close to breakdown.

Other people contributing to this volume might not feel that things have slipped as far as I think they have. I can offer two explanations. Firstly, I have no need to spin things: I am not running for political office, do not seek anyone's vote and have no more need to strike an optimistic pose than I do a pessimistic one. But I would also plead age. Now in my late 20s, it is my generation that has experienced the effect of the breakdown that our parents' generation so often worked towards. Our parents knew what they were rebelling against: mine has no idea. Student artists are often told that they have to know the rules in order to break them. It often seems that my generation – and certainly the one coming up after us – has never learned the rules. It has left them groundless and baseless.

Even when they were rebelling against Britain and Britishness, our parents' generation knew what Britishness was. Their rebellions were against a distinct and strong culture. They had a compass by which to orient themselves, perhaps especially when they were orienting themselves in opposition to that culture. Such a compass simply does not exist for my generation. It makes pride in a sense of Britishness a particularly hard thing to express. This is even more the case because when pride was felt by earlier generations in this country it was often – as George Orwell among others observed – done with a reserve which was itself, as an attitude, distinctly British. Perhaps we should not be surprised that a patriotism that expressed itself most clearly when it expressed itself most quietly would be especially susceptible to erosion.

All nations have pasts through which their presents can be identified and their futures imagined. Our past in Britain has been many things, but it was summed up in shorthand and made most visible by the great institutions of our country. Among them were our armed forces, Parliament, the monarchy, the established Church, the law courts, the great schools and the great universities. All were recognisable, and their significance acknowledged. Such symbols spoke for a wealth of collective history, endeavour and belief. Yet today they have something else in common: for they have all, in recent years, been subjected to the most sustained and devastating attack of hooligan iconoclasm by a political and artistic class that believed itself to be outside the Establishment but that has for at least a generation now actually been that Establishment.

Other factors have contributed to the fragmentation. Future generations are likely, I suspect, to study with bafflement the current push-me pull-you situation of Britain. For at the same time as becoming inexorably more integrated into a grand continental alliance that aims to (at best) blur our national identity, mini-nationalists are attempting the Balkanisation of Britain. Like many people, I find myself in the position of continuing to describe myself as British at a time when increasing numbers are choosing to describe themselves as Welsh, English, Scottish, Europeans (rather presumptuously I feel) or even (almost beyond presumption) 'citizens of the world'.

Today we often talk of Britishness as though it is a separate thing from

Englishness, Welshness, Northern Irishness or Scottishness. But truly it is, or was, greater than the sum of our parts. Stepping above mini-nationalisms to a union of manageable size as well as historical legitimacy, it made us into something not just politically greater, but – through our successes during times of trouble – more deserving of greatness.

Perhaps it is also as well to get out of the way at the outset the other major factor that cannot be ignored.

Even after a generation-long onslaught on our past and our institutions, a strong British identity might have survived in a society made up of the descendants of people who had lived here for generations and felt that they had a stake in the society. But there was never much likelihood that a weak national identity could long survive the period of unparalleled mass immigration that this country has seen since the last war and which has, partly for good but also for ill, transformed Britain utterly in the course of a lifetime. The speed of immigration has been so swift since the last war that many immigrants have felt absolutely no need to try to integrate and become British. It is no use denying this fact or ignoring it. It is one of the major reasons why this debate has arisen. We now have many millions of people in Britain who may not feel – and may feel they have no need to feel – that they have any commitment to this country or any real stake in its future.

It was the German Muslim Bassam Tibi who coined the term *Leitkultur*. It suggests a useful starting point in which to find our way out of the disintegrating relativist multicultural (rather than multi-racial) nightmare into which we have either been dragged or stumbled. *Leitkultur* denotes the dominant culture in a society. It does not deny or denigrate the presence of other cultures or other ideals. But it suggests an orbit around which other cultures and identities within a society can orient themselves. Though they may have very different attributes, in such a society there is no doubt about the central orbit. To change to a musical metaphor: the core culture is the theme. Multiple variations can be played on that theme, but the theme itself remains recognisable.

In Britain, our dominant theme has become not just unrecognisable but also increasingly undiscernible. Many people now have no idea that there ever was a theme. On occasions, the situation is worse: if you do recognise the theme you are likely to be told that you should not have done so. We have come close to losing our core culture because it has – in careful order – been abused, then denied, until finally any and every other culture has been identified as having greater claims to greatness than it.

In *The Fire Next Time*, James Baldwin wrote:

> To accept one's past – one's history – is not the same thing as
> drowning in it; it is learning how to use it. An invented past
> can never be used; it cracks and crumbles under the pressures
> of life like clay in a season of drought.

As others have related elsewhere countless times, in Britain we have created a selective and masochistic invention of our past. It is one in which schoolchildren are more likely to be taught guilt at the horrors of the slave trade than pride in its abolition, in which the study of counter-cultural trends supersedes, and often exists without any knowledge of, the cultural trends that it formed in reaction to. It is a culture in which our own past is held up to a scrutiny and consequent denigration afforded to no other culture or country. Earlier generations reacted to a culture they often perceived to be jingoistic. They have replaced it with a culture that is jingoistic only in its self-denigration. Everyone has their own favourite example of this: Eid celebrated, Christmas denigrated; St Patrick's Day parades promoted, St George's Day parades ignored. The masochistic period we have been in was one in which the British were presumed to have been born into some kind of guilt, while everyone else was born into innocence.

My favourite depressing example of these sentiments came in September 2005 in Leicester Square when leading representatives of the worlds of politics and the arts gathered to uncover Marc Quinn's statue of the artist and thalidomide victim Alison Lapper. Unveiling the statue in a square surrounded by Nelson, Cunningham, Napier and numerous other military heroes, the then mayor of London, Ken Livingstone, declared that he had 'no idea' who most of the people commemorated in the square actually were. Ms Lapper herself said, 'At least I didn't get here by slaying people,' while Alan Yentob of the BBC stated that 'It's better than a load of generals that no one gives a fuck about.' These were bold claims. But they revealed the zeitgeist among our phony-underclass elite. Among the military heroes commemorated in Trafalgar Square are the man who saved the British from the tyranny of the French, the naval commander who saved us from the tyranny of the Nazis, and the general who, among other things, forbade the burning-alive of Indian widows on their husbands' funeral pyres. This is not simple ignorance of our past, but a demonstration of our elite's loathing of it.

The combination of this elite-spurred self-loathing (what Roger Scruton has termed 'the culture of repudiation') with the short selling of our culture by those who talk of Britishness as if it, and we, had been born yesterday presents an unappealing buffet. It is no surprise that many people reject what is on offer. I would myself. Those who promote the culture of repudiation present us with a masochism that is so extreme as to be suicidal. As it happens, this masochism, though common among our 'elites', is mercifully not a fetish that is more widely practised, so extricating ourselves from it should be easier than it might otherwise be.

We are emerging out of the wreckage that has been created for us with a range of options. Simplest and most likely to succeed among them is to restate our theme: to reacquire the ability to simply state where we stand, say what our values are, draw the line on what we will tolerate and what we will not. We must learn again how to make value judgements. For instance, migration between the Third World and Britain has been one-way. There is a reason for this. We must relearn – in terms of liberalism, tolerance, culture and tradition – why it is that this country attracts where others repel.

The generation now in power and those coming to power will have some role in leading us in this. But they will not find the task easy. They will be learning or relearning what all small-'c' conservatives learn at some point: that it is easier to pull down than it is to build up, easier to destroy than it is to create. If mention of even small-'c' conservatism puts up the backs of some, perhaps I might recommend André Comte-Sponville's thoughtful recent pronouncement that 'only by transmitting the past to our children can we enable them to invent their future; only by being culturally conservative can we be politically progressive'.

If we are to create Britishness again it will have to be a conscious effort. And it will have to go to the heart of the greatest things we have to offer. We will, among other things, have to relearn pride in our institutions by learning what they are. We will have to do that again from the bottom up – by relearning how we got here. We will have to, among other things, teach history in an informative, factually based way that helps people to understand the symbols of our past that stand around us, ensuring in the process that we shore up such institutions for future generations.

Attempts to describe Britishness by diminishing ourselves to items of ephemera will not do. Occasional lists are published in order to try to sum up Britishness in just such a fatuous way. Fish and chips, queuing, vacuous celebrity 'culture' and all the other take-it-or-leave-it 'British identity' tokens are trotted out. All are attempts to avoid the question and in the process sell our culture and traditions desperately short.

Those who currently seek to build our culture on the most generalist terms are trying to rebuild it on wide but shallow ground. We need to do better than this. For a culture to endure, it must know its roots and shore up its foundations. A strong culture is built on solid ground, not whimsy.

We are engaged in a culture war. If we want to recover our pride and our sense of common identity, we cannot evade the past. But nor should we simplify it. We should not simplify it to be unadulteratedly wonderful, but nor should we flatter those who pretend it is exclusively bad. By and large, if you look around the world today, the countries that remain our allies and those who lead the world are members of the Anglosphere. To them we have contributed much of our law, our culture, our outlook and our language. The English-speaking economies are disproportionately highly represented in the lists of the world's most successful economies, the countries with the greatest economic freedom and the countries with the greatest political freedom. The British tradition of liberty, the achievements of the British Enlightenment and our development of representative parliamentary democracy are not small achievements. They stand as among the most significant and meaningful achievements of our species.

These are not facts that we should use as an excuse to make other people feel bad, but it is certainly no reason to be made to feel worse than anyone else ourselves.

We must also be better at admitting how we got to where we are. There are reasons why our culture has emerged in the distinctive – and more tolerant than most – way that it has. Whether you hold the Christian religion to be true or not, Christianity has been central to the life and culture of our country. Its near-disappearance from our public life and the privileging of other religions over the national faith has led to a strange disconnect between generations. The first reason that this disconnect has occurred is an unawareness of the fundamental differences between religions. For instance, it is important – if you cherish religious freedom in the state – to know that Islam has never had its 'render unto Caesar' moment, but that it is from just such primary Christian tenets that we find the seeds of rights that we enjoy.

But other factors play into this disconnect, and not least a disconnect from our collective culture. You simply lose many young people today if you say 'render unto Caesar' or 'camel through the eye of a needle'. They look at you with a strange stare, rarely wanting to admit their ignorance, but not entirely persuaded that you haven't just started gibbering. An atheist friend recently described to me her disappointment in reading Oscar Wilde's fairy stories to her niece and nephew, getting to the end of the story of the Selfish Giant and being greeted at the pay-off with a bemused grunt. The stigmata of the child at the end of the story meant nothing to the children, and so the whole story was meaningless.

It is no wonder that so many people cannot be coaxed into art galleries to see anything but the most sensationalist and one-dimensional art when the experience of seeing stories central to our national development can be as confounding as confronting the myths of ancient Greece. An annunciation or ascension is all very well, but it is a bit disorienting if the stories are as vaguely known as tales from Ovid. Our past is connected to us via multiple currents, and when one of those currents is cut off the whole shines less brightly. If you don't know the foundations, the intricate details are often impossible to appreciate.

Perhaps those searching for a way in which to restate Britishness today might look to those composers in the late nineteenth and early twentieth centuries who took pains to re-find British music and renew it in modern form. Many of us first discovered our folk-song through twentieth-century realisations by Vaughan Williams, Benjamin Britten and others. We must find a way to teach our religious and cultural past with the purpose of connecting young people to that past. It does not have to be at the expense of learning about other cultures, but with the knowledge that only by knowing where you are starting from can you get anywhere.

Knowing our religious and artistic culture is important because such knowledge pollinates other parts of our collective identity. It speaks not least, for instance, of our landscape. You hear the landscape of our country in Elgar and Finzi, Butterworth and Gurney. Listening to Howells' *Hymnus Paradisi* the other day, I was struck again by the string music after the soprano's 'And my cup shall be full'. The paradise music is the sound of the hills and brooks of Salisbury and Gloucester. It is the same British mystical literalness that Stanley Spencer displays in *The Resurrection, Cookham*, with the resurrected clambering out from their tombs and getting onto the boats on the Thames which will bear them to paradise.

It took an immigrant, T.S. Eliot, to best sum up this relationship in 'Little Gidding', reflecting on the way in which, through conversing with the past in the chapel and the rural hamlet, 'history' and 'the timeless moment' become 'now' – our past and our present uniting.

To anyone unversed in our music or literature, let alone our religious past, our landscape may not provoke these reverberations. But for those who are steeped in it, it is impossible to say whether the countryside echoes the art or the art the countryside. For someone who knows neither our art nor our countryside (as is the case with many people growing up in inner cities), the alienation must be complete. Britishness would become – as it apparently has become – entirely relative, rather than a store of tradition, history and feeling that has seen us through worse times than this, has predated us and will outlive us.

It is the sense of belonging in a tradition, rather than the contemporary attitude of being encouraged to feel above tradition, that orients a person. There is no reason why this feeling cannot be open to anybody who lives here. It simply has to be taught, encouraged and nurtured instead of being ridiculed, diminished and denied. To do this we must think seriously about what it is that we wish to impart – what we wish to leave behind. 'Citizenship lessons' have the opportunity to continue to be fatuous things if they avoid telling truths about our past, or attempt – and I think particularly of Scotland here – to construct an invented past. But if we get it right, and if we teach the truth of our country – our rich and, most importantly, specific traditions – then even now it might not be too late to turn our culture of repudiation around and save the generations to come from the work of ruination that an older generation, high on the adrenalin of destruction, so eagerly began.

In 'Church Going', Philip Larkin unpicks his habit of dropping in to see country churches, places that can even draw non-believers such as himself, if for no other reason than to mingle with the past. I have always felt this pull strongly, and rarely manage to pass a country church without stopping to nose around. Nowhere else is the language of the dead, and the ability to hear echoes from them, more possible than in the places in which our history was formed, recorded and, hopefully, sustained.

The other day I was in the grounds of the ruined cliff-side cathedral in St Andrews and – as almost always happens – was brought up short by an inscription at one grave in particular. It was the tombstone of a young airman killed in action in 1944. The quotation below his dates was from Shelley's 'Adonais' on the death of Keats: 'He has outsoared the shadow of our night'.

Nowadays I quite often get asked whether I'm patriotic, and am always alert to a momentary hesitation before I reply. The words have been so skewed for my generation that I note a hard-to-shrug-off uncertainty. When I reply, I find myself replying quietly.

Like everyone who has tried to acquaint themselves with the lessons of history, I know I don't feel nationalistic. Displays of collective pride in which the speaker himself has had no part – like the 'we' description used in 'we [my team] won the game' leave me cold. Claiming a part of achievements in which you had no part has always struck me as presumptuous, if not perverse. But this is the question that a nation, more than a football team, needs to ask its would-be supporters. Do you feel that you have a stake in it? When a success is achieved, even if on this occasion it was not by your direct input, was it achieved by the collective will to which you contributed yesterday, gave today and promise tomorrow? When that feeling of belonging is encouraged then the collective 'we' means something. It means you have a stake in success and in failure: a stake, in short, in our collective future.

I admitted earlier that I hesitate before confessing to patriotism. But standing on a windswept outcrop of the Scottish coast the other day, reading an English poet, at the grave of a man killed in one of Britain's many battles against totalitarianism, I felt pride, yes, but that other, more familiar feeling also came washing over me. Not the patriotism that so many British people have always been embarrassed by, nor the nationalism that most people end by being shamed by. But a quality that is somehow much more British and that I suspect goes much deeper into who we are and what we might continue to be. That strange yet explicable feeling: not so much pride, more like gratitude.

17

NATIONAL IDENTITY
AND THE HISTORIANS

J.C.D. CLARK

NATIONAL IDENTITY IS A SLIPPERY SUBJECT. AS AN HISTORICAL topic it looks at once different from, say, the Whig Party, the Methodist Church or industrial growth, all of whose stories can be, on one level, narrated or counted. By contrast, national identity is subjective: Britishness is a perception, not a thing. The historian does not record national identity as such, but only what people in the past assumed or asserted national identity to have been. Such assertions were always political; appropriately, present-day claims that national identity in the eighteenth or the nineteenth century 'was' *this* or *that* can be equally political, designed by the historian-politician or the politician-historian to provide a sanction for steering national policy in some particular direction. This makes the subject extraordinarily important, but also an area of history fraught with danger and vulnerable to mediocre scholarship and to passing fashion. Historical writing is always political; equally, there is always a distinction between good and bad history.

To understand group identity historically we must first appreciate that it was not always the same, or as recent, as nationalism. 'Nationalism' is the proper name for a new ideology, formulated in continental Europe in the early nineteenth century, which ascribed to a 'people' an essential and indelible identity based on their genetic inheritance and homeland – in brief, 'blood and soil' – and assumed their natural self-realisation in a nation state. But this formula was only the latest in a series of formulae down the centuries about what it was that individuals had in common, and none of these formulae had any special status ('patriotism', similarly, was a political slogan of the 1730s, not the acceptable face of a timeless 'nationalism').

Moreover, 'nationalism' was accepted to different degrees in different places in the British Isles: most in Ireland, less in Scotland and Wales, least in England. Many commentators in each still often described their identity differently, for example by reference to shared 'liberties' and common history, a constitutional tradition of representative government and the rule of law. Nationalism, like all ideologies, also experienced a trajectory: because it was a distinct ideology, it had a lifespan. By the late twentieth century, it was widely condemned; but its renunciation did not then release individuals into a new cosmopolitanism or pan-European idealism. On the contrary, this fading of nationalism could allow the re-emergence of older ways of seeing collective identities.

Group identity, then, was expressed differently over time; it conforms to no 'ideal type'. It also works in different ways at different levels. At the local level of street and field, prosaic things can suggest place and home, like the smell of the land: everywhere different, everywhere inescapable, nowhere definable. At this level, prominent themes have been a shared awareness of accents, of food and drink, or of antipathies to other local groups, often denominational. So it is in Liverpool, Glasgow, or South Tyrone; and here the term 'community', where it can really be observed, has less appealing connotations than in *bien-pensant* discourse.

Localities have seldom generated 'regional' consciousness, which, in the English case, has been in decline since the age of the Anglo-Saxon Heptarchy. A few localities venerated local saints, recognised there as figures of extraordinary spiritual power, whose fame nevertheless hardly spread further, like the north-east's St Cuthbert (*c.*635–87); but such cults hardly underpin the administrative vision of today which seeks to re-invent 'regions'. Most local things never achieve wider unifying significance. When English 'regions' were devised, part of an EU strategy to weaken national governments, they had to be run by appointed officials who were not subject to democratic election. They could seldom draw to any important degree on pre-existing 'regional' awareness. Equally, however, there was little 'regional' protest. 'Local' identities, then, are not the natural building blocks of 'regional' ones.

At the wider geographical level of England or Scotland, Ireland or Wales, identity was often discussed, when discussed at all, in terms of shared historical experience or (less often) symbols of that experience. These symbols can be very miscellaneous. They can be physical objects like Scotland's Stone of Scone, on which Scottish kings were crowned from the time of Kenneth mac Alpin (reigned 840–58) until the stone was taken to Westminster Abbey by the English King Edward I in 1296. They can be a place, like Ireland's Tara in Co. Meath, ancient centre of kingship, or England's Glastonbury Tor, reputed burial site of the Holy Grail. They might be an artifact, like England's Drake's Drum, reputed to beat with a ghostly drumming at moments of national peril or triumph. They might be a battle, like Ireland's Battle of the Boyne (1690), evocative for both Catholics and Protestants. They might be cultural, like Wales's tradition of poetry and choral singing, or Catholic Ireland's Gaelic culture, only recently being appreciated by English-speaking historians. Or they could be heroes credited with group survival, like England's dimly remembered and much mythologised King Arthur, or its very real King Alfred (849–99); Scotland's William Wallace (d.1305); or Ireland's Daniel O'Connell (1775–1847). Yet in England, Scotland, Ireland and Wales there have been strangely few such symbols: these peoples have not greatly indulged in saluting flags, pledging allegiance, singing marching songs, or the idolatry of founding documents, although they have done a little of each. Their symbols have also been most effective at national level alone. 'Regional' identities, then, have not been the natural building blocks of 'national' ones.

At wider levels of political organisation, it becomes harder again to devise symbols that win instinctive approval among disparate groups. The Union of England and Wales in the 1530s was achieved under the Tudor dynasty, but it made little of its Welsh origins; the Union was made to work in Wales through the more mundane means of the English common law and local Justices of the Peace. The personal and dynastic Union of Scotland and England in 1603 was troubled under the Stuarts, but was to be more so under the houses of Orange and Hanover. The parliamentary Union of the united England and Wales with Scotland in 1707 was yet harder to express symbolically, although the redesigned Union flag was one icon that emerged from this episode. The parliamentary Union of 1801 between these three societies and Ireland was a still more difficult task, and unionist image-makers were hard put to it to devise lasting symbols: that failure had something to do with the independence of southern Ireland in 1922.

Yet the identity of the UK today seems almost massive in comparison with more general commitments. At this wider geographical level, the League of Nations (founded 1919), the United Nations (founded 1945) and the European Union (originating in the Treaty of Rome of 1957) found few enduring symbols within the UK; the attempt to integrate the UK further into the EU from the 1980s was hampered by attachment to what were sometimes used as symbols of national independence, the pound sterling and imperial measurements, and by the failure of the EU to generate compelling alternative symbols. 'National' identities, then, are not the natural building blocks of international ones.

These absences indicate that peoples with ancient identities have less need of emblems, and opinion-poll research within them shows people's marked difficulty in naming such icons; it is newly invented nations that perform implausible public rituals to reassure themselves of their unity, like the Americans after 1783 and the French after 1789 (in neither case effectively). And why single out any particular list of emblems? Each individual has a highly selective gallery of memories, meaningful to that person but often, when most moving, most private; the historian has few means of establishing a lowest common denominator.

Galleries of significant things differ in the public as in the private arena. Some people have fashioned images of national history in libertarian terms, from the Peasants' Revolt (1381) through the Levellers (c.1645–9) and the Tolpuddle Martyrs (1834) to the Liberal or Labour parties. Others observe that the British do not become more tolerant over time, only intolerant of different things, and instead idealise the strong state and its champions. For the mass society of the late nineteenth and twentieth centuries, professional sport came to take on the role of expressing character and recording achievements (and cathartic defeats); but the working of professional sport tends to show divisions and conflicts rather than commonalities.

Societies have long sustained many ways of seeing themselves, often inconsistent. Consequently, 'History' does not teach unambiguous lessons: it does not prove the EU to be either an impossible loyalty, or a natural next step; it deals in the balance of probabilities, and in the stubborn persistence of diversities. Britishness has recently been contested, as Scottishness, Englishness, Irishness and Welshness always were; that may be evidence either for its increasing importance or its weakening in the minds of the population. It might, thirdly, be unrelated to need: because there are few or no agreed definitions of 'Britishness' does not mean that the native population shares less in common than it recently did. Historical debate and real life are not the same things.

A problem with relating Britishness to symbols of identity is that, however significant and moving to insiders, symbols are open to derision by people outside the group. The British Isles have a long history of mutual satire between and among the English, Scots, Irish and Welsh, a genre in which national stereotypes were worked out with worrying insight and exploited to the discomfiture of less self-aware neighbours. Sometimes this process of stereotyping went beyond jest to hatred and violence; and this has been much more true on a European level. Stereotypes and symbols can be unpredictably subversive of political projects as well as supportive of them.

If state-building had ever depended primarily on symbol or ceremony, it would never have got far. Politics has also to do with the hardest self-interest. England's unity was established under the Anglo-Saxon kings by military success and the duller achievements of coinage and a monetised economy, the rule of law and centrally directed militia service, features hardly found elsewhere at that time to that degree. Ireland's attachment to the Union of 1801 had been strengthened by her growing prosperity in the eighteenth century and booming agricultural exports to Britain during the French Revolutionary and Napoleonic Wars. Wales and Scotland were tied into the Union by participation in the coal and steel economy, quickly flourishing in the Welsh valleys and on Clydeside. Even today, the economic benefits of size are manifest at all levels of the economy, whatever the centrifugal forces exerted by sentiment.

If so, present-day polemic itself is the thing that most needs careful historical analysis. 'Identity' has recently been too often treated by certain historians as the set of traditional illusions that encouraged conquest, or whose dispersion led to the reversal of conquest. Thus it was implied that Britain or the United Kingdom, being assembled by force, could not possess an identity; that the UK was merely an anachronistic dynastic survival. This assumption ignores the fact that present-day Wales, Ireland, Scotland and England are each themselves the result of their own bloody fusing of their component parts in eras long preceding the Union of 1707, yet their identities are robust even in our era of major social change.

This durability of identities seemed questionable when 'nationalism' appeared to require the nation state. Some historians from the 1970s rightly demonstrated that the UK was not such a state (not assembled, like Germany or Italy, in an age of nationalism) but a 'composite monarchy' put together in the old order of dynastic Europe. Such states can be surprisingly effective. But others could seize on these results to demand constitutional reconfiguration in the direction of Scots or Welsh independence. This 'composite monarchy' argument, drawn from sound constitutional history, was used to promote a dubious argument of the inevitability of 'break-up', an argument echoing a low-level postmodernism. The current cliché is that Britishness is of recent invention and shallowly rooted, shaped by circumstance, so that changing political goals (including fuller integration into the EU) are not hindered by ancient identities.

Yet, as we have seen, this is problematic. As the Oxford philosopher R.G. Collingwood famously argued, all history is the history of thought. To say that a nation is an imagined political community is therefore true, but unimportant. If so, it seems that the current 'crisis' of Britishness has been got up by the bourgeois intelligentsia. Identities in these islands are, on the contrary, very old; always changing, yet strangely always themselves.

True, some groups or individuals did have a powerful role in devising images of their country, like the London-based Society of Cymmrodorion (founded 1751), whose members shaped an understanding of Wales, or Sir Walter Scott (1771–1832), who framed the dominant imagery of nineteenth-century Scotland. Postmodernists exploit such examples to discredit national identity as 'invented'. But for the historian, for whom it is also a truism that everything is at some point done for the first time, the question is why the images of such authors as Scott were so persuasive and so widely received. The 'invention of tradition', a recently fashionable phrase, is a deeply loaded one.

Scottishness and Welshness (like Irishness in the nineteenth century) were by no means obviously strong enough to bear the novel weight that is now to be placed on them by those who hope to see Scotland and Wales take their places as Peoples' Republics in a newly regionalised EU. Scots and Welsh introspection about the 'meaning' of Scottishness and Welshness too often uncovered diversities as well as commonalities, and sometimes revealed an historical consciousness some aspects of which were as recent as England's if not more so.

In addition, Englishness was rather awkwardly strong, too strong to accept demotion to equality within a 'community of communities' (another loaded phrase, devised by the advocates of mass immigration). Not for nothing had England often managed to stand proxy for Scotland, Ireland and Wales: for good or ill, England was the larger player. In this recent argument, Englishness had therefore to be deliberately denigrated, weakened to the point where it could be treated as just one instance among many. Opponents of Englishness (some originating outside England, others in the English provinces and driven by a provincial desire to deride what they took to be a metropolitan, 'establishment' version of their country's past) were in effect drawn to argue: 'My practices are genuine custom, your practices are invented tradition. My identity is authentic, your identity is false consciousness, our shared identity is elite mystification.' Since it was politically welcome in some quarters, this argument was in those quarters found persuasive. But it soon became apparent that its historical basis was problematic.

Scottishness, Irishness, Welshness and Englishness could be more intractable than they had been thought to be, and less amenable to enlistment in any particular political project. The existence of these anciently rooted identities, moreover, did not always prevent the existence of identities at the higher level of the UK or the EU, just as supporters of a local football team could identify also with their national squad. 'Britishness' had considerably more strength than its postmodern critics allowed; not because it was an essential identity, existing independently of shared historical experiences, but precisely because it was embedded within them. Britain and Britishness were not 'invented' in the everyday sense of that word; they developed, building on much older forms of self-awareness. Nor were they 'forged'; they were genuine embodiments of the everyday life-experiences of everyman and everywoman over many centuries.

Users of academic history should therefore distrust a recent fashion, an adaptation of the 'declinist' thesis much heard from the 1970s that belittled British economic performance as showing the 'decline of the industrial spirit'. From the economic recovery of the 1980s this thesis became problematic and in the 1990s was defended by relocating it to the territory of national identity. In this deprecatory vision, the English (and, by extension, 'the British') are depicted as a xenophobic people whose national identity was much more recent than they thought it to be, and therefore only skin deep. Their nationalism (runs this argument) was created negatively, by affirming an allegiance to 'Protestantism' against an alien external enemy, 'Catholicism'. In the fashionable social-anthropological jargon, which may in reality add nothing to the historical analysis, Catholicism was described as the 'Other'. Protestantism (and, by implication, Christianity itself) was therefore only a temporary expedient, not a substantive commitment. In the absence of a genuine religious or ideological cargo, the 'Other' was opposed by military means; this promoted a crude xenophobia that had a disastrous impact at home, stifling early moves towards democracy and social justice at the time of the French Revolution.

A blinkered, prejudiced and militarily inspired nationalism (continues this interpretation) led naturally into a nineteenth-century imperialism that, not coincidentally, had the same characteristics. Because it was so shallowly rooted, it quickly degenerated into ceremonial and vanity, pride and pomp, show and display. All this went with a thoughtless deference to rank, a worshipping of race, and an elevation of men over women. These damaging prejudices lasted long into the twentieth century. They made Britain both imperialistic abroad and hierarchical at home, the interlocking system of class and empire surviving past its time but finally collapsing together. It was always a weak system in the nineteenth and twentieth centuries, not least because of the invented nature of its eighteenth-century foundations. Such a system nevertheless survives as a foolish Euroscepticism as Britons regress to a narrow and prejudiced insularity even after their Protestantism has been rightly destroyed by secularisation. So runs a currently fashionable version of Britishness. But this scenario has many flaws.

First, it ignores Scotland, Ireland and Wales, each of which have their own identities, extending back many centuries and often robustly resistant to claims about decline, whatever the fortunes of empire or Protestantism. The scenario just outlined was really a re-expressed ploy to denigrate Englishness and so to achieve certain ends within English politics more than a genuinely scholarly attempt to understand how group identity worked in each of these four component societies or to identify commonalities within the British Isles and to trace their historical evolution.

Second, this scenario treats 'nationalism' as a timeless category. Yet, as we have seen, nationalism was only one doctrine that sought to put a new spin on collective self-awareness, a phenomenon that long preceded nationalism and continues to be influential after nationalism is in decline.

Third, the reliance that this theory places on 'Protestantism' is problematic. Group identities in England, Wales, Ireland and Scotland long preceded the Reformation. Even after the 1530s, divisions within what came to be called Protestantism were often more important than the commonalities. These differences led to conflict between Presbyterians, Covenanters, Episcopalians, Puritans, Separatists, Millenarians, High Churchmen, Nonjurors, Low Churchmen and Latitudinarians. The decisive act of separation from a Protestant Britain was that of the Thirteen Colonies in 1776, most of which were as, or even more, Protestant.

Fourth, Catholicism was not always, or necessarily, identified as the 'Other'. Britain was able to ally with many Catholic continental European countries at different times and for different purposes. The English-speaking world sustained lasting debates about the meaning of the Reformation and its significance for relations with continental Churches and states. If the EU today is welcomed by some in Britain despite being predominantly Catholic, that is not a reflection of a newly weakened British identity.

Fifth, the postmodern preoccupation with symbol and ceremony misses the element of practical self-interest in people's sense of group solidarity. Nations, like empires, were run by sceptical realists, not by forgers of identities, any more than subjects at home or in the overseas empire were credulous believers in forged identities. The implication that the 'common people' were merely deceived by manipulators and spin-doctors is profoundly condescending; but it also misses the substantial reasons why people often identified with their polity in peace, and fought for it in war.

If Britishness after the Unions of 1707 and 1801 can be reconceived as consistent with much older foundations, this insight can be carried forward to revise the recent orthodoxies on the nineteenth and twentieth centuries. Recent historians of empire have shown how not just Protestantism but Anglicanism continued to matter in defining the nature of the empire and providing a rationale for its administration. Class and gender roles had much to do with religious beliefs, little with empire, and a religious dimension persisted. Even the First World War has recently been identified as a war of religion. A popular war like that in the Falklands (1982) evoked demonstrations of group solidarity that astonished the chattering classes, however much unpopular wars from Suez (1956) to Iraq (2003–) showed opinion divided.

Undeniably, however, the British Isles offer a rich repertoire of images and instances ready for deployment by those intent on invoking 'History' as a ratification of their present-day purposes. They forget that a unitary 'national identity' is a notion of recent coinage: most societies for most of their history managed without debating their assumptions about what they had in common. The reality is that historical scholarship on the newly defined (or 'invented') question of national identity is still only at an early stage. Some of it is excellent, but some is of very modest intellectual calibre, or is not securely based on evidence, or is written by historians whose research is in other areas; not coincidentally, historians of all periods tend to discover the origins of 'national identity' in their own small patch of the past. Much writing therefore shows a transposition to this new field of old grudges and familiar agendas. That, of course, is why it is welcomed.

Historians have scarcely yet begun to address the largest issues; for example, those created by the mass immigration of actively disaffected religious groups.

This omission says much about the intellectual origins of recent debates on identity. In the face of such an immature and unsatisfactory historiography, one must advise the public: *caveat emptor*. In many areas, it would be appropriate if historians used five seldom-encountered words: 'we do not yet know'. It is worth discovering whether politicians whose knowledge was primarily of economics have recently encouraged historical theories that they hoped would facilitate integration into the EU, only to find that those ideas were more effective as solvents of the UK. These are not just theoretical problems. The historian who pronounces inept formulae becomes only the sorcerer's apprentice; but for the politician, programmes premised on flawed history, as on flawed economics, are doomed to disaster.

18

A MUSEUM OF BRITISH HISTORY: THE TIME HAS COME

KENNETH BAKER

EVERYONE SHOULD HAVE A CLEAR IDEA OF WHAT HAS HAPPENED in our nation's history – how we got from the past to today. This is not romantic nostalgia but a practical recognition of how our society and our country works today – or, in some cases, does not work. It also helps children to understand what it means to be British. In France and America, history reinforces their national pride. America, indeed, does have a Museum of History in Washington, as does Germany in Berlin, and President Sarkozy plans one for the centre of Paris, 'to reinforce French identity'. Such a museum in this country would show the position of Britain as a world power and as a European power, as well as what, over the centuries, it has given the world. It would also demonstrate how Britain came together as a nation.

National pride should not just be a matter of cheering cricketers and rugby and football players. In modern times, the basic freedoms that we live by – free speech, no arbitrary arrest, free democratic elections and universal suffrage – are the gifts we have given to many parts of the world. These didn't simply come about; they emerged from centuries of struggle in which men and women suffered and even died. The museum would also show how over hundreds of years we have absorbed peoples from all races and all religions, and how they have enriched our country. They came to us because they liked freedom, fair play, tolerance and the respect for others' opinions and rights. That's something to be proud of.

We shouldn't be ashamed of celebrating our achievements. For a little island, we have done a lot. Take our inventiveness: in the seventeenth century, a physician in London, educated in Padua and Cambridge, discovered the circulation of blood, and a philosopher from Grantham, gravity. In the eighteenth century, the Industrial Revolution – all those engines, spinning-jennies, pumps and pistons – changed the history of the world. A north-eastern engineer invented the first railway engine, a Scottish electrical engineer the first television, an engineer in Rugby the first jet engine; a doctor in Paddington discovered penicillin and two Cambridge scientists DNA; and a British computer specialist invented the World Wide Web.

It is a rich and fascinating story. In sport, for example, many of the games played around the world originated in Britain. In music, we range from Purcell, Gilbert and Sullivan and Elgar to the Beatles, the Rolling Stones and Elton John. In our built heritage, from castles and the glory of the mediaeval cathedrals and parish churches to Adam, Nash, Barry and Norman Foster. Our forces fighting in Afghanistan and Iraq come from across the United Kingdom, just as the armies of Marlborough, Wellington and Montgomery did.

The museum would also recognise that the English language has become the main means of communication around the world thanks to the British Empire, and we must stop apologising for that. Karl Marx said, 'The question is not whether the English had a right to conquer India, but whether we are to prefer India conquered by the Turk, by the Persian, by the Russian, to India conquered by the Briton.' All our children should also be led to a greater appreciation of the immense wealth of the English language in poetry, plays, and storytelling.

We have many national and local museums all telling part of our nation's story, but not the whole of it. The British Museum is brilliant on Roman Britain, but has little else of our history since the fourth century AD. The V&A has wonderful galleries on the furniture, clothes, textiles and lifestyles of England through the centuries: all individual pearls, but there is no string attaching them to other pearls. It's amazing that there is no museum that tells our political history. I would like to see a museum that recreates the Putney Debates between Cromwell and the Levellers, the Fox–Pitt debates on war, the Gladstone–Disraeli debates on empire, the Lloyd George and Balfour debates on the House of Lords and the suffragettes, the Iain Mcleod and Nye Bevan debates on the Health Service, and the Thatcher and Kinnock debates on Europe.

It is important for our young people to appreciate all this since history is slowly dropping out of the National Curriculum. As pupils can now give up history at 14 – the only other country in Europe that allows that is Albania – a third of state schools do not teach history after the age of 14. This decline is not just sad; it is wrong and harmful.

Well, does history matter? My answer to that is a resounding 'yes'. A people that has little knowledge of its past will lack the confidence to cope with the problems of today and the possibilities of tomorrow. That is why over ten years ago I tried to establish a Museum of British History. I assembled a team of 15 historians, with cross-party trustees like Denis Healey and Roy Jenkins. We identified a site in central London, appointed an architect, produced a feasibility study and business plan, and the Millennium Commission shortlisted us for a grant of £50 million towards the total cost of £110 million. But when Tony Blair won the general election in 1997, the museum was dropped from the shortlist: he wasn't 'into' history. I tried to interest the Millennium Dome, but was told that the minister in charge, Lord Falconer, had decreed there should be no history under the Dome. It is now rather more encouraging, for Gordon Brown has said, 'I am so excited by Lord Baker's proposals for a new National Museum of British History.'

Today it is even more important and necessary because as a result of devolution there is a tendency for England, Scotland, Wales and Northern Ireland to go their own ways. While we must be fair to each of the four countries, it would be an act of great political and historic folly to abandon the United Kingdom. It has been an immensely successful political, economic and cultural entity – we should celebrate its success and ensure its endurance.

If we get a Museum of British History in London – and I think it should be in the capital – I would like to see every pupil from every part of the United Kingdom at primary level and secondary level visit the museum at least once. It must have all the latest communications technology to make the story compelling and exciting, so that these visits are remembered and every child, student, adult or tourist will leave with a greater understanding of the people and events that have shaped the life of Britain over the past 2,000 years.

19

THE SCEPTER'D ISLE: CULTURE AND POWER IN AN OFFSHORE SETTING

ARCHBISHOP ROWAN WILLIAMS

I. AN ISLAND STORY

British identity, like any other regional or national identity, depends first and foremost on history: we are who we are because of where we have come from. Saying this doesn't mean that we look uncritically at our past as simply the heroic and triumphant story leading up to the climax that is us as we now are. But it does mean that we shall understand why we do what we do and value what we value only as we try and see clearly some of the processes that have got us where we now are – with our present problems as well as our present virtues.

And because our cultural climate is not very friendly to taking the past seriously, it is all the more important to try and trace these processes – to try and discover how we have *learned* to be the way we are. Without this, we have very few landmarks for working out why this or that aspect of our life in British society might be worth holding on to, which bits of the picture were discovered slowly and with difficulty, which are fragile, which are likely to last. To talk about 'British values' without this labour of understanding the past is to risk vacuous generalities. It must be a matter of working out why we have come to value certain kinds of human excellence or social stability – not as unique to Britain but as things of general human value that our history has brought to the fore in particular ways. So a lot of what follows will be about history – and not least history in its connection with geography.

Britain is an island – or, if we must be precise, an archipelago: a largish island surrounded by a lot of small ones. Because of this, in the earliest traceable history, it is a place where migration more or less stops; some, not all, migrant groups went on to Ireland and halted there, but a great many settled for good in Britain. Being an island, Britain was never all that easy to migrate into, but a surprising number of groups did; it was also not all that easy to mount a military invasion, though the Romans managed it, with very qualified success. For nearly 400 years, a good deal of Britain was part of an international state, the Roman Empire. After this, a confused period of internal migration and further settlement by Germanic groups from Europe followed. The island's cultural divisions, notably between lowland and highland, were accentuated. But the Germanic groups coalesced quite rapidly into a culture unified around the Christian mission from Rome and a network of related political and legal habits – kingship, a loosely Germanic common law. There was a steadily growing unity among the Germanic kingdoms, though the north and west remained largely untouched, linguistically and politically. The cultural mix was complicated by a fair amount of Scandinavian settlement, ending decisively when a dynastic quarrel in the eleventh century led to the seizure of power by a well-organised military elite from France.

For the next 400 years, during which this elite subdued the Celtic kingdoms to the west (including parts of Ireland) and tried unsuccessfully to do the same in the north, the English state was part of a patchwork of dynastic possessions extending over considerable tracts of France, though the extent of these possessions was steadily reduced. Religious rupture in the sixteenth century combined with a new concentration of power in the monarchy (a united Anglo-Scottish monarchy by the early seventeenth century) and its central administrative organs to create a self-consciously independent nation; and a remarkable burst of naval and commercial enterprise established a significant network of international trading posts, gradually evolving into dependent territories. Once again, we find ourselves looking at a roughly 400-year period, during which the empire developed and declined. The twentieth century's two horrific global conflicts destroyed both the imperial ideal and the economic 'ballast' that had secured high levels of prosperity. Britain became again a destination for migrants, from both the old imperial territories and the newly fluid Europe.

II. DEFEAT AND PERSISTENCE

This breathless sketch prompts one or two thoughts about the conditions of a British moral sensibility. The first is that this is a history characterised by *unsuccessful victories*. 'Conquests' occur, but their effect is curiously muted. After the end of four centuries of Roman rule, Celtic language and political structures slipped back into the vacuum with surprisingly little trouble; the language had been mildly Latinised and the culture of the courts was not at all unsophisticated or insular, but – in comparison with France – the impact of Rome had been limited. The Germanic settlements had more immediate success in replacing the language, but ethnographical research points to a high level of continuity in population, and the Christian mission softened the cultural divides. The Norman Conquest was a brutally effective episode from the point of view of governance, yet within two centuries the Germanic-based vernacular was already pushing the once-dominant French dialect to the margins. The Reformation failed to establish a decisively new religious system, and the survival of mediaeval practice – and even theology in some respects – continued to cause conflict, combining with economic and social unrest to generate one of the worst episodes of civil strife in British history. And the victors in that conflict were to lose again within less than two decades. The empire offered the tantalising image to Britain of a unique fusion between global dominance and small-scale domestic prosperity; but the attempt to defend this led to its dismantling and a complex legacy of nostalgia and guilt.

In an island, there is nowhere else for the defeated to go. Of course defeat leads to exile for some (Scottish and Irish memories will confirm that beyond doubt); but the impression you have from this national story is that the defeated have not been expelled or eliminated and have therefore been around in the memory and awareness of the 'conquerors'. They have been around, ready to step in when the dominant power recedes. The language, place names and even folklore of the defeated have all remained. In one of the great paradoxes of British history, the legendary defender of the Celtic kingdoms against Germanic migrants became the 'King of All England' in the developed cycle of stories about King Arthur. In many contexts, mediaeval Catholic religion refused to be tidied away, despite a campaign of unprecedented violence and re-education; and in our own day, as has often been said, it is a diffused half-Catholic folk piety of candles and flowers and sacred places, rather than Bible-based Protestant devotion, that survives as the spiritual environment for a great number of people who don't have any formal religious allegiance (remember the manifestations of popular religiousness after Princess Diana's death). The empire has vanished, yet its residual reality is massively visible in the patterns of migration and settlement that have changed especially the urban face of Britain in recent decades. British military dominance was 'defeated' in the old imperial territories, yet Britain retains its pull and some of its cultural authority, even at the same time as its own culture is being modified by its former colonial dependants: a tangled pattern.

III. PATIENCE AND STRANGERS

Unsuccessful victories: consciously or not, they produce the recognition that victory is fragile and that it has the potential to deceive. They also carry the awareness that the defeated are still there to be lived with, even negotiated with. The 'Others' will not simply go away, but obstinately stay there to remind you that they too are a part of your own story. What has been for the moment silenced or buried works patiently back to the surface. Hegel wrote of the 'cunning of reason', the way in which the overall shape of intelligent human development finds its way infallibly through the chaotic chances of actual history; our island history suggests that there is a 'cunning' in defeated cultures, a capacity to infiltrate, inflect and change what thinks of itself as the dominant voice.

Anyone who has read the poetry of David Jones will recognise these themes. Central to Jones's enterprise is the reading of contemporary experience through the prism of a hugely varied cultural history, picking up in all sorts of quite unexpected places the track of buried belief and habit, so that – in his masterpiece, *In Parenthesis* – the soldiers in the trenches of the First World War are seen as shadowed by, almost embodying, the Celts and Angles battling in the sixth century or Malory's Arthurian knights or even the Homeric heroes, as well as the deeper patterning and figuring of the story of Christ's crucifixion and the liturgical enacting of that in Catholic worship. History does not go away; arguably, in a not very roomy island, its not going away will be especially visible or tangible.

It creates a habit of living with ironies. If conflict is never just finished, if the 'Other' is never just silenced, we can't avoid being aware of the fact that what we live with is both provisional and also remarkably durable. The British state maintains, in the face of a lot of rationalising argument, a number of institutions and customs that embody a long past and seem to exist at right angles to anything like a defensible modern polity – the monarchy, the established Church, aspects of legal practice and convention and so on. They have survived; it would be wrong to say that therefore they can't change – but equally wrong to say that we could or should be creating a new polity that would embody a 'final', rational form for political, religious or legal practice that took no account of what these historic institutions stand for. The functional and rational analysis that seeks to begin again from Day One ignores the 'cunning' of culture that I have described, the capacity of what has been buried to return. If we are able to accept without undue anxiety the doubtful 'rationality' of some of our institutions as a significant part of our corporate life, we are in effect accepting that there is more at work in that corporate life than our conscious plans and hopes. We may also be accepting that this dimension is necessary if we are to avoid hectic and unrealistic attitudes to our society that cause deep but largely invisible damage to our unconscious awareness of continuities and landmarks, the sort of awareness that is needed for the health of individuals and communities.

But there is a genuinely *moral* dimension that makes these attitudes and habits more than casual phenomena. Being conscious of the incompleteness of victory and the persistence of the defeated within a limited territory imposes a degree of patience and of acceptance of the 'Other' that pulls sharply against totalising, monophonic and monopolistic politics – against tyranny and the reduction of persons to functions in a national scheme, a national operation. This is not simply to say that irony breeds tolerance; in itself, that is not really a very interesting moral observation, and at times it can be a recipe for just shrugging our shoulders. It is more to suggest that a history of unsuccessful victories generates the *humility* that allows that we have something to receive from the other, including the defeated 'Other'. It is not a 'value' that appears very strongly in the lists of desirable values that are generated in the educational establishment from time to time – though it is instructive and rather encouraging that some participants in the network of 'values-based' schools in the UK do mention it. It is a much misunderstood virtue, being associated with self-denigration by many people. But, seen as a habit of realism and receptivity, it is a profoundly positive thing. And what I am proposing is that there is a way of telling the story of British history that might help us grasp what it means and why it is worth fostering.

Being an island from which it is difficult to escape implies that you cannot avoid making terms with the defeated. It can thus also mean a developed habit of slightly detached acceptance in respect of the quirks of our historical landmarks; and this, fully nurtured, becomes one aspect of a habit of humility. This, perhaps, is one dimension of British history that shapes a genuinely

149

moral climate – not in virtue of any innate quality in an ethnic group but simply because we have lived where we have lived. Other nations no doubt find their way to this and other virtues through different historical tracks, but this seems to be the one we have been provided with.

IV. STATE LAW AND MORALITY

But this is not the only morally interesting spin-off from our history, and I want to turn much more briefly to a second reflection on the making of a moral climate, this time to do with what is currently the sensitive subject of the relation between religion and the state. As mentioned above, the mission sent from Rome in 597 to establish the Christian Church among the Germanic or Anglo-Saxon kingdoms in lowland Britain had a massive impact on the collective self-consciousness of these kingdoms: 'English' identity was shaped around common loyalty to the Church structure set up by Augustine of Canterbury and his colleagues and successors, so that Bede's great *Ecclesiastical History* is really an account of how the 'English', despite their diverse tribal and royal allegiances, came to see themselves as a single people (notably, alas, over against their Celtic neighbours, for whom Bede has no time at all).

As the English monarchy developed, its symbiotic relationship with the Church continued. The monarch was anointed (this was unusual in Western European practice at this point) and acquired just a little of the sacral mystique of Byzantium as a result; but this did not mean any simple dominance of the Church by the ruler. A study of the history of English law shows how secular and religious practice in jurisprudence interacted in ways that significantly modified both. A strong Church could and did throw its weight into the scales against monarchical absolutism (Archbishop Langton's role in Magna Carta); the debacle over Becket had left the Church's immunities reinforced, and, despite the deep ambiguities of this in terms of the threat to universal civic and legal equity, one result was to keep in play a sense that the law of the state remained accountable to standards external to its own life.

Conversely, the impact of common law on ecclesiastical practice meant that ecclesiastically inspired drives for conformity on the model of the mediaeval Inquisition did not find much sympathy in England. Mary Tudor's reign was widely and rightly seen as an example of foreign practice intruding on traditional local patterns, and common lawyers were among those who resisted some of the juridical ambitions of Charles I and Archbishop Laud. Church lawyers helped to refine the laws of evidence in civil cases and civil lawyers restrained inquisitorial ambitions; the use of judicial torture was comparatively restrained by the end of the Middle Ages. And although the English Reformation upset this balance colossally by the declaration that the monarch was the supreme judge of appeal for Church matters, this revolutionary move itself could not have happened without the previous history of close, sometimes conflicted but often mutually constructive, relation between civil and ecclesiastical jurisdiction. And the seventeenth-century clarification of the monarch's responsibility to the law built upon some aspects of that older sense of the limits to executive absolutism (in spite of the efforts of some religious ideologues of the period to defend a 'divine right' significantly alien to earlier Christian ideas of monarchy).

The point is that the peculiar variety of constitutional monarchy that has survived in Britain has its roots in a historical argument, sometimes amicable and sometimes not, between state and Church. Their relation in England first and then in the United Kingdom was different from the relation that existed elsewhere – partly because (the island phenomenon again) the Church had always had some distinctive features and a slightly greater distance from the political agendas of the Church in Continental Europe, and partly because of the close involvement of the Church from the seventh century onwards in the legitimating of the monarchy and the consolidation of the sense of an 'English people'. So the idea of law that became pervasive in Britain was never a purely 'Roman' one, with a predominant concern for uniformity and a careful centralised architecture, but one that presupposed the liberties of diverse groups and maintained the acknowledgement of a responsibility on the part of the entire political-legal apparatus to abiding and absolute principles.

This heritage allowed the United Kingdom to move increasingly towards a high level of religious toleration (resisted, it must be granted, by many or most in the established Church) without formal secularisation. It meant also that the English 'Revolution' of the seventeenth century could present itself as the outworking and development of immemorial customs and liberties, not as a radical new beginning; a stark contrast with both the French Enlightenment, with its timeless rationalism, and the French Revolution. And, to focus once again on the specifically moral issue, the legacy of this is both a continuing sense of the state's duty towards religious conscience as an element in its own legitimacy, and a legal and public tradition hostile to the idea that 'reasons of state' can be allowed to suspend civil liberties and moral decencies; the courts continue to work on this basis.

V. CONCLUSION

I have not been trying to unearth anything like an essence of British identity, let alone a set of clearly demarcated British values; only to outline how some features of our history as an island cluster of nations and eventually an island state have worked to reinforce certain attitudes and habits that we can argue to be of broad moral worth. Defining and promoting 'British identity' is a serious enterprise only if it is about finding sources of general moral energy that make for a just and truthful society. My suggestion has been that at least two areas of our national history point in such a direction (there will be many others that other analysts can explore, but this is a start). The unavoidable need to accept both the persistence of the 'Other' and the ambiguities of victory generates that mixture of irony and humility that offers the chance of a realistic, adult perspective on our political and personal lives; and the intertwining of religious and political-legal concerns has meant the emergence of a Church whose impulses to coercion have been chastened and a legal tradition strongly alert to the claims of conscience and suspicious of *raison d'état*.

If in the present context we want to see a recognisably British identity survive, we could do worse than reflect on what is needed to keep these themes alive. But my entire argument here has been based on the assumption that you will not keep principles alive unless you keep telling the story of how they came to be articulated. How to teach British history continues to be a contentious question, especially in an ethnically and religiously diverse society. But we badly need some common sense here. Insisting on historical perspective, and even on the positive appreciation of aspects of our history, is not the same as a triumphalist declaration of national superiority. Sadly, we have reacted (understandably) against such triumphalism, against the uncritical glorifying of Parliament, Crown, Protestant Establishment and Empire common in an earlier generation, with an embarrassed apology for our past or an equally unbalanced focus on our historical sins and failures (the horrors of the early Industrial Revolution, the slave trade and genocidal brutality in contexts like Tasmania).

The challenge is to cultivate clarity and truthfulness about the whole range of our history – but also, and without embarrassment, to teach about and to value the ways our history has driven in certain moral insights. It is no favour to any minority in this country to pretend that Britain has no history and no worthwhile institutions. Indeed, if I am right in what I have been suggesting, our capacity to relate creatively and not fearfully or repressively towards minorities and migrants depends on our being properly self-aware about some of the cultural and religious strands in our past that resource this capacity. To speak affirmatively about our Christian heritage and our internal British plurality of language and tradition becomes part of what we owe to those who have arrived more recently in these islands – not an assertion of superiority but an exposition of why welcome is possible.

20

A CATHOLIC PERSPECTIVE ON BRITISHNESS

CARDINAL CORMAC MURPHY-O'CONNOR

INITIALLY, TWO WORDS LINKED WITH BRITISHNESS COME TO mind: myth and nostalgia. The former because of the various attempts throughout history to identify a mythical past as the source of British identity: the legend of King Arthur, for example, gave earlier generations a national myth of kingly virtue and the promise of the once and future king who would return when we needed him. There is also the strange legend evoked every year on the last night of the Proms when Blake's hymn 'Jerusalem' is sung: that the merchant Joseph of Arimathea visited England to buy tin from Cornwall and brought with him the child Jesus, whose feet then 'walk[ed] upon England's mountains green' – the land of Britain was thus sanctified by the direct presence of God made flesh and became holy ground. We should not lose these stories, unreliable though they are, but they cannot bestow meaning as they may once have done to this island race.

The second word, nostalgia, evokes a rural Britain of villages and warm skies – even warm beer – a harmonious and confident community that was at the same time the world's greatest imperial power, a comfortable and stable paradise from which we were expelled by the traumatic world wars of the twentieth century: since then the gates of Eden have been closed to us, but at least we have our costume dramas to console us. We should not drink too deeply from the wells of nostalgia, because this history was not rosy-hued for everyone. W.H. Auden's cautionary words in 'In Praise of Limestone' are relevant here – that the seemingly calm, settled Britain is not the sweet home that it seems. Britishness is not one unchanging thing across the centuries, susceptible of clear delineation; it changes as the population and context of life in these islands changes. A British identity cannot be simply geographical, a product of this landscape, these waters and this weather: it is also a product of culture and cultural change, progress and decline, uncertainty and conflict. We may be at one of those points of redefinition of Britishness.

It is not accidental that the question of Britishness is being raised at this time. According to Linda Colley's influential argument, the concept of Britishness in the eighteenth century was invented by a Protestant nation in order to unify these islands, promote trade, consolidate the monarchy, foster an empire and make the country strong enough to resist Catholic Europe.[1] So too now: the question of Britishness is being raised by politicians in order to cope with the possible threat to our identity by too rapid an incorporation of other peoples within our shores and by nationalist movements among the Scots and the Welsh. Is our government suddenly concerned about Britishness because we have lost confidence in a programme of multiculturalism and because politicians are worried by Scottish Nationalist threats to the Union? The third factor, of course, may be the question of the relation of Britain to an expanding and centralising European Union and the fear that Britishness may become simply a regional identity within the European republic. We fear that nations will dissolve while regions will endure – hence the concern to identify a British national identity, unified and confident, capable of handling these things.

It is with a heavy heart that a Catholic like myself can only agree when someone says that what we describe as Britishness can be traced back to the civil war and the Acts of Union. Indeed so, and the presence of Catholics in this historically Protestant state was for a long time problematic, particularly and most severely in the north of Ireland, where Catholics suffered a discrimination that should have been removed before bitterness erupted so murderously there. Catholics in these islands know only too well that this country has promoted a version of Britishness that denied them liberty of religion and human rights simply because they held that the authority of the Pope is central to the Church founded by Christ. Within the recent past, for example, many Irish people coming to Britain read signs outside factories and houses that said 'No Irish need apply'. As a British citizen born of Irish parents, these issues have been very close to me.

156

The distinction George Orwell makes between patriotism and nationalism appeals to me: patriotism, he says, speaks of a devotion to a place and a way of life 'which one believes to be the best in the world but has no particular wish to force upon other people'.[2] It is 'of its nature defensive, both militarily and culturally',[3] and is therefore presumably non-aggressive, posing no threat to other nations or peoples – a good thing by all accounts. There is surely in our country a deep natural patriotism expressed through a reserved, often unspoken, love of places, people, customs, stories, heroes and a liking for 'the way we do things around here' (the late Archbishop Derek Worlock's definition of culture). This is surely part of British identity at its best.

Orwell distinguishes this laudable, decent pride from a nationalism that he characterises in considerably darker terms: for him, nationalism is inseparable from the desire for power; it is 'power hunger tempered by self-deception'; a nationalist thinks solely or mainly 'in terms of competitive prestige'.[4]

Now, is the concept of Britishness a patriotic or a nationalist one? You may judge that the question hardly merits a reply because Orwell characterises both categories in morally opposite ways, and who would commend his picture of nationalism? But the question does need to be asked because versions of national identity have been used to foster hatred and xenophobia. Catholics, as I said above, know this only too well. If the idea of Britishness is to have a future, it must not be surrounded by an aggressive nationalism that will twist it. In a parallel way, 'Englishness' should not become the badge of xenophobes: it should be rescued and developed positively. In this we are extremely fortunate in having a monarch who acts as a unifying symbol and points to values and loyalties that embrace everyone in our country. Nor may it be inappropriate here to mention overlapping and complementary identities – people are British before they are European; Scottish or Welsh before British; indeed, a Londoner or a Mancunian before being subsumed into the wider British concept.

So just what is Britain for? Things must have a purpose if they are to command a loyalty that is worth dying for. And let me begin to answer it in an indirect way by taking a sentence from the writings of Julian of Norwich, the fourteenth-century mystic, which I will develop in relation to our discussion here. She writes: 'In the self-same point that our soul is made sensual, in the self-same point is the City of God ordained to him from without beginning.' I take her to be saying that when our soul – the constitutive aspect of the self that makes us who we are – is linked to our bodiliness, namely at the moment of our conception, we are directed towards the community that is formed by

God's presence among us. Our identity, *ab initio*, brings us membership of the community that God creates through his self-gift in Christ, a community that Julian, following St Augustine, calls 'the City of God'.

If Julian is right, then all the social groupings such as tribes, clans, peoples, nations, and so on that we create through our cultures are small glimpses of the great community to which we belong, the City of God that begins, according to Augustine, with the death of Abel at the hands of his brother Cain, that takes shape in Israel's election as God's people and is then extended through Christ to all the peoples of the world. The Christian vision of reality is that the destiny of all is social and collective: all humanity is to be 'in Christ', in the body of reconciled humanity that the Lord creates through his death and resurrection.

In other words, the communities that human beings make among themselves have only one purpose: to embody the qualities of the human family that God creates through his teaching and presence. You can see that if I think in this way, it is clear that I cannot accept a secularised version of any social order and consequently that I find it impossible to accept that Britain and Britishness should be construed in ways that eliminate or marginalise the religious dimension. Britain should not be a God-free zone, and Britishness must not be interpreted as a religion-free secularism.

The political unit 'Britain' can command our allegiance only if it actually promotes an identifiable social good that advances humanity towards its union in God. Its value is not to serve the interests of a particular group. If you ask the question, 'What is Britain for?' – and I take it that this is the pressing question, given the variable pressures towards internal separation on the one hand and incorporation within the greater unity of the European Union on the other – I would answer that the only proper aim for Britain is to foster the flourishing of the human race by embodying practices and policies governed by law and justice, directed by fairness and respect for all, guided by Christian values and teachings, in respectful engagement with the range of human religions and cultures. I want to see a deeply Christian Britain that can be a home for all the communities it contains.

This is not generally accepted. I detect an uncertainty among politicians about stating confidently that the values that inspire Europe and, indeed, Britain are grounded in Christianity. You will remember the recent disputes about the Charter of Fundamental Rights of the European Union, when the French prime minister Lionel Jospin insisted on the deletion of references to Europe's Christian heritage from the preamble. But it is encouraging to hear that the German chancellor Angela Merkel has renewed her criticism that the constitution does not explicitly refer to Europe's Christian roots. She said that she regretted that the draft constitution for the 27-member European Union did not include a mention of God or Christianity:

> I would have liked to have seen a clearer declaration on the Christian roots [of Europe]. No one doubts that they significantly shape our life, our society. I wonder, can we maintain the formative aspects of Christianity for day-to-day politics if the political sphere does not stand by them?[5]

It is a question worth pondering as the issue of the European Constitution returns to the political agenda in 2009. This takes in the question of values and diversity. Diversity needs to be acknowledged as a fact in Britain today: in other words, if you belong to Britain, you should accept a set of core democratic values; and the hope, of course, is that these values will take precedence over values associated with particular cultural (and religious) identities within Britain today. It is hard to disagree with the most common words used to describe the bedrock of values on which our nation is built, such as liberty, democracy, tolerance, free speech, pluralism, fair play and civic duty.

Yet they are strangely disappointing. Only these, I ask? Now, it is hard to be against them – there is a touch of old-fashioned decency, pipe-smoking and cricket-playing about them – but is this list sufficient to underpin Britain's moral and social life? By no means. The problem with essentially liberal perspectives like this is that while they may regulate how individuals or groups are to relate to one another, in themselves they are not sufficient to identify what our life together is for. Liberty or tolerance in themselves cannot be the goal or telos of a society; it may govern how relations are to be governed within that society, but a society like Britain does not exist simply in order to be free.

We seem to be in a position today in which the only compelling moral value that merits absolute respect is tolerance. Gertrude Himmelfarb, a philosopher much admired by Gordon Brown,[6] identifies liberty as the only moral principle that commends general assent in the Western world.[7] Himmelfarb is disturbed by the way we have moved away from a concern with virtues to a concern for values:

> It was not until the present century that morality became so thoroughly relativized and subjectified that virtues ceased

to be 'virtues' and became 'values' . . . Values as we now understand that word, do not have to be virtues: they can be beliefs, opinions, attitudes, feelings, habits, conventions, preferences, prejudices, even idiosyncrasies – whatever any individual, group, or society happens to value, at any time, for any reason. One cannot say of virtues, as one can of values, that anyone's virtues are as good as anyone else's, or that everyone has a right to his own virtues. Only values can lay that claim to moral equality and neutrality.[8]

In similar vein, Pope Benedict XVI notes that 'we prefer today to speak of values rather than of truth, in order to avoid coming into conflict with the idea of tolerance and with democratic relativism'.[9] I think that Benedict is right on this matter, and I commend to our political leaders a closer reading of Himmelfarb's view that the shift from virtues to values may signal a cultural acceptance of moral relativism that is not a good basis for British life.

With this line of thinking, am I advocating the creation of Britain as a theocracy? Not at all: Jesus took no interest in using political systems to validate and advance his religious vision, and neither should the Church. Too often there have been alliances of 'throne and altar' that have been deeply problematic and that Catholic Christianity ought to eschew. Rather, I am commending to our politicians the notion that the state has a moral purpose and that Britishness ought to be characterised by its moral quality rather than by pragmatic self-interest. Let me again quote Pope Benedict:

> Thanks to the path taken by Jesus Christ, Christian faith has dethroned the idea of a political theocracy. In modern terms, it has brought about the secularity of the state, in which Christians live together in freedom with members of other persuasions. They are bound together by the common moral responsibility that is based on the very essence of man, on the essence of justice. Christian faith distinguishes this reality from the kingdom of God, which does not and cannot exist in this world as a political entity. Its task is to transform the world from within by means of faith, hope and love. Under the conditions of the present age, the kingdom of God is not a secular realm but an appeal addressed to human freedom and a support offered to reason so that it may fulfil its own task.[10]

What Pope Benedict says in this paragraph is carefully phrased: Christians are to live together with members of other persuasions (personal and religious) in a common bond created by our shared moral responsibility to promote the human good of all and the conditions of fairness and rightness that we subsume under the category of 'justice'. Politics, the Holy Father goes on to say, is 'the realm of moral reason, since the goal of the state, and hence the ultimate goal of all politics, has a moral nature, namely, peace and justice'.[11] Now, however we interpret Britishness at the end of this time of consultation, these remarks of Pope Benedict about morality and justice point us to central aspects of how it needs to be construed.

I want to insist that the life and perspective which Christian faith introduces is not an obstacle to human social flourishing. It is one of the repeated claims of our contemporary atheists, God bless them, that belief in God is an obstacle to human achievement and flourishing. Not so, I want to argue. The philosopher Bernard Lonergan says that what religious faith gives us is a sense of being called by God to an authenticity that overcomes evil with good and that commits our communities to seeking the widest possible human good as the horizon within which our efforts are set. He goes on to say:

> Decline disrupts a culture with conflicting ideologies. It inflicts on individuals the social, economic and psychological pressures that for human frailty amount to determinism. It multiplies and heaps up the abuses and absurdities that breed resentment, hatred, anger, violence. It is not propaganda and it is not argument but religious faith that will liberate human reasonableness from its ideological prisons. It is not the promises of men but religious hope that can enable us to resist the vast pressures of social decay.[12]

Indeed so. We must ask one final question: is Britishness now to be construed in multicultural terms in the post-Protestant, post-imperialist future ahead of us? Before we slide effortlessly towards these sunlit uplands, let me suggest that things are not so simple. Again I turn to Pope Benedict, whose remarks on the cultural ideal of multiculturalism in our modern European context are worth noting. He suggests that the rapid espousal of multiculturalism can sometimes be 'a refusal to accept that which is one's own or indeed be a flight from that which is one's own'.

But Pope Benedict's comments do not end with this. He acknowledges that there is a value in multiculturalism, but he suggests that '[it] surely cannot survive without reverence for that which is holy. This involves encountering with reverence that which is holy to another, but we can do this only if the Holy One, God himself, is not foreign to us'.[13] In other words, if we want to foster multiculturalism, we need to have a deep reverence for God within the living practice of our own religion. Only then will we be in a proper position to engage with the way in which the Holy is approached within another tradition. We ought to foster a respect and reverence for the different religious communities in our towns and cities. But we will do this best if we ourselves know God through our own Christian faith. If we lose the sense of who we are under God, how can we welcome and understand those who worship God in different ways?

If this approach is correct, then a genuinely British multiculturalism will not be a secularising project that unhooks Britain from its Christian roots, but something best conducted from within Christian faith and life. Solid Christian practice, grounded in the Scriptures and conducted with intellectual openness and rigour, might be the best context from which to foster a Britain that promotes the good of all and is of service to all the communities of the world. And it might actually be the best way in which our country can move into the next stage of its history. So my vision of Britishness is that we create a deeply Christian Britain that can be a home for all the communities it contains.

With these comments, I have tried to bring some Catholic Christian perspectives to bear on the question of Britishness and to ensure that certain central things are not forgotten.

1   Linda Colley, *Britons: Forging the Nation* (New Haven: Yale University Press, 1992).

2   George Orwell, 'Notes on Nationalism', *Essays* (London: Penguin, 2000), 300.

3   *Ibid.*

4   *Ibid.*

5   'Merkel Wants EU Charter to Make Reference to Christianity', *Deutsche Welle* (21 January 2007). Available at: http://www.dw-world.de/dw/article/0,2144,2320266,00.html

6   Gordon Brown contributed the introduction to the British edition of Himmelfarb's *The Roads to Modernity: The British, French and American Enlightenments* (London: Vintage, 2005).

7   Gertrude Himmelfarb, introduction to John Stuart Mill, *On Liberty* (London: Penguin Classics, 1985), 7: 'In an age which prides itself on its liberation from all absolutes, which has succeeded in making the very word "absolute" sound archaic, there is one concept that has very nearly the status of an absolute. That is the idea of liberty . . . the idea itself continues to exercise that ultimate authority which once belonged to the idea of God, nature, justice, reason or the ideal polity.'

8   Gertrude Himmelfarb, *The De-Moralization of Society: From Victorian Virtues to Modern Values* (London: Institute of Economic Affairs, 1995), 11–12.

9   Cardinal J. Ratzinger, *Values in a Time of Upheaval* (New York: Crossroad, 2006), 55–6.

10 *Ibid.* 114.

11 *Ibid.* 24.

12 Bernard J.F. Lonergan, *Method in Theology* (London: DLT, 1971), 117.

13 Ratzinger, *Values in a Time of Upheaval*, 149.

21

COVENANT AND THE REMAKING OF A NATIONAL IDENTITY

SIR JONATHAN SACKS

JEWS KNEW TOLERANCE WHEN THEY SAW IT. THEIR LIVES, OR THE lives of their grandchildren not yet born, depended on it. That is why they loved England. Even the most ultra-Orthodox, in London's East End or Stamford Hill, seemingly remote from England's manners and mannerisms, called it a '*malkhut shel chessed*' ('kingdom of kindness').

An Israeli of the old school telling me about the tensions between the British and Jews in the then Palestine in the 1930s and '40s stopped in the middle of his diatribe and said with a wry smile, '*Aval ha–Anglim hem gentlemanim*' ('But the English are gentlemen'). Even to say it, he had to use the English word. For Jews, Britain epitomised a deep-down decency, a refusal to let hate be the final word, a residual, understated, yet unshakable, humanity. For many years, I did not know how rare this was and is.

Jews' love of England was not blind. They knew its faults, its snobbery, its fastidious class-consciousness, its anti-intellectualism. They recognised the anti-Semitic undertones in writers as different as John Buchan, G.K. Chesterton and T.S. Eliot. My late father was there when Oswald Mosley and his Blackshirts marched in the East End of London in the 1930s. But they also recognised the philo-Semitism of an Arthur Balfour and a Winston Churchill. They admired the British sense of fair play. Beneath its sometimes cold exterior, they knew, beat a pulse of liberty and justice.

They knew that the English could be as susceptible as anyone to prejudice in its many guises. It could be heard around genteel dinner tables or boisterously in pubs. But not in public discourse. Political parties did not win elections by campaigning against immigrants or minorities. England lacked a rhetoric of hate. That was the difference, and it was all the difference. Somehow the body politic in England had built up an immunity to the darker forces of human nature. I say this because we are in danger of forgetting it, and what a nation forgets, it loses.

In the first half of the nineteenth century, a spring breeze of optimism blew over the new nation states of Europe. Fresh words and sensibilities were in the air. Europe was the home of the Enlightenment, rationalism, science and a flowering of the arts. The keyword was progress. Politics was shaking itself free of old establishments and hierarchies. Wordsworth caught the mood unforgettably in his response to the French Revolution: 'Bliss was it in that dawn to be alive / But to be young was very heaven!'

For Jews and other minorities – in England, Catholics and Dissenters – the prospect of civic equality was at last within sight: the right to attend university, enter the professions, even to be elected to Parliament. Emancipation, though it did not come soon or easily, was at least on the agenda. In 1789, the French National Assembly had declared that 'All men are born and remain free and equal in rights.' Civic disabilities based on class or religion were about to become a thing of the past.

Yet it was precisely at this time that a new and deadly prejudice was born. In 1879, the German journalist Wilhelm Marr gave it a name: anti-Semitism. By the time the nineteenth century was at an end, it had become clear that the hopes of the Enlightenment and the promise of emancipation had failed, at least for Europe's Jews. The Viennese journalist and highly assimilated Jew Theodor Herzl understood this instantly when he witnessed the Parisian crowds outside the École Militaire after the initial verdict in the Dreyfus trial, shouting '*à morts les juifs!*' ('Death to the Jews!') The reality, when it came, exceeded his worst nightmare.

I mention this not because I believe that Jewish suffering is the only suffering with a claim to our attention. All prejudice is dangerous, whoever holds it and whoever it is held against. Rather, the fate of nineteenth- and early twentieth-century Europe is a reminder that national character and culture are not minor matters, idiosyncrasies, random mutations in a world of moral relativity. At moments of crisis they can make the difference between life and death, freedom and tyranny, decency and evil, courage and complicity.

Why, when a whole continent from Paris to Moscow was convulsed by *die Judenfrage*, the Jewish question, was Britain – not quite, but almost, alone – immune? Was it its famous empiricism, its refusal to go down the continental road of polysyllabic philosophical obscurantism that befuddled the brains and anaesthetised the consciences of generations of intellectuals? Was it its long tradition of individualism that saved the British from the madness of crowds and mass incitement to hate? Was it the difference, remarked on by J.L. Talmon and Friedrich Hayek, between British liberalism, with its respect for tradition, and continental liberalism, with its revolutionary desire to make the world anew?

Could it have been British mercantilism, the much derided character of England as a 'nation of shopkeepers'? In European history, trade has been the tutor of tolerance: witness Venice in the sixteenth century and the Netherlands in the seventeenth. It was the City of London, England's financial centre, that first welcomed Jews and first elected one, Lionel de Rothschild, to Parliament.

It may have been any of these things. But there was one other difference between nineteenth-century Britain and the rest of Europe that deserves attention, namely their respective attitudes to civil society. Britain, like the United States, valued the 'little platoons' of family, congregation, neighbourhoods, friendly societies and charities. Alexis de Tocqueville saw this as the single most striking feature of American political culture. He called it 'the art of association' and saw it as the necessary underpinning of a free and democratic society.

A generation before, Edmund Burke had said the same about Britain. Families, he wrote, were the birthplace of 'public affections'. What was wrong about continental political philosophy for Burke was its focus on the abstract, atomic individual, with rights but no sense of connectedness and belonging, no attachment to place or locality, history or tradition. Politics, Burke understood, is about people, not just ideology, and people need a 'thick' identity, nurtured in family and community, if they are to retain the better angels of their nature.

For Burke and de Tocqueville, civic associations mediated between the individual and the state. They forged bonds of friendship and trust. They created what today we call 'social capital'. They were local, personal, intimate and humanising. They were an ongoing education in moral responsibility and reciprocity. They represented society with a human face.

The continental tradition was far less minded to see virtue in the little platoons. Rousseau saw the family as a distraction from politics, something that stood in the way of the total identification of the citizen with the *volonté générale*, the collective will, of the nation as a whole. Hegel saw civil society, *bürgerliche Gesellschaft*, as the arena of self-interest as opposed to the higher ethical life of the state. The failure of a political culture to make space for civil associations leads, not immediately but at times of crisis, to what J.L. Talmon called 'totalitarian democracy'. That, I believe, is one reason why anti-Semitism did not enter the mainstream of British debate between 1850 and 1950 as it did elsewhere in Europe.

The Jews of Britain, knowing what was at stake, understood the reciprocity of any social order. They strove to integrate. They adapted. They made strenuous efforts to belong and look as if they belonged, and if they did not, the more established Jewish community did not mince words in telling them to do so. 'If they intend to remain in England,' wrote the *Jewish Chronicle* in 1881 about the new wave of Jewish immigrants from Eastern Europe, 'if they wish to become members of our community, we have a right to demand that they will show signs of an earnest wish for a complete amalgamation with the aims and feelings of their hosts.'

Morris Joseph, minister of the (Reform) West London Synagogue, told the new arrivals that they had a 'duty to leave behind them the ideas and habits that were tolerated in Russia'. The Jewish Lads' Brigade was formed to anglicise its charges, iron out 'the ghetto bend' and, as Sharman Kadish puts it in *A Good Jew and a Good Englishman* (1995), 'instil into the rising generation all that is best in the English character, manly independence, honour, truth, cleanliness, love of active health-giving pursuits'. Educational establishments like the Jews' Free School trained their pupils to be model Englishmen and women. The headmaster, Louis Abrahams, urged parents to reinforce the message of the school:

> Strengthen the efforts of the teachers to wipe away all evidence of foreign birth and foreign proclivities, so that your children shall be so identified with everything that is English, in thought and deed, that no shadow of anti-Semitism might exist, that your boys and girls may grow up devoted to the flag which they are learning within these walls to love and honour, that they may take a worthy part in the growth of this great Empire, whose shelter and protection I hope will never be denied them.

They had role models, most notably Sir Moses Montefiore, an observant Jew, president of the Board of Deputies of British Jews, Sheriff of the City of London, a well-known figure among the general public and a close personal friend of Queen Victoria. On his 99th, and again on his 100th, birthday, *The Times* published leaders in his honour. The latter, from 24 October 1884, is a particularly fascinating document. It speaks of Montefiore's philanthropy to Christians and Jews alike. It pays tribute to the synthesis he had created between his two identities: 'He has been the victorious defender of persecuted Jews because he was the perfect English gentleman.' The article ends with a call to the rest of the Jewish community to follow his example: 'the determination to show, by his life, that fervent Judaism and patriotic citizenship are absolutely consistent with one another.'

It would be wrong to romanticise. The Jews of London's East End and other inner cities were often destitute, unskilled and living in cramped tenements. Many of them worked in sweatshops under conditions that shocked Victorian social reformers like Charles Booth and Beatrice Webb who came to observe them.

They had to run the gauntlet of hostility. The *East London Advertiser* spoke of 'the swarms of foreign Jews who have invaded the East End labour market'. In 1903, the MP for Stepney, Major Evans-Gordon, said at a constituency meeting: 'There is hardly an Englishman in this room who does not live under the constant danger of being driven from his home, pushed out into the streets, not by the natural increase of our own population, but by the off-scum of Europe.'

Within two generations, the 'off-scum' had made their way in British society, creating businesses like Marks & Spencer, Tesco and Shell Petroleum; clothing stores like Moss Bros and Burton; writers like Harold Pinter and Peter Shaffer; theatre and film producers, politicians, cabinet ministers, academics, soldiers, judges, philanthropists, poets, philosophers and Nobel Prize winners. Jews knew what they owed Britain – their lives – and they sought to give back all they could.

Integration carried a price. Jews had to understate their Jewishness and sometimes make compromises with their Judaism. They lost much of their own rich culture. One example: Jews had spoken Yiddish – a hybrid Jewish vernacular – for a thousand years. In it they expressed some of their deepest spirituality, their most lively literature, their irrepressible humour. They lost it in a single generation because parents – mine included – did not teach it to their children. They wanted them to speak English, become English, and leave the habits of the ghetto behind. Without massive efforts in recent years to re-educate Jews in Judaism, the community might have disappeared almost entirely, robbing Britain of the distinctive contributions that Jewry, like every other minority community, brings to the common good.

This narrative, I admit, has a musty, sepia-tinted, Victorian feel about it. After two world wars and the Holocaust, we have come to distrust the nation state and the very idea of national identities. This, however, is a mistake of historic proportions. It fails to take note of the vital distinction, made by George Orwell, between patriotism and nationalism. Nationalism, which he opposed, is 'inseparable from the will to power'. Its purpose is to secure ever more prestige for the nation: 'Nationalism is power hunger tempered by self-deception.' Patriotism, by contrast, he defined as 'devotion to a particular place and a particular way of life, which one believes to be the best in the world but has no wish to force upon other people'. That is the difference between arrogance and pride. Pride means valuing others because you value yourself. Arrogance means devaluing others so that you can have a high opinion of yourself. National arrogance is unforgivable. National pride is essential.

Three forces are today threatening the very concept of national identity. The first is the sheer diversity of the populations of every European state. When I visit British schools, especially in inner cities, I meet pupil populations drawn from as many as 50 different language and ethnic groups, each with its own customs and history. Never before have people been more mobile. Walk down the average British high street and you will meet more cultural difference than a seventeenth-century anthropologist might encounter in a lifetime.

The second is communications technology. Migration once meant leaving one culture to make your home in another. It no longer does so. Today anyone can watch television and read the press of his or her country of origin courtesy of satellite television and the Internet. Benedict Anderson, in his *Imagined Communities*, argued that national identities were created by one medium of communication: the newspaper. Today they are being fragmented by another: the Internet. Newspapers are national; the Internet is global. Whether any national culture can survive this transformation is far from clear.

The third is the doctrine of multiculturalism. Britain once encouraged integration. Multiculturalism promotes segregation. So the Cantle Report into the northern mill-town riots of 2001 concluded, and so did Trevor Phillips of the (then) Commission for Racial Equality; David Goodhart, editor of *Prospect* magazine; and John Sentamu, the Archbishop of York.

I have set out the argument in detail in *The Home We Build Together* (2007). The Dutch, who were the first to embark on the multicultural experiment, are now its greatest critics. Introduced to increase tolerance, they say, multiculturalism in fact radically diminishes it. The difference, they explain, is that a tolerant society ignores differences. A multicultural society makes an issue of them at every point.

It may simply be that the nation state is nearing its end. In a world of global interconnectedness, it is too small for the big problems and too big for the small ones. Philip Bobbitt argues that the nation state has already died and in its place has come the market state, a place where people transact the business of life but not one with which they identify or to which they belong.

I do not share this view. If the nation state goes, there is nothing to take its place. We have none of the mechanisms or sensibilities to create a system of global governance. Even the European Union is too diffuse to replace its constituent member states. Disaggregating nations into regions or localities – bringing back, in effect, the Europe of the Middle Ages – would encourage a parochialism wholly inadequate to the challenges of our time.

If we are to sustain the social virtues – the feeling that we share a fate, that we have responsibilities to others, including those who do not share our religion, and that there is a common good to which we bring our distinctive gifts and contributions – then we will continue to need national identities.

A key insight was articulated by Alasdair MacIntyre at the end of his masterwork *After Virtue* (1981), when he drew a parallel between our age and the decline of the Roman Empire:

> A crucial turning point in that earlier history occurred when men and women of good will turned aside from the task of shoring up the Roman imperium and ceased to identify the continuation of civility and moral community with the maintenance of that imperium. What they set themselves to achieve instead – often not recognising fully what they were doing – was the construction of new forms of community within which the moral life could be sustained so that both morality and civility might survive the coming ages of barbarism and darkness.

In other words, when the groups that make up a society turn inward, a civilisation is at risk of coming to an end. For some years now, many if not most of Britain's subcommunities have been turning inward. That is a danger signal of major proportions.

If my argument is correct we are faced with two propositions: (1) that the nation state is at risk, and (2) that its continuation is essential if we are to counterbalance the relentless individualism of a consumerist society with the social virtues on which our collective well-being depends. If this is so, then a third proposition follows: we are going to have to do something Britain has not done in peacetime for many generations. We will have to engage, consciously and actively, in society-building. We can no longer see this as something that happens inevitably, as if by an 'invisible hand'. This has implications for our political culture.

As I explain in detail in *The Home We Build Together*, there have been throughout history three broad types of society: organic, hierarchical and covenantal. Organic societies are those with a long sense of shared history. Hierarchical societies are built on status, class or caste. Covenantal societies are created when people come together in an act of collective self-determination. A covenant is an open-ended commitment on the part of individuals, each respecting the dignity and integrity of the others, to share a fate and destiny. In it they undertake a moral bond of loyalty and responsibility to do together what none can do alone.

Covenant played a large part in the politics of Europe – in Switzerland, the Netherlands, Scotland and England – in the sixteenth and seventeenth centuries. Only in the United States has it remained central to public discourse from the beginning (the Mayflower Compact, 1620) to today. The reason is obvious. As a nation populated by wave after wave of immigrants and asylum seekers, America has had to engage in society-building in almost every generation. Renewal is part of its political culture. Barack Obama understood this and framed his rhetoric around it, subtly evoking the cadences of Abraham Lincoln and Martin Luther King. He won the presidency because he was able, in an age of anxiety, to construct a compelling narrative of hope. Covenantal societies are built on the politics of narrative and the language of hope.

England, by contrast, once its civil war was over, relied on the two other modes, organic and hierarchical: tradition and class. But by now these have lost almost all their force. That is why the concept of covenant deserves to be revisited, together with all that goes with it: a national narrative, civic rituals and the enlisting of the many groups – religious, charitable, educational and community based – that make up the still dense texture of our civil society.

It cannot be done, say the sceptics. In fact it can, and we have one striking example. Since 27 January 2001, Britain has observed an annual national Holocaust Memorial Day. This has a central national ceremony, together with local events in virtually every city and town. Each brings together civic leaders, representatives of the major faiths, politicians of all parties and community activists of all kinds. The mere fact that it exists, and that speeches are made, means that a national Holocaust narrative (as opposed to a Jewish one) is in the making. If it can be done in Britain for something that lies in the past and did not happen in Britain, then it can be done for the present and for Britishness itself.

Britain, it is said, acquired an empire in a fit of absent-mindedness. It is in danger of losing its identity the same way. Granted all its imperfections, Britain stayed sane while much of Europe lost if not its sanity then certainly its humanity. Britain's culture and character helped write the history of law-governed liberty. We cannot lose them now without endangering the future of freedom. We must remake our national identity, in covenant, together.

22

A DAY OF BRITISHNESS

JOHN O'FARRELL

IT SEEMS BIZARRE THAT THE PATRON SAINT OF THE ENGLISH IS someone who is famous for killing an animal. If St George had done the deed in this country, he'd have faced angry protests from weeping demonstrators demanding the setting up of a dragon sanctuary. The government would have been forced into banning the hunting of dragons with saints, while the Countryside Alliance claimed that the mythical reptile actually enjoyed the sport. Britain should have patron saints who excelled in things with which we can identify: St Cuthbert, for example, the patron saint of queuing. Or St Botolph, who Christian legend has it bravely defied the Romans and organised a petition against the Watling Street bypass.

The meaningless days of long-forgotten saints is the closest we British have to national days, even though St George wasn't English and St Andrew wasn't Scottish, while St Patrick was about as Irish as the people wearing leprechaun hats in the Irish pubs around Leicester Square. Perhaps the reason that the United Kingdom lacks a meaningful national anniversary is that we have never had a proper revolution. It looked possible for a moment when the BBC axed *One Man and His Dog*, but the British have never felt compelled to suddenly overthrow all the landowners and chop all their heads off. We were far more vicious than that; we made them open their homes to the public, providing llama rides for the kiddies and disappointing displays of agricultural machinery.

Without a set day on which to do it, irregular expressions of national pride tend to be celebrated by fragmented sections of the population; the England football fans celebrating a victory over Germany are not the same people who wave Union flags at royal weddings (maybe because the royals probably supported Germany anyway).

But we badly need a day on which we celebrate what it means to be British, when we focus for a moment what is best about this country. I recently wrote a complete history of Britain and was struck by how our concept of national pride used to revolve around the Glorious Revolution of 1688, of the supremacy of Parliament and the political freedoms enjoyed by the ordinary English or Scottish citizens. Democracy is Britain's greatest gift to the world, and the Mother of Parliaments should be the focus of what we celebrate when we reflect upon what we stand for. Centuries before any other major power, we were evolving the concept of elected governments, of ruling by consent rather than coercion. Surely this is worth commemorating more than the fact that a fifth-century Turk killed a dragon (which, apart from anything else, he didn't).

For some time now there has been discussion about a possible autumn bank holiday, running alongside a search for a date on which Britain might celebrate its collective identity. But our national day is staring us in the face; we already celebrate it! The Americans let off fireworks on 4 July, the French let off fireworks on 14 July, while English teenagers chuck around illegal air bombs for six weeks either side of 5 November. The day that Parliament was saved should be celebrated as our national holiday. What's more British than standing outside in the drizzle and watching expensive fireworks fizzle out? What is more symbolic of British cuisine than an over-cooked jacket potato and warmed-up red wine with cloves floating about in it?

Making 5 November a bank holiday – 'Parliament Day' – means that we would be taking much of what is already in existence and combining it to provide a focus for progressive patriotism and the democratic tradition of which Britain should be far more proud. By timetabling the State Opening of Parliament for the same day, we would at a stroke create a national patriotic celebration that would combine royal pageantry and tradition with the firework parties taking place all over the country to create a real sense of celebration and history. (The State Opening of Parliament was, of course, the target of the conspirators.)

Some might worry about the possibility of a vague anti-Catholic residue surrounding 5 November, but this would wither with the new focus on Parliament and democracy. In any case, the reason that sixteenth-century progressives were anti-Catholic was because to them Catholicism was synonymous with the dictatorships of the French and Spanish monarchies. It comes back to the concepts of freedom and parliamentary supremacy and the Glorious Revolution; 5 November was, of course, the very day when William III (arguably our first constitutional monarch) landed in Britain at the invitation of MPs and Lords. Perhaps the anti-Catholic echoes of that date could be laid to rest by simultaneously repealing the archaic Act of Settlement – finally making it legal for Catholics to marry into the royal family.

The first king of Scotland to rule England was of course saved from death on that date – so this would also be a celebration of the beginnings of the Union. By fixing the State Opening of Parliament for 5 November, 'Parliament Day' would also become a celebration of our constitutional monarchy. It might feel contrived for a couple of years, but before long we would think that we always celebrated our national day on the night that Parliament was saved and the day that the monarch still arrives at the Palace of Westminster. To give it real value it should always be on the fifth; the French or Americans would never shift their national day to the nearest Monday. And having the new bank holiday on the day of the State Opening of Parliament would have one other populist bonus: the only people who would have to turn up to work would be the royal family and all the MPs!

Britain has given the world a great deal down the centuries. Its favourite sport, its language of choice, industrialised capitalism and, of course, the Teasmade. We are a modest nation, not prone to excessive patriotism or blowing our own trumpet. For example, you'd never find us publishing a whole book full of British people saying how great we all were – oh, hang on a minute . . . But for one day a year it might be worth stopping to think that above everything else, the system of government to which most of the world aspires, one in which we elect our representatives, in which we have freedom of speech and association, was pioneered right here. 'Parliament Day', 5 November, could be just that. And for those cynics who cringe at the idea of a British government attempting to do anything patriotic or new, well, they can have their own reasons for a party on 5 November: 'Look, it's the best possible date for a national celebration – it's the last time the government found any weapons of mass destruction!'

23

IN PRAISE OF VAGUENESS

ANTHONY KING

ONE NIGHT A LONG TIME AGO, I STOOD ON THE PLATFORM OF Ottawa's Union Station and waited to board an overnight train to New York. From New York I was booked to sail on one of the great Cunard liners to Southampton. From Southampton I would take the train to Oxford to take up the Rhodes Scholarship I had recently been awarded. With me on the station platform were my mother and my then fiancée, and I distinctly remember wondering, as I stood there with the two of them and my big leather suitcase, whether I would ever return to Ottawa or even to Canada. I had certainly made no decision either to leave or to return. I just wondered, and I did even that for only a moment.

I was a Canadian, of course. I knew that perfectly well. My parents were both born in Canada. I was born there, too, and I grew up in Canada, went to school there, took my first degree there and had what people told me was a Canadian accent. Furthermore, in case there was any doubt, my blue passport told me I was a Canadian – not only that, but also in those far-off days 'a British subject', '*un sujet britannique*'. But I have since come to realise that I had no very vivid sense of being a Canadian. It was part of my identity, an integral and formative part, but it was by no means an intense part. I did not feel desperately Canadian. I felt strongly about all kinds of things – about the Toronto Maple Leafs hockey club, about Jackie Robinson, the first black player recruited to an hitherto all-white American baseball team, and about the terrifying McCarthyite witch-hunts in the United States – but I did not feel strongly about being a Canadian. My status as a Canadian was just a fact about me: a benign fact, certainly not a fact to be ashamed of, but ultimately just that, a fact, like being tall or having brown hair.

It now occurs to me to wonder why my sense of nationality was so matter-of-fact, because I realise that of course tens of millions of people feel very intensely American, Russian, French or whatever. Perhaps citizens of small independent nations tend to feel less intensely about their nationality; one seldom meets a fervent Norwegian. Perhaps being brought up in a country that has never been invaded makes a difference. In my case, it may have had something to do with the fact that my parents, although Canadian-born, had friends and relatives in both Britain and the US. My father had studied to be a painter in France. He and my mother had honeymooned there. Both knew French and more than a modicum of German. Just as I never felt intensely Canadian, I did not grow up feeling that other countries and other peoples were foreign or 'Other' in the sense of being alien or hostile. They were just different – to me, intriguingly so.

My experience of Oxford, and soon of Britain as a whole, had the same quality. Although I was *un sujet britannique*, I did not feel British, but equally I did not feel non-British, let alone un-British. It also turned out that my being a Canadian was merely a fact – usually not a very interesting fact – to most of the people I met. I was never 'integrated', in the sense that anyone did or said anything to integrate me: I just did integrate, unselfconsciously and rapidly. Putting it another way, there was no line between me and the British: no line that I had to cross if I wanted to become one of them. I was here; they were here; and that was that. My suspicion is that the British I encountered were so secure in their own identity that they never gave the matter a moment's thought. They knew who they were, and they never felt their identity to be under threat – or only a minority of them did – even when, beginning in the late 1950s, hundreds of thousands, and then millions, of people from elsewhere started to arrive in their midst. It never ceases to amaze me that this insular and hitherto homogeneous population has absorbed so many millions of immigrants, many of them Asian or black, with so little fuss. There have been troubles, of course, and angry voices have been raised, but only sporadically and on nothing like the scale that was once predicted.

Now, however, there is anxiety about British identity and 'Britishness'. Or, rather, there is anxiety about it in some quarters. Most of the locals, certainly in England, seem as little concerned about such abstractions as they ever were. I remember a few years ago driving up a hill in Essex behind a car with a 'Buy a British apple' bumper sticker on its rear end. The car was a Mercedes. Or, as someone wrote not long ago to a British paper: 'Being British is about driving in a German car to an Irish pub for a Belgian beer, then travelling home, grabbing an Indian curry or a Turkish kebab on the way, to sit on Swedish furniture and watch American shows on a Japanese TV.' The British Academy has never sought, in the manner of the Académie française, to impose Britishness rules on people's use of the English language; it is as porous as it ever was. No one doubts – or at least few doubt – that Amir Khan and Christine Ohuruogu are British, however exotic their names. It is said, and is probably true, that Britain has one of the highest rates of interracial marriage in the world.

So what is the problem? Why the current concern about Britishness that has inspired this volume? It appears to have three sources, each familiar in its own right.

One is the widespread sense, which I share, that British society is less cohesive than it once was. Families break up far more frequently than they used to. Family members neither pray together nor even share meals together. Teenage pregnancy is far more common than in the past. The use of hard as well as soft drugs is on the rise. Alcoholism and binge drinking are rife. People are more suspicious of each other and of institutions than they used to be. Incidents of casual insensitivity and outright rudeness are more common than in the past. Pregnant women are left to stand in crowded railway carriages. All the evidence points to a decline in the incidence of duty, as distinct from self-regard, as a driver of individuals' behaviour. British society is far from being 'broken' – that is a gross exaggeration – but it is certainly chipped and cracked at many points.

Another source of people's concerns about the state of modern Britain is, of course, the fact that substantial numbers of newcomers to this country – and their children and grandchildren – evidently reject Britain's Enlightenment values of rationality and tolerance and, worse, are prepared to condone violence and even to employ violence in order to give vent to their alienation and disdain. Although most Muslims living in Britain are far from being extreme rejectionists, most of those who are extreme rejectionists are, or claim to be, Muslims. It does not really matter that members of many immigrant communities choose to live somewhat apart; Irish immigrants did that in the nineteenth century and Jews before then. What really matters is that a minority of Muslims – albeit a small minority – preach doctrines of religious and cultural hatred and are prepared to blow up their fellow citizens. For the first time in centuries, we have in Britain 'an enemy within'. The police and MI5 find themselves cast in the role of Francis Walsingham's spies.

The third source of people's concerns relates to the future of the United Kingdom itself. A majority of the Irish pushed off decades ago, and there is at least a possibility that the Scots as a whole will join them, at which point the country would presumably have to be renamed the United Kingdom of England, Wales and Northern Ireland (though the inclusion of 'United' in the new name might sound a trifle odd). At the moment, opinion polls suggest that in a referendum north of the border on the issue only a minority of Scots, possibly quite a small minority, would vote for outright secession. That is presumably why, although an SNP administration is currently in power at Holyrood, no such referendum has been held. But that could change, and supporters of the Union on both sides of the border are right to be concerned. What Iain McLean of Oxford has dubbed 'primordial unionism' – the belief that the Union is good in and of itself, irrespective of any tangible benefits it may bring – is on the wane. Indeed, it has probably already largely disappeared.

Now the central point about these three sources of concern about the condition of modern Britain – loss of social cohesion, domestic terrorism and the possibility of Scottish secession – is that they have precious little, if anything, to do with each other. Any one of the three could exist, and to a large extent does exist, wholly independently of either of the others. Loss of social cohesion, to the extent that it is being lost, plays scarcely any role in fuelling 'Islamic' terrorism, a worldwide phenomenon, let alone the enthusiasm of a minority of Scots for independence (even Scottish secessionists do not imagine that independence will do much, if anything, to solve Scotland's endemic drugs problem). Similarly, domestic terrorism contributes little or nothing to either Britain's loss of social cohesion, a phenomenon that long predates the 2007 attacks at Glasgow Airport and in London, or the desire among some Scots for independence, a desire wholly unrelated to terrorism and dating back to at least the late 1960s and the discovery of 'Scottish' oil. As for the desire for Scottish independence, not even the most splenetic Englishman blames it for either Britain's nationwide loss of social cohesion or the emergence of domestic terrorism.

The three are thus separate, almost wholly so. Yet, bizarrely, all three are frequently addressed as though they somehow comprised a single phenomenon reflecting what might be called 'a shortage of Britishness'. If only there were more Britishness about the place, it is claimed, the UK would be more socially cohesive, less subject to the threat of domestic terrorism and less likely to fall apart politically, with Scotland claiming its independence. However, as the Duke of Wellington famously said in a different context, 'If you believe that, you'll believe anything.' Or, alternatively, if anyone does believe that, their reasoning would appear to be circular – tautologous and therefore otiose, the solution defining the problem.

Consider the array – one might almost say the potpourri – of ideas that have been advanced for promoting Britishness. It is fair to ask of each whether it would address any of the three concerns listed above and, if so, which. It is also fair to ask whether it would be likely to be effective, in practice, in addressing one or more of these concerns. Would it actually work?

The array of ideas on offer, from Lord Goldsmith among others, is long and diverse:

- encouraging people to fly the Union flag more often
- inaugurating an annual 'national' holiday
- offering financial incentives to people who do voluntary work
- encouraging immigrants to learn English
- staging citizenship ceremonies for schoolchildren
- restricting the vote in UK elections to full British citizens
- creating a new National Youth Community Service
- paying more frequent and fulsome tribute to the men and women of Britain's armed services.

A casual perusal of this list immediately reveals a number of difficulties. Although several of the ideas on offer are undoubtedly worth considering in their own right – for example, finding ways of encouraging immigrants to learn English and creating a National Youth Community Service – few of them, if any, seem likely to increase social cohesion (drunken football fans often drape themselves in the Union flag), to discourage domestic terrorists (all of whom know English and are recorded by the police and MI5 speaking English) or to discourage avid Scots from seeking their nation's independence (every Scot speaks English and is fully conscious of the contributions made by Scottish regiments to the British Army's historic exploits). The main effect of inaugurating a new national holiday would be to make those who already feel patriotically British feel even more so and to give everybody else a day off. The main effect of doing more to pay tribute to the services rendered on our behalf by Britain's soldiers, sailors and airmen would be, one hopes, to make those particular men and women feel better appreciated than they are now; but there is no reason to think it would do much, if anything, to instil more profound feelings of Britishness in the whole population, let alone to reduce teenage pregnancy, forestall London bombings or turn Scottish nationalists into UK loyalists.

In other words, none of the items on the list addresses all three of people's real concerns; most of them address only one, and all of them are likely to have only minimal effect. Indeed they are liable to be a distraction, directing attention away from what really needs to be done to promote social cohesion, defeat domestic terrorism and persuade a majority of Scots that, after all, the Union is worth preserving. There is no single, overarching problem of 'Britishness' and, even if there were, there is no reason to suppose that all or most of the above-listed suggestions would be likely to have more than a marginal effect in making people feel more British than they do now. Even if they did have that effect, such measures would in most cases be less effective than measures designed not to address the largely non-existent problem of Britishness but, rather, the very real problems of binge drinking, Muslim alienation and Scottish nationalism. The best way to make Scots want to remain citizens of the United Kingdom is not to make them feel more 'British' – whatever that may mean – but to remind them of the great things that the Scots, Welsh, Irish and English have achieved together, which they would not have achieved separately, and to point out that outright secession might not actually be to their advantage, whether economically or in any other respect.

Moreover, in all of this there are real downside risks: that, if implemented, some of these suggestions would achieve effects precisely the opposite of the ones they are meant to achieve. To generate feelings of insiderishness is to run the risk of generating feelings of outsiderishness. The marginalised Muslim youngster forced to attend a citizenship ceremony may as a result feel more British, but he may on the other hand come to feel even more marginalised, to feel that he is on one side of a line, with the majority of the population, the 'real British', on the other side. Seeing the Union flag flying everywhere could well have the same effect (as in 'there ain't no black in the Union Jack'). Scots could easily be made to feel, not that feelings of Britishness reinforce feelings of Scottishness, but that the one is being set up to diminish the importance of the other. Britishness has survived for more than three centuries substantially as a blur, on the whole an amicable blur. Sharpen it up and it might come to have a cutting edge, one that would cut two ways.

One of Britain's strengths through the ages has been its vagueness, its porousness. People have wandered in and made their home here or else wandered out. There have never been tests of ancestry, race, linguistic competence or, despite Norman Tebbit's best efforts, sporting affiliation. All sorts of people have fought on this country's behalf; one has only to look at the war memorials and military cemeteries in Singapore or North Africa. The British long ago gave up worrying about people's religious faith. For their part, the English more than a century ago gave up trying to suppress the Welsh language and to transmogrify Scotland into 'North Britain'. All four of the United Kingdom's peoples have adapted astonishingly well to the UK's having become, within two generations, a large-scale immigrant society. There is a lot to be said for not asking too many questions about what all this means. It means just what it is: one of the world's most open and attractive societies.

I began with several paragraphs of autobiography. I probably ought to end with a confession. I am not a British citizen. I have never become one even though I have lived (and loved) all of my adult life in this country. Why have I not taken out British citizenship? In part, because of laziness: as a Canadian of my generation, I have the vote and have never felt any real need to become a British citizen. In part, because of a strong – and one might say typically British – dislike of form-filling and bureaucracy. In part, because I quite like being an insider who is also, ever so slightly, an outsider. Also, I have always been struck by the fact, and impressed by the fact, that so long as I am here and do my bit no one seems to mind, or even notice, that I still carry my blue passport.

Of course, if I have to take out British citizenship to remain here and continue to be entitled to vote, I will certainly do that (assuming I can pass the exam). But will that make me feel more British? I doubt it. Will that make other people look on me as being more British? I doubt it. In my view, the traditional absence in Britain of hard and fast lines dividing Britons from non-Britons, and different types of Britons from each other, still has much to commend it.

BELONGING AND BEING BRITISH

MICHAEL WILLS

IT MAY SEEM RASH FOR ANY MODERN GOVERNMENT TO INTRUDE on questions of identity, as who we think we are has become so intensely personal. And it may seem particularly perverse to focus on such issues when for at least 20 years general elections have turned on practical issues of public policy – defence in the 1980s, public services more recently and the economy throughout. And even more so as this is written, as the world is going through the sharpest recession in living memory.

Of course, politics is instrumentalist and voters see it as a means to an end. Their assessment of what's in it for them, who'll manage the economy best, and deliver the most jobs, the highest living standards, the lowest mortgage rates, the best NHS and the best schools, all help determine general elections. So why has the government led by Gordon Brown embarked on a discussion about a British 'statement of values', and now?

Because our national identity matters. Who we think we are shapes both public policy and decisions in the polling booth. Voting is not simply a consumer transaction. It's also an expression of identity. And a robust, inclusive expression of identity could help meet pressing challenges of social cohesion, including those posed by mass global migration and terrorism, in strengthening the Union that, for all the problems, has served the peoples of these islands well for centuries, and in reinforcing the self-confidence this country needs to get through the tough times that lie ahead.

In the twentieth century, identity politics drove new political movements, speaking the language of insurgency, challenging the conventional organisation of politics around beliefs and policy programmes (with political parties as briefcases for such beliefs and programmes) and organising instead around a shared identity – usually one expressed as being oppressed and exploited.

But that talk of rainbow coalitions was not exactly the new departure it was often claimed to be. Identity has always driven politics, if not always so explicitly. Whenever material issues have been bundled up into an ideological contest between competing systems of values, politics has become as much about identity as about self-interest or policy. Those who sign up to a system of values are saying something about what sort of person they think they are. Class, for example, is an identity. Class politics is not simply a battle for economic power. It is also a conflict between different views of identity. Working-class conservatism was fuelled by a different sense of identity from that offered by nineteenth-century working-class liberalism and twentieth-century working-class socialism.

And when such working-class voters migrated to Mrs Thatcher's Conservative Party in the 1980s, they were expressing a view not just about taxation and council-house sales and CND but also about their aspirations for themselves and their families, an assertion of the individual against the state. And when they migrated back to Labour in the 1990s, they were expressing an alternative view about how they wanted their country to be and their place in it, a view rooted in a sense that the atomisation of society had gone too far, that there was a proper place for the collective in our polity. That there was such a thing as society.

Today, many cast their vote because they feel their chosen party embodies values that define who they are, feeling that how they vote says something about the kind of person they are. They want to feel their vote validates them. That helps explain, for example, why so many vote, consciously, against their own economic self-interest: the prosperous who vote for parties who'll tax them more, the poor who vote for parties that will cut taxes on the better-off and cut the public services on which they themselves depend.

But identity is important also on a still more profound level, defining the territory within which politics operates. Democracies depend on a covenant between the individual and the state, between government and the governed. Democratic politics can only take place within a framework of common purpose and a sense of shared destiny between voters. It is this that creates a moral community, not necessarily defined by geography or class but rather by shared sentiments of mutual and reciprocal respect and obligation, only possible where there is some sense of a shared identity. Any moral community flows from the sense of identity of its members – where they feel they belong, to whom they feel they owe their loyalty and from whom they feel they derive rights. Without such a moral community, based on a shared identity, a democracy can be neither stable nor sustainable. Without it, election results won't be accepted as legitimate. Voters who don't feel they belong together, tend not to stay together.

If a sense of identity is important in shaping voting behaviour and in underpinning any system of democracy, then how people identify themselves matters.

For most of us, our identity is plural. It derives from our personal history, our family and our friendships, our neighbourhood, region and country. Gender, age, sexuality and ethnicity can all shape identity. Few of us feel any one of these characteristics define us exclusively. And their relative importance will ebb and flow over time in response to changing circumstances. And so too our sense of the moral community to which we belong will ebb and flow. At one time, we will feel most intensely our obligation to a parent or partner. At others, it will be to victims of a tsunami or famine on the other side of the world.

But politically the nation state remains the anchor of belonging. So much of what roots us, politically, economically and culturally, flows from the nation state – our systems of education and justice and our public services of health and broadcasting. So many of the ties that bind us, that root us in our own place and time – the shared language, culture, social and political institutions and norms – are derived from the nation state. Where we feel we owe our loyalty and from where we feel we derive our rights focuses our politics. The yearning to belong has always been a motor of history, threats to a sense of belonging even more so. And the nation remains a focus for that sense of belonging.

This is not axiomatic. The importance of national identity has been called into question by the great global transformations of the last 50 years. In this country particularly, much of what constituted our national identity and made our parents and grandparents identify with Britain is being contested by five great and intertwined changes.

The rapid dissolution of the British Empire after the Second World War removed the institutions and symbols that had been instrumental in defining Britishness since the late nineteenth century. Profound economic and technological change, driving the phenomena of globalisation and growing interdependence, has been turning economies outward and global away from the inward and national. Growing interdependence has in turn driven institutional change as nation states rely increasingly on multilateral institutions such as the European Union, NATO and the World Trade Organization to pursue their national interests, with a resulting decrease in the centrality of national institutions, hitherto a cement for national identity.

Accompanying this has been cultural change, particularly among younger generations, as a new global consciousness takes root. The growing ubiquity of air travel and television and the global embrace of the Internet have made culture more outward-facing and diluted the dominance of specifically national media.

At the same time, rapid social change and the individuation of politics, deriving from individual characteristics such as gender and sexuality, have been turning consciousness inwards to the individual and not outwards towards the nation.

To many it seemed that the locus of identity was, at the same time, being stretched out to the world and focused in on the self, leaving the nation isolated and lonely in-between. The imagined community once populated with monarchs and the British Grenadiers now shares space with Tom Cruise and Starbucks and dreams of self-fulfilment.

But, for all this, the nation survives and remains a locus of political identity. In a 1999 survey for the Smith Institute, 70 per cent said they believed a strong sense of national identity was very important or quite important in judging a country's success. Partly this is a result of historical inertia – change is often less apparent to the people who experience it than to the media and politicians who comment on it – but significantly it is also a result of the destabilising effects of rapid global changes that appear to threaten it. Such profound changes make people seek to root themselves in the familiar. It is not surprising that the dreadful shock of what happened on 11 September 2001 caused such an upsurge in patriotic feeling among Americans as they sought a mooring in the unexpected and savage storm.

And so national identity becomes a central issue for politics. Many of the concerns that excite public discourse are driven by questions of national identity. Concerns about immigration are cultural as well as economic. When the Archbishop of Canterbury dominates the airwaves by speaking about sharia law, the questions he raises about the place of religion in our public life bear as directly on national identity as on the position of Islam. The strong reactions – for and against – Lord Goldsmith's suggestion for an oath of allegiance, the agonies the Conservative Party have put themselves through over Europe for 20 years, the alienation of young Muslim men, the arrival of a minority nationalist administration in the Scottish Parliament: all these issues derive their potency from views about national identity – and disputes about it.

More generally, the redistribution that is inherent in the tax system is only sustainable within the framework of a politics founded on a shared identity and community of interest, where citizens are committed to reciprocal rights and responsibilities. And the electric sensitivity about anything to do with the monarchy flows from its role as an emblem of the nation and our national identity.

National identity is an important political issue not simply because it's unavoidable but also because a robust sense of it, shared widely, will be a source of national strength in the years ahead. The cohesion, solidarity and political stability it can foster are essential if societies are to meet the challenges created by the speed and extent of global economic change, driven by extraordinary technological revolutions, and radical social change, transforming the norms and patterns of behaviour that have characterised human relationships for centuries. Tackling these challenges will require hard choices and difficult decisions, particularly as we go through an unprecedented recession, and a society lacking a shared purpose and sense of identity will find them harder to take, diverting precious energy into purposeless friction, bickering instead of building. If people are to seize the opportunities of change rather than being submerged by its challenges, then they must have confidence in their future. Unless people believe that tomorrow can be better than today, they will be unlikely to take the risks to make sure it is. And a rooted sense of belonging is crucial to that confidence.

In January 2008, the Ministry of Justice commissioned Ipsos MORI to carry out a survey to explore what sources of identity gave people a sense of belonging. Two thousand people were asked in face-to-face interviews how strongly, if at all, they felt a sense of belonging to Britain; to England, Scotland or Wales; to their local area or neighbourhood; their own age group; their religion or faith; and their ethnic group. The continuing importance of national identity, and British national identity, leaps out from the data:

- 45 per cent said they strongly felt a sense of belonging to their religion or faith

- 69 per cent said they strongly felt a sense of belonging to their ethnic group

- 70 per cent said they strongly felt a sense of belonging to their own age group

- 78 per cent said they strongly felt a sense of belonging to their local area or neighbourhood

- 80 per cent felt a strong sense of belonging to Britain

- 82 per cent in England felt a strong sense of belonging to England

- 91 per cent in Scotland felt a strong sense of belonging to Scotland

- 95 per cent in Wales felt a strong sense of belonging to Wales.

Of course, there are variations from these national figures within sub-groups. For example, 81 per cent in England felt a strong sense of belonging to Britain, compared with 87 per cent in Wales and with 70 per cent in Scotland, and it's worth noting that, for all the focus on the role of the Union in Scotland, 71 per cent in London felt a strong sense of belonging to Britain: virtually the same percentage as in Scotland.

What emerges strongly from these findings is the strength of British identity as a source of belonging. And this is true across age, gender, region and ethnicity. Of black and minority ethnic respondents, for example, 75 per cent said they felt a strong sense of belonging to Britain.

And this feeling is resilient. Despite all the learned commentaries about the growth of national sentiment in England, Scotland and Wales and the detachment of minority groups, 54 per cent said their sense of belonging to Britain had stayed the same over the last five years, 16 per cent said it had become stronger and only 28 per cent said it had become weaker. And again, there aren't significant variations across age, gender, region and ethnicity. For example, 54 per cent of whites compared with 48 per cent of black and minority ethnic respondents said their sense of belonging to Britain had stayed the same over the last five years.

These figures are significant. For the new Labour government that came to power in 1997, devolution was seen as essential to preserve the Union by better reflecting its new realities. But for years opponents have argued that devolution has wounded, perhaps fatally, the Union and that multiculturalism has fragmented national cohesion. But while it is true that English, Welsh and Scottish sentiment has strengthened and that, for example, twice as many black and minority ethnic respondents felt a sense of belonging to their religion or faith as white respondents, being British nevertheless remains central to a sense of belonging for the great majority of the peoples of these islands. There are many and complex reasons for this resilience, but, among other things, it must point to the importance of the pluralism that defines being British.

For our national identity is essentially plural. The nation state is the United Kingdom, a union of different nations, joined since the end of the Second World War by distinctive cultures from Asia, Africa and the Caribbean. It is this pluralism that distinguishes our British identity from the other allegiances we feel to one or other of the constituent parts of the United Kingdom.

As an institution, the Union is important in shaping and defining much of what is important about being British. The unions of nations over hundreds of years has demanded a tolerance and openness to others, accustoming us to the plural identities that lie at the heart of being British. It is intrinsic in the nature of the Union that we have multiple political allegiances: we can comfortably be Scottish and British, or Cornish and British, or Geordie and British, or Bengali and British. And research has consistently shown how comfortable the British people are with such plural allegiances. Our British identity is different from our English or Scottish identities or our Bengali or Cornish identities because it is quintessentially plural. And therefore inherently inclusive. And, as a result, attractive to all those who resist, for whatever reason, identifying themselves exclusively in a single category. Of course, a few will resist plural identities, but the rest of us are clearly comfortable with them and welcome them.

That is why the commentators who insist on positing the rise of Scottish or English national sentiment, or indeed any other kind of identification, as undermining an identification with being British are mistaken. These identities are not alternatives; they can exist alongside each other – and do so. What matters is that they exist and they are significant.

The Union has served the peoples of these islands well. We share a common history (and a common destiny, shaped by intimate bonds of friendship and kinship): 20 per cent of the population of Wales was born in England, 7 per cent of the population of Scotland was born in England, 745,000 people born in Scotland live in England: equivalent to 15 per cent of the Scottish population. The Union is an institutional expression of admirable values: tolerance and openness.

And the Union offers a guarantee to the peoples of these islands – that need will be met equitably throughout the UK, and sustainably over the long term.

In these times of rapid and profound economic and social change, plenty and need are likely to shift, and go on shifting, throughout the UK as year follows year. The shared sense of identity and destiny, embodied in the Union, ensures that the better-off, at any given point, will look after the needy members of our moral and political community. And the global economic crisis has driven home the problems of going it alone for any of the constituent nations of the United Kingdom.

It is clear that the vast majority of the people of these islands feel British, but that doesn't necessarily have implications for public policy. Why should politicians feel the need to intervene in this area of public life?

Since the initial announcement that the government believed it was important to try to find a statement of values expressing our British national identity, that could bind us together, voices from the Left and the Right have been insisting that we shouldn't be doing this. That somehow it's un-British to assert a British identity. That it'll exclude those who don't want to sign up to being British. That it's not needed, and it's a waste of time and money. That the focus of public policy in this area should be elsewhere, using other mechanisms to engage with alienated Muslims and combat the separatist nationalists in Scotland and Wales. That it can only end up being banal or vacuous.

In my view, these arguments are mistaken. Of course, separatist nationalism must be taken on, and it is and it will be. Nor would any British statement of values be an alternative to encouraging expression of other identities. This government's measures of devolution were designed to encourage such expressions, and I believe that we need to go further in expressing identities in England. But these can, and should, exist alongside a British statement of values. And, of course, new ways must be found to engage with alienated young Muslims, and they are and they will be.

But the formulation of a statement of values has a broader purpose: to bind the country together. The profound changes we are living through – great global migrations of people and capital, social and economic transformation, cultural volatility and flux – all, inevitably, create pressures on identity and our sense of ourselves. And these are likely to intensify. At such a time, it's important we do everything we can to support cohesion and assert what binds us together rather than focus on what differentiates us.

And there's nothing novel about such an approach. Most advanced democracies have responded to great changes in their national life by developing ways to express their national identity. Throughout much of its history, this country has vigorously discussed what it meant to be British. It was only in the years after the Second World War that we went through a period of introspection, lacking in self-confidence, when such discussions were often regarded with embarrassment. We are now more successful and self-confident as a country, and the time is ripe to find a way to express who we believe ourselves to be – in a way that is inclusive and commands broad support. And if other countries can find ways to express their sense of themselves that are not banal or vacuous and, indeed, often find ways of doing so that are inspiring, I see no reason why we should not also be able to do so.

And if government doesn't lead this discussion in an inclusive process, there is a risk that others will do so in a divisive and destructive way. National identity matters to people. If there isn't a national process to discuss it, in ways that include everyone on these islands, then a vacuum will be left in public discourse and there is a risk that it will be filled by sectarian views and even poisonous ones.

Of course, any free-standing list of values will be too abstract and general to be that helpful in locating British identity. But people feel British, and we have to find a way to describe and express that. If no one believes any longer in nineteenth-century definitions of blood and soil – and very few do – then we must look elsewhere. I believe that our identity resides fundamentally in our shared values, expressed through our history and our institutions, in an evolving conversation with each other. That is why the search for a British statement of values must also explore how they should be expressed.

The test of success will not be whether we secure some predefined notion of a British statement of values – or even one at all. Rather it will be whether we can hold an inclusive discussion where the British people come together to discuss what binds us together. Ever since we announced the search for a British statement of values, the government has made it clear that, for us, the process of discussion and deliberation is as important as the outcome.

Any statement of values must not be imposed by government. Unless the process is driven by the people themselves, it will never take root. So we are developing an innovative constitutional process where the key decisions will be made by the British people themselves, in a series of discussions up and down the country, accompanied by print material and online forums, on what it means to be British, what's best about it, what best expresses what's best about it. This will all be fed into a deliberative process with representative groups of citizens on the main questions: should there be such a statement of values? If so, what it should be? And, finally, what it should be used for? Their decisions will then go to Parliament for a final decision.

This is a risk for the government, as it cannot control the process. But we believe only such a process whose ownership is located among the people themselves can have any chance of success. And the risk only becomes a serious one if you believe the British people don't want to talk about what being British means to them – and I believe many, many do – and if you believe the British people cannot arrive at a shared view of what binds us together. And I believe they can. We can.

25

1688 AND ALL THAT

MICHAEL GOVE

BRITISHNESS IS A CONVERSATION ANYONE CAN JOIN. BUT IF the conversation is going to continue to make sense, then it helps to know the rules.

No discussion of British national identity is possible without an understanding of the unique history of these islands. No discussion of British identity is possible without a meaningful engagement with how that identity has been most durably expressed – in specific institutions and through the greatest of our arts, our literature. And no discussion of British identity will ultimately make sense unless it takes into account the quirky, ungovernable, chaotic and cherishably subversive side of our nature. Something most politicians hate.

But before I launch into a discussion of the merits of Macaulay versus Colley, or offer thoughts on the role of the Argyll and Sutherland Highlanders or Jane Austen in shaping national consciousness, or even ruminate on what the *League of Gentleman* and *Peep Show* can tell us about Britishness now, it's probably best to get the Gordon question out of the way.

This volume is produced in collaboration with the prime minister, and it is very kind of him to assent to my inclusion in his Festschrift. His thoughtful interest in historical debate, and wider intellectual gifts, do him great credit. But those virtues should not be allowed to obscure the very political reasons for his frequently trumpeted interest in the question of British national identity.

The prime minister is acutely aware that his position as a member of the United Kingdom Parliament for a Scottish constituency places him in a difficult position now Scotland has its own parliament. As a life-long Unionist, I am anxious to defend the right of MPs from any part of the United Kingdom to serve in Her Majesty's Government. But the prime minister is clearly sensitive on this point. Scottish Labour voices deployed anti-Unionist rhetoric in the past, attacking reforms of education as 'the Englishing of Scotland's education' and denying the legitimacy of the United Kingdom Parliament when the Conservatives lacked a majority north of the border.

Since the establishment of the Holyrood Parliament, there has been growing concern among English voters that Scotland enjoys more favourable treatment than other parts of the United Kingdom while, at the same time, Scottish feelings have moved in a separatist direction with the election of an SNP administration in Edinburgh. I deprecate both trends, but they clearly only make the prime minister feel even more sensitive about his own position. Which is why I'm not surprised he's commissioned this volume.

While it's understandable that the prime minister as an individual should feel concerned about his own personal position, and want to make the case for Britishness for reasons of career self-defence, there are also other, broader, reasons why the leader of the party that has been in power for the last decade would want us to venture onto this political territory.

Over the last ten years, the UK government has surrendered a growing number of powers to transnational institutions, most notably the European Union. The decision to turn up the volume in a debate about Britishness is clearly designed to draw attention from this diminution of national independence.

And, over the last ten years, concerns about multiculturalism, integration and community cohesion have grown. The debate has moved from the seminar room to the streets following the horrific terrorist violence of 9/11 and 7/7. The failure of this government to tackle proselytising extremists in its early years and the continuing failure of the Home Office to correctly identify the challenge to our democratic structures from Islamist ideologues is a major security scandal. But moving the debate from the particulars of how Islamist ideology should be countered to generalities about Britishness and extremism is another way of dodging responsibility.

It is, at bottom, impossible to consider any engagement on the part of the prime minister with the question of Britishness without referring to the specific political calculations that drive his actions. Gordon Brown is not a man known for spontaneity or a devil-may-care attitude or free-ranging chit-chat. While Britishness is a conversation anyone can join, when he arrives at the table he expects others to fall silent.

Indeed, looking at the whole run of the prime minister's career, it is clear that he has seldom expended mental energy on any activity that is not designed to bolster his political position and advance his partisan agenda. I'd be grateful if any reader can give me a single example. This single-minded approach to public life has its fans. But it's important for the rest of us to note that the prime minister is someone who cultivates his hinterland not as a garden in which he can take delight and think freely, but an allotment in which every square inch has to be put at the service of digging for victory.

The prime minister's tendency to instrumentalise every intellectual concept he engages with and bend it to his immediate political need is all too apparent in the speeches he has made on the subject of Britishness.

A narrow, partial and distorted account of Margaret Thatcher's premiership is deployed, in which her views are caricatured, in order to present the Labour Party in a more flattering light. British foreign policy in the nineteenth century, when a succession of prime ministers sought to avoid permanent continental entanglement and stood aloof from Concerts, Holy Alliances and *Dreikaiserbunds*, is presented as somehow a prelude to ever-closer European integration. A specific set of virtues is attributed to Britain – creative, adaptable and outward-looking, believing in liberty, duty and fair play – which serve the prime minister's purposes, but which might, with equal justice, apply to the Dutch or Danes, diaspora Jewish communities, Israel itself, America, Ireland, the Czech Republic, Georgia or Estonia. Britishness as a concept is flattened, desiccated, drained of specifics and then reduced to a set of freeze-dried ingredients that the prime minister can reheat whenever he wants to sound as though he's got something meaty to offer. Instead of genuinely recognising the glory of the British national character in all its rich, quirky diversity, the prime minister has done Britishness a disservice by making it a narrower, blander, less intriguing thing.

Any of us can, if we're tempted, place just one interpretation on British history.

I am a strong believer in pursuing a forward foreign policy in the War on Terror. I am, depending on your own position, a muscular liberal, a hawk or a neocon. One can look (and I have) to past British politicians for inspiration in this regard. Whether it was the destruction of the Danish fleet at Copenhagen during the Napoleonic Wars or the French fleet at Oran during the Second World War, we've always been willing to engage in pre-emptive action to stop weapons of massive destruction falling into the wrong hands. Whether it's been Canning's support for the independence of Latin American countries in the 1820s, or Palmerston's encouragement of liberal movements in mid-Victorian Europe, or Gladstone's defence of the rights of the Bulgarians, or our 1914 guarantee of Belgian neutrality, or Churchill's denunciation of Munich, or Margaret Thatcher's support for Solidarity, or Tony Blair's role in liberating Iraq, there has been a consistent, activist, democracy-promoting, strain in British foreign policy. And I support it.

But one can't ignore the powerful alternative current which has also been there in British foreign policy. The majority of British opinion in the early eighteenth century was not outward-looking, our expensive participation in the War of the Spanish Succession was unpopular and anti-war feeling propelled the Tories to electoral victory in 1710. Walpole knew that an avoidance of entanglements abroad was key to his power-cementing policy of peace and prosperity. Some of the most powerfully popular political figures of the last 200 years, from Charles James Fox through to John Bright and David Lloyd George, were eloquent champions of non-intervention abroad. Munich was a hugely popular treaty at the time. Disarmament was the dominant cry of the liberal-left for most of the 1920s and '30s. Even today the default position of the majority when it comes to intervention abroad is 'leave well alone'. I deprecate that trend and that tendency, but I can't ignore its historical reality any more than I can ignore the geographical reality of the Pennines and the Cairngorms.

The attempt to flatten Britain's past into a warrant for just one way of looking at the world is poor history and partisan politics. But that, I fear, is where the Brown view of Britishness takes us. Instead of a conversation with our ancestors, in which the prime minister seeks to learn from a diverse range of views, he tries to marshal our predecessors into a celestial choir who are there solely to sing his praises.

In place of a narrow view of Britishness that serves one set of party political ends, I would, tentatively, suggest it's better to develop a fuller and richer understanding of our history, at all levels.

The first duty of politicians is not to conscript a set of historical actors into one camp or another for contemporary partisan battles but to ensure that all our citizens have a fuller understanding of what actually happened in Our Island Story. The current history curriculum does not provide students with a coherent sense of the narrative of British history. Ofsted's July 2007 study *History in the Balance* reported that pupils' knowledge and understanding of key historical facts was not good enough; their knowledge was fragmented:

> Young people's knowledge is very often patchy and specific; they are unable to sufficiently link discrete historical events to answer big questions, form overviews and demonstrate strong conceptual understanding ... Young people's sense of chronology is relatively weak and they are generally unable to ... relate a longer narrative or story of the history of Britain.

Key Stage 3 – the first three years of secondary education in England, Wales and Northern Ireland – is supposed to furnish students with a working knowledge of British history, but despite the best efforts of history teachers that just isn't happening. The pressure placed on school timetables by a proliferating range of obligations means that many schools are opting to fit the Key Stage 3 history curriculum into just two years. That means many students stop learning about history at 13.

A study by a group of academics for Anglia Ruskin University revealed that very few pupils are ever taught anything about the late Middle Ages, the creation of Parliament, the Wars of the Roses or the period broadly from the Restoration to the French Revolution. So crucial events in the history of Britain and British institution-building, like the Glorious Revolution or the Act of Union, are foreign to most students.

Again, as Ofsted has pointed out, 'in practice some events are treated very lightly, if at all. Moreover, some aspects that are taught in depth ... are not set in broader contexts'. There is a 'focus on limited areas of history without overall coherence'.

Recently London University's Institute of Education asked a number of GCSE history students, that's to say those 16 year olds who had deliberately chosen to pursue historical study, to write an account of British history over the last 2,000 years. As Jonathan Howson, the academic leading the study, reported:

> Some of the students simply couldn't do so. They said things like, 'I wasn't born yet so I can't remember' or they did not even attempt to answer the question ... Many listed topics, events, people and colligations like the Industrial Revolution without

any particular order to the list and with no distinction made between the items listed. A few students tried to construct an 'and then' narrative starting usually with the Battle of Hastings and simply bolting on events thereafter. This effort always ended abruptly at the point where it became clear that the task ahead was enormous or due to the emergence of significant knowledge gaps.

Any politician serious about Britishness would want the next generation to understand the story of past generations. That simply isn't happening at the moment, and until it does then the government's good faith is in question.

One thing British history does teach is the importance of institutions in giving shape, voice and character to national identity. From the Anglican episcopate of the late seventeenth century to the officer class graduating from Sandhurst at the beginning of the twenty-first, it has been from explicitly traditional institutions that the defenders of British liberties have sprung.

And there is a special irony here for the prime minister.

In Macaulay's *History of England*, the trigger for King James II's downfall is his attempt to interfere with one particular historic institution – Magdalen College, Oxford. James's efforts to bend Magdalen, and Oxford, to his will, to interfere in their self-government for his own ends, was the moment when Stuart conservatism crossed the line once more into incipient absolutism and provoked revolt.

More than 300 years later, in what became known as the Laura Spence Affair, Gordon Brown also tried to interfere in the internal workings of Magdalen College and Oxford University. Basing his case on a partial and erroneous interpretation of the facts, the prime minister tried to argue that Oxford had operated an admissions system built on old-fashioned prejudice. As Magdalen's then president, Tony Smith, pointed out, the college was and remains in the vanguard of widening access. The truly significant thing about the debate was not, however, Oxford's success at attracting new students, but the prime minister's failure to appreciate that the British approach to great institutions involves respecting their independence. Newman's 'Idea of a University' was a 'self-governing community of scholars', while Brown's 'Idea of a University' seems to be a subordinate arm of his government.

The prime minister doesn't want a conversation with the independent institutions that define, and enrich, British civic life. He just wants them to obey orders.

The idea that successful institutions should each have their own distinctive character at arm's length from the centralising state is inimical to the Brown approach. Whether it's his government's restriction of academy freedoms for schools that want to be self-governing, the target and inspection regime forced on local government or the new infant curriculum with its 600-plus targets now being imposed even on private and voluntary nurseries, this government is only willing to let a thousand flowers bloom if they reach the regulation height and the petals are the departmentally approved colour.

This drive towards conformity and control is, in itself, out of kilter with British traditions, but what makes it worse is the extent to which it undermines those specific institutions that have helped nurture and protect Britishness over the years. Whether it's been the amalgamation of historic regiments, the drive to create a layer of regional government supplanting more familiar allegiances, the abandonment of village post offices, the uprooting of existing GP practices or the elevation of planning decisions to a remote and unaccountable level, there has been a running-down of social capital that weakens all the ties that bind.

At its best, British political culture, indeed all of British culture, is raucous, contumacious, disputatious – lumpy, loose and baggy. It is characterised and enriched by institutions and individuals that aren't necessarily very congenial to the likes of me. Whether it's republicans from Tom Paine to Ronan Bennett, vulgarians from Gillray to Russell Brand, Puritan cranks from the Long Parliament or *The Guardian*'s Society page, they all reflect the fact that diversity isn't just about background, it's about attitude. Recognising that British success has been built on respecting diversity doesn't just mean welcoming successive waves of immigration – it also means appreciating that your side sometimes gets it wrong.

That's why I began by arguing that Britishness is a conversation – our national identity involves learning from others. And the more one considers the prime minister's style of government, the more it appears that he treats Britishness as though it were a lecture – an opportunity to sermonise, harangue or instruct, but rarely to listen.

The British Conversation has been going on for centuries. And, as I mentioned at the beginning of this brief essay, of all the arts in which the British have excelled, the one which defines our character best is the most conversational of them all – literature.

Britain's visual artists, however glorious, don't rank with the Italian Renaissance and Flemish masters who occupy the highest positions in that pantheon. Our composers and musicians, however brilliant, can't compare with the Russian, Italian and, above all, German, geniuses who gave music its finest expression in the nineteenth century.

But in literature – from Shakespeare to Shelley, Austen to Eliot – English voices, together, make up the world's most impressive cultural output. And to this day, the most vital and impressive creative writing in the world takes place in English, if less often in England.

To understand Britishness in the round, you need to know its literature – and that's no small thing.

You'd probably have to start with a grasp of Chaucer and knowledge of the contribution of the great Scots makars, Henryson and Dunbar, as well as the power of mediaeval Welsh literature. Then you should have a working knowledge of Shakespeare – with a sense of what each of the major tragedies teaches us, an understanding of the history plays, a knowledge of the Roman dramas, a feel for the comedies and an appreciation of the subtle genius of the late plays – and then an appreciation of the glories of seventeenth-century verse, Donne, Herbert, Milton and Marvell specifically, then a sense of the Augustan voice, with a handle on what Pope, Swift, Defoe, Addison, Steele and the writers of the early eighteenth century offered before Johnson, Fielding, Richardson and the later Augustans got into their stride.

You'd then need to appreciate the force and power of the Romantic movement – Wordsworth, Byron, Keats and Shelley especially – as well as the distinctive Scots contribution to this period – from Burns through to Hogg and Scott.

After that, it's necessary to get a sense of how the novel developed in its nineteenth-century golden age – Austen, then Thackeray, Dickens, Trollope, George Eliot, Thomas Hardy and Henry James – as well as knowing about the big Victorian poets – Tennyson, Browning, Arnold – before diving into the twentieth century, with Arnold Bennett and H.G. Wells, the Georgians, the war poets, the great Modernist voices – Eliot, Yeats, Woolf and Joyce – the writers of the Scottish Renaissance, such as McDiarmid and Muir, and then on to Auden and MacNeice, Dylan Thomas, Waugh, Larkin and Betjeman and, well, up to you after that . . .

Now how much of that can we expect a well-educated 18 year old to be comfortable with these days? Shakespeare, Austen, Hardy, Larkin and the war poets, at a pinch . . .

It is striking how much of our English literature curriculum is now taken up with study of contemporary writers, at the cost of engagement with genuinely great minds. The assumption that school students can only properly be excited by encounters with living writers who are 'culturally relevant' is a pre-emptive surrender to ignorance. Education should be an introduction to the best that has been thought and written. When so much of the very best that has ever been written is in our language, and defines our culture and nation, then to deny proper access to these treasures is a crime. And yet that is what we do to generations of young people, who grow up in ignorance of the most interesting, challenging, wise and hilarious voices ever to participate in the British Conversation.

I realise I am now at grave risk myself of turning into that classic figure from English literature, the curmudgeon, and I have no desire to become too uncanny a replica of the old Tory squire parodied in the first *Spectator* who denied there'd been any good weather since the Revolution. While I gravely regret the impoverished nature of the education we are giving young people, in particular with regard to our history and our literary culture, I am also delighted that the times through which we're living are rich in promise and adventure, experiment and innovation.

I'm also glad that, whatever else may change, for good or ill, one of the classic, quintessential, qualities that goes to the heart of Britishness remains robust. Our humour.

It has been argued that fascism could never have taken root in Britain because we would always have seen the inherent risibility of preening egotists taking stiff-arm salutes, and civilians in black shirts and Sam Browne belts. And it's certainly the case that there is an inherent subversiveness to British humour that is instantly recognisable. The mix of darkness, bizarre invention and riotous impiety which characterised *Monty Python* is there, in essence, in the *League of Gentlemen* and *Peep Show*.

As ever with humour, it's dangerous to attempt over-analysis. But it's sufficient to say that the British comic voice is instantly recognisable in a certain ironic, quizzical, mickey-taking tone. It's a register that you can catch in conversation, that is impossible to render precisely in print, but that hovers somewhere between the sardonic and the self-deprecating. Imagine Stephen Fry or Paul Merton on form, or John Bird and John Fortune together and you have it. No understanding of the British Conversation is possible without hearing their voices in it. And I suspect the one thing they are, all, saying now, is, that's enough from you, sonny, let someone else join in this conversation you've been banging on about, someone who can actually make us laugh . . .

26

REFLECTIONS

SARFRAZ MANZOOR

I AM LOOKING AT A PHOTOGRAPH OF MY LATE FATHER, TAKEN ON a rare return visit to his childhood village in northern Pakistan. My father, Mohammed Manzoor, left Pakistan in the winter of 1963, arriving into an icy snow-bound Britain as a twenty-nine-year-old man who had recently married my mother and left her and two very young children to seek a better life for them all. In the eleven years he spent away, he returned only three times, and I was conceived on the last of those visits back home. It was not until the spring of 1974 that my father was finally able to raise the funds to bring his wife and children to this country. Mohammed Manzoor was employed on the production line at the Vauxhall car factory, working every overtime shift he was offered to try and ensure there was food on our table and clothes, usually second-hand, on our backs. It was years before he had the money to return to Pakistan, but sometime in the 1980s, in an effort to locate and secure a husband for my older sister, he flew back to Lahore, and it was on that visit that the photograph I am looking at was taken. It shows him sitting, rather stiffly, on a rope bed alongside his sister, her husband and assorted relatives. Everyone apart from my father is wearing traditional Pakistani clothes, who, in contrast, is wearing a white shirt and dark tie underneath a grey woollen overcoat. He looks so incongruous sitting next to his relatives, as if he has been transported from another photograph entirely. However, it is not the clothes that are most memorable about this photograph: no, the thing I find most compelling is the look on my father's face. He looks into the camera with a gaze that is sorrowful and quietly proud, sad and superior; it is the look of someone who realises that he no longer belongs in this place and cannot quite hide his relief at this fact.

My father had a complicated relationship with his homeland; to his children it was a nation he relentlessly mythologised, and yet he also complained bitterly about it. Even as a young boy I had concluded that if Pakistan had been as singularly wonderful as he suggested, my father would surely not have left. In Britain, he worked in a factory, but when he visited Pakistan, the gold-embossed business cards he took with him did not read 'Mohammed Manzoor, factory worker' but rather 'Mohammed Manzoor, investment consultant'. This was presumably because my father enjoyed trading in stocks and shares: although a solid Labour man, he was willing to try anything honest to help his family. The business cards were largely about maintaining an illusion and the stories that he told us about Pakistan were also myths intended to keep us on the virtuous path, but what is most striking about the photograph is the honesty captured in my father's expression, the recognition of that inarguable truth: that you can never return home again.

I was born in Pakistan and came to this country, carried in my mother's arms, as a two year old. In the years that I have spent growing up in Britain – as a small boy, a teenager and an adult – I have wrestled with questions of identity and belonging, trying to answer the question, 'Who do you think you are?' I knew I could not return 'home' to Pakistan; indeed, I had no memories of Pakistan, and so it was difficult to call it home at all. But was Britain really my home? My father offered a straightforward response: we were Pakistanis who happened to have British passports. And yet the truth, as the photograph of him back in Pakistan revealed, was that we were not the same as the ones who remained at home. Leaving the motherland changed my father, and it changed who his children became. This was not something that the first generation of immigrants easily conceded. In my father's case, he was concerned deeply at the impact that coming to Britain would have on his children. His great fear was that we would become seduced into believing that we were British, which, in his eyes, meant a diminishing of being Pakistani and Muslim. This binary reading of identity was instilled in me as a child, and if you had asked me as a young boy who I thought I was, I would have replied that I was Asian. I would have denied that I was British, but if you had caught me in an honest moment, I might have admitted that the reason I was denying it was to prevent the embarrassment of someone else denying it to me. These were the years of Norman Tebbit's 'cricket test' and a prime minister who had spoken about this country being 'swamped' by immigrants. I would watch the Conservative Party political conferences and see the pink-faced delegates waving the Union Flag and singing 'Land of Hope and Glory', and I could see in their faces that this was not a land that they imagined had a place for the likes of me. It was only natural that I returned their apprehension with my own: I proudly failed the 'cricket test' and in any sporting contest would support any team but England. This was not because I genuinely hated Britain but rather because I did not feel that I truly belonged to this country. Like so many second-generation immigrants, I was lost in an existential no-man's-land, searching for an identity to rightfully claim as my own.

In the immigrant narrative, the first generation remains rooted to the motherland and the second generation is torn and conflicted. The third generation, the one whose members are now in their teens and early 20s, are usually more confident of their new identities, and yet in the case of young British Muslims, it is members of this generation who seem the most strident in rejecting a British identity. Their answer to the question of 'who do you think you are?' is that they are Muslims who happen to be living in Britain. When I was growing up, Islam was only one constituent element of my identity; the rise of religious identification among Muslims is not only a reflection of a greater attention to Islam since 9/11 but also, I think, evidence that these young people have found a sense of belonging in their faith that this country has failed to provide. The debate around Britishness has sceptics who suggest it is politically motivated or inherently futile; yet for me, asking questions about what it means to be British is absolutely critical, because it is only by asking those questions and being clear about what it is to be British that we can persuade others to find a sense of belonging. When I was young, I believed that there was a contradiction between being brown-skinned and British. I read British history and did not see my story and thus accepted that I would always be an outsider: tolerated, but never accepted as truly part of this country. I thought, for example, that Asians such as myself had only been in this country since the 1950s. If I had known then, as I know now, that in fact the history of Asians in Britain stretches back 400 years, I would have felt more confident in asserting that this was my country. If I had known, or been taught, about people like Dadabhai Naoroji – an Indian who was elected to the British Parliament in 1892 – or if I had known about the efforts of Indians fighting alongside the British in both world wars, I would have felt a greater sense of belonging to Britain. But I did not know, and I was not told, and thus I never appreciated the ways in which my family's story was, in fact, as British as that of any of my white friends. In considering what a modern version of British identity should be, it is important to stress, then, that while Britain is an ancient land, an appreciation of history must not make us blind prisoners to the past. History is crucial in helping bind a nation together, but if that history is too narrow, it risks alienating rather than binding. This does not mean rewriting the past, it means delving more deeply into our shared history. A modern British identity, then, does not ditch the past; it retrieves these hidden stories. It rescues the role of people like my grandfather, who fought in Japan with the Allies; it remembers the role of Asians in creating today's Britain in everything from cuisine to their contribution to the National Health Service, and in recalling this, it reminds young British Asians today that their stories are part of a great British story.

As I learned more about the roles played by Asians in British history, so I became more comfortable with the notion that British history was also my history. But a modern British identity needs not only to retrieve the past but also to feel less despairing about the present: we need to celebrate more and worry less. It is sometimes forgotten that the immigrants who came to this country, like my father, came because there was something that appealed to them about Britain. There was, of course, often an economic motivation, but it was not only money that appealed. In the spring of 2008, I was in Wolverhampton for a newspaper feature about the 40th anniversary of Enoch Powell's 'Rivers of Blood' speech. The intention was to speak to Asians and blacks who recalled the speech, to gauge its impact and legacy. It was while I was in Wolverhampton – where Enoch Powell was a Member of Parliament – that I met Mirza Baig, who had left Pakistan for Britain more than 40 years ago and had worked as a community activist during the '60s. I wanted to ask Baig about Powell and racism and the impact of the notorious speech, but instead Baig wanted to share with me his love of poetry. He showed me poems he had written while still in Pakistan, and quoted with some relish his favourite lines by Tennyson. He had developed his fondness for poetry while at school in Pakistan, and when he had come to Britain he had been excited at being able to discuss poetry with the English. 'I would sit with my English friends and recite poetry and they would be stunned,' he told me. 'They would say "we don't know these poems".'

Two thoughts struck me as I sat listening to Baig. The first was that to most people who saw him walking down the street, they would see only an elderly Asian man, short and stocky, and they would project onto him any number of stereotypes. Very few would imagine him a lover of English poetry, and the conclusion I draw from that is that too often we view people only through the prism of their perceived difference, thus reducing them into convenient but over-simplified caricatures. The second thought I had was that Baig reminded me that for many immigrants, the culture and traditions of this country were part of its great appeal. The lesson from this observation is that British identity should not have to have an apologetic tone; rather it should stand stout and proud. Britishness should be big enough not only to welcome the role of blacks and Asians in British history but also to celebrate, for example, the Last Night of the Proms without embarrassment.

As well as celebrating the best of British, we also need to be worry less about the supposed threat from Islam to British values. This concern is rooted in the notion that Islam is antithetical to mainstream liberal values and, scanning newspaper headlines about terrorist plots, protests about cartoons and novels and so on, it is easy to conclude that Islam cannot sit easily with Britishness. I believe otherwise. Historically, there have been, as Zachary Karabell writes in *People of the Book: the Forgotten History of Islam and the West*, many examples of Muslims, Christians and Jews co-existing peacefully. It is not Islam that is at the root of tension, but the *interpretation* of Islam. I was given a striking illustration of this recently when I was invited to a 'flashmob iftar'. An iftar is the evening meal that marks the end of the daily fast during the month of Ramadan, and it is traditional to celebrate it with family and friends. One young British Muslim had the idea of sharing the evening meal with the homeless, and he coined the term 'flashmob iftar' to describe an event where Muslims come with food to share with the homeless and less fortunate. I attended such an event in London's Lincoln's Inn Fields and saw hundreds of young Muslims, young women in hijabs and young men in beards, welcoming the entirely white homeless and sharing their pilau rice and samosas. When I talked to the Muslims, they all said that their actions were inspired both by being Muslim and by being British. Their religion instructed them to help the needy, and their sense of British identity led them to the homeless in Holborn: for them, then, there was no contradiction between being British and Muslim.

But just as concern for the supposed 'clash of civilisations' is misplaced, so there is also a danger that well-intentioned sensitivity can do more harm than good. Britishness should not be concerned that every expression of difference is damaging, but it should also be intolerant of intolerance. When I was a boy, I remember my older sister not being allowed to go to school because the uniform required her to wear a skirt, and my father was insistent that this was not acceptable. She did not attend school for a full three months, until a compromise was reached and she was able to wear trousers. This seems another world from today, where a female student can take the British government to a European court for not allowing her to wear a jilbab. This is progress, but at a price, and it seems to me that we need to be more confident about asserting the limits to tolerance – for example, in terms of excessive reaction to perceived insults to Islam or demands for sharia law.

In questions of identity, symbolism matters. Britishness is not only about ideas but also about icons – so which icons and institutions symbolise my version of Britain? It was reflecting on this very question that first crystallised my own identity and provided the answer to the question of who I thought I was. I may have been born in Pakistan, but the simple fact is that everything that I have achieved has been because of this country: it was Britain's education system in which I went to school, its economy that has employed me, its culture that has entertained and inspired me, and its health system that took care of my mother when she had a stroke. My patriotism is, then, a pragmatic one rooted in an appreciation and respect of such institutions as the health and education services and the BBC. It was because of these institutions that I realised that I had a stake in this country, and even today they underpin my sense of Britishness.

Imagine standing in front of a mirror and seeing before you a stranger. Now imagine speaking to that stranger, and seeing them open their mouths and hearing a voice that is not your own. That was how it felt to be a young Asian when I was a boy. Whether it was on television or in Parliament, in books or in business, I searched in vain for my reflection, or someone who looked like me, and everywhere I was invisible. It was that invisibility that drew me towards supporting any team but England, because I could not see where I fitted into this country. The current debate about Britishness may seem like a discussion about abstract concepts such as identity and belonging, but at its heart it is about Britishness as a mirror that reflects every single citizen in this country. The ideas that I have expounded draw from history and law, politics and culture, but they have one unifying ambition: to construct a compelling vision of what it means to British. This vision draws upon the past, but is not weary of the present; it celebrates difference, but strongly defends cherished principles such as the rule of law and freedom of speech; and it acknowledges that there need not be any incompatibility between being Muslim and British.

I began this essay by recalling the photograph of my father in Pakistan and suggesting that the image captured the truth that you can never go home again. My father's generation had it tougher than their children in many ways, but in one way they had it easier: no matter how many years he lived in Britain, my father always knew that Pakistan was home. It is the fate of the second and third generations to be rootless, and with that there is restlessness, a searching for a sense of home. It is that restlessness that faith speaks to, and the success of Islam among the young is partly because they have found answers in religion to their profound questions of belonging. If we want these young people to feel a greater attachment to Britain and to feel a stronger sense of belonging to this country, the challenge is to construct a compelling argument for Britishness. I believe that this is possible, but it can only happen if the vision we have of what it means to be British is broad enough that it invites everyone and no one is alienated. That, then, should be our aspiration and our ambition: to formulate a vision of Britishness that is a mirror into which all those who gaze see their own reflection staring back at them.

27

GREAT BRITAIN:
A DISINTEGRATING KINGDOM?

GEORGE CAREY

IN MARCH 1945, DIETRICH BONHOEFFER, THIRTY-NINE YEARS of age and one of the most outstanding theologians of the twentieth century, awaiting execution for conspiracy to kill Adolf Hitler, penned a poem entitled 'Who Am I?' It is a troubled poem. Bonhoeffer questions his very identity and the mutability of the self, wondering how he appears before others and asking himself if he changes day by day. He compares himself to a 'contemptibly woebegone weakling' and a 'beaten army' fleeing from a 'victory already achieved'. This powerful image mirrors Bonhoeffer's own confusion. Mocked by his own questions, he clings to the deepest reality of all: that he is only truly known by God ('I am thine'). There are few things more upsetting than the disintegration of a personality or experiencing a family member suffering from dementia and helplessly observing their sad decline into confusion and loss of personhood. Although there is nothing to suggest that this was Bonhoeffer's experience, he was nevertheless facing certain death and asking fundamental questions about himself. Happily for him, he found his identity in his relationship with God, facing the most awful experience possible with calm equanimity.

But what about a nation suddenly facing a similar lack of confidence in itself – questioning its identity as a people, wondering if there is anything distinctive at all in its being, and losing hope in its collective being?

Such seems to be the case of Great Britain. In recent years, a steady stream of books, articles and TV programmes have raised questions to do with Britishness. This engagement with our identity as a nation owes much to our uneasiness and anxiety over a number of rapid changes – devolution, multiculturalism, 9/11 and growing ethnic populations. In 1999, Professor Norman Davies concluded his huge book *The Isles: A History* with the words 'the break-up of the UK may be imminent'. Recent surveys, such as those in Nick Johnson's *Britishness: Towards a Progressive Citizenship*, seem to bear this out, showing that the proportion of people who consider themselves British has fallen from 52 per cent in 1997 to 44 per cent in 2007. According to Andrew Marr in *The Day Britain Died*, the impact of devolution introduced by New Labour in 1999 strengthened the regional at the expense of the national, with only 18 per cent of Scots identifying with Britain, 27 per cent of the Welsh doing the same and only the English with a more substantial number at 43 per cent. According to Paul Kingsnorth in his March 2008 *Guardian* article 'Fending off England', 'Britain is dying' and devolution is the main cause, with the English waking up belatedly to the fact that, unlike the Scots, Welsh and Northern Irish, the settlement has left the English with few constitutional rights. Kingsnorth states:

> The English, meanwhile, have the worst of both worlds. Instead of our own elected parliament or assembly, we have unaccountable 'regional assemblies' – eight of them, which make major decisions on housing, spatial planning and transport, among other things, with no recourse to the people they claim to represent. Meanwhile, at Westminster, Scottish and Welsh MPs can make decisions about the future of England for which they will never have to answer to their constituents.

The result, according to Kingsnorth, is that England is the only nation without any form of democratic devolution, leading to ill feeling and an increasing preference for placing English before British identity.

Central, of course, to the questions concerning our identity is the issue of immigration and the perceived danger to identity that successive waves of migrants represent. To a real degree, however, we have always been a 'mongrel' people. Our island home has been invaded countless times over the centuries – we think of Jutes, Picts, Celts, Romans, Saxons, Vikings, Normans and many others. Very rarely have we actually welcomed them, but they have settled down and integrated with us, usually successfully. Today, throughout the world, peoples are on the move in great numbers. In Europe, waves of new citizens are arriving from Third World countries and are placing great strain on public services. Many of these newcomers settle down successfully. Trevor Phillips, chairman of the Equality and Human Rights Commission, remarking on the presence of new peoples in the UK, notes that in London alone there are now 42 communities of more than 10,000 people of foreign heritage.

The crisis of identity arises as newcomers seek to express aspects of identity – heritage, ethnicity, faith – that make them different from their neighbours. This usually creates no problem whatsoever. What does create resentment and social disturbances are people who seem unable to make the transition from 'guest' to 'citizen'. A 'guest' is a transitory dweller who does not intend to stay among us; a citizen is one who puts down roots, pays taxes, votes and shops with the rest of us.

What, then, are the boundaries that give identity its richness? We might wish to separate cultural and religious identities from issues to do with human rights. Most will agree that customs to do with dress, daily prayers and food laws such as those regarding halal meat are inoffensive matters that do no harm as long as they are not imposed on others. Indeed, they may enrich diverse communities. Of greater importance are inalienable values that make us equal in the sight of the law. No newcomer has the right to challenge those laws that have been hammered out over many centuries: laws such as equality of women with men, of equality in marriage, the protection of children, the right to be educated and so on. We do not insist on assimilation, but there has to be integration. When culture is used to defend things that are abhorrent to our values, such as forced marriages, honour killings, female genital mutilation or child abuse, then these illegalities must be challenged as injustices, as indeed they are.

Professor Todd Gitlin, in Johnson's *Britishness*, argues that British citizens have the right to demonstrate opposition or support for their government's policies in Iraq, but it is also obvious that they do not have the right to use violence to do so. On the whole, British experience has been very good in this regard. The Jews are most probably the oldest recognisable group among us, and their contribution to the nation has been outstanding and exemplary. We have been enriched, likewise, by Hindus, Sikhs, the Chinese and many other national and ethnic groups.

However, there is much concern that some Muslim newcomers do not show the same interest in integrating with the wider population, and their instinct to remain separate threatens community life.

BRITAIN IN HISTORY

But before a verdict can be delivered on the demise of Britishness, we need to go back to the beginning. Where did the concept arise? What were the forces that led to the formation of the United Kingdom and to what extent are they relevant for today?

Most people are unaware that Great Britain is a fairly recent concept. It goes back a mere 300 years to the 1707 Act of Union, when Scotland joined with England and Wales. The Westminster Parliament declared 'there would be one united kingdom by the name of Great Britain'. There had been, of course, an earlier Act of 1536, which made Wales and England one. Now the three kingdoms would be united under one Protestant ruler, one legislature and one system of free trade, which Daniel Defoe described as a union of policy, not a union of affection. Indeed, it has to be admitted that 'affection' could hardly be used to describe Anglo–Scottish relations. War rather than peace had been the state of play for many years, and attitudes towards the Act of Union, both north and south of the border, ranged from suspicion to paranoia. Linda Colley, in her magnificent book *Britons: Forging the Nation, 1707–1837*, described Great Britain at the beginning of the eighteenth century as rather like the Christian doctrine of the Trinity, 'both three and one and altogether something of a mystery'. However mysterious the Union was to many Scots and English, it was not long before Scots merchants found that the larger market now open to them was the gateway to national prosperity, and, of course, it also meant that the smaller yet innovative market of Scotland was now accessible to the English. Shrill English complaints began to be heard about the Scots taking over. By 1750, the Scottish economy was growing faster than England's by a third and was increasingly being seen in the prosperity of Scottish cities and towns.

However, commercial profit was not the major reason for the Union. It is often forgotten in our more secular days that the primary bond of all three kingdoms was the Protestant religious settlement over and against Catholic Europe, especially France. France was to be feared as a larger, more populated country than the UK, with a more powerful army. But the reason why France was feared was because it represented what many saw as the repressive religion of Catholicism. Although Scotland had significant pockets of Catholic sympathisers, usually from the gentry, the vast majority of Scots were enthusiastic supporters of the Reformation. As Colley makes clear, it was Protestantism that defined the character of Great Britain. From the Act of Union in 1707 to the Battle of Waterloo, Britain was involved in successive dangerous wars with Catholic France. War and a shared religious allegiance permitted a sense of British national identity to emerge. To be sure, it was an identity that was founded more on sentiment and imagination than reality. Britain was seen as specially chosen of God and, as elect, was mandated to keep its Protestant faith pure and unsullied by any truck with Catholicism. This was expressed in its self-understanding as well as by law.

Looking back objectively, we may see today how selective imagination played a powerful part in idealising the role of Great Britain. The Protestant almanack for the year 1700 places the most significant historical moments as the creation of the world, the Incarnation of Jesus Christ, the reception of the Gospel in England, Martin Luther's thesis of 1517, the first deliverance of England from popery under King Edward VI, the second deliverance from popery under Queen Elizabeth I, the horrid design of the Gunpowder Plot and the third deliverance from popery under William and Mary. This selective reading of history was based as much on fear as it was on fantasy. Colley quotes Ernest Renan, who observed acidly that, 'Getting its history wrong is part of being a nation.' The legal side of an imagined Protestant polity that saw itself as elect, standing in opposition to a threatening and powerful Catholic Europe led to the exclusion of British Catholics from state office and from the electorate until 1829. For most of the period 1707 to 1829, Catholics in Britain faced discrimination in education, property rights and freedom to worship. They were treated as potential traitors, indeed, as 'un-British'.

If Protestantism defined the identity of Great Britain and if the growing alliance of the kingdoms secured the profitability of the UK through commerce, the inner spirit of Britain was formed by what was to be called 'parliamentary democracy'. Of course, the democratisation of Parliament took a long time coming. Although Britain was well on its way to developing a constitutional monarchy by the early eighteenth century, it was not until 1867 that working-class men could vote. It took the suffragettes' courage, as well as the vigorous support of others, to secure suffrage for women in 1928. Nonetheless, central to British identity have been elements of representation, fairness, freedom and equality before God; unlike France, which went overnight from being an absolute monarchy with feudal privileges to a republic repudiating aristocracy and the power of the Church. In spite of many similar challenges to those that

France experienced, Britain was able to remain one nation with a monarchy and established Churches.

BRITAIN TODAY

The purpose of this historical excursion is to suggest that, in spite of the fact that the identity of Britishness was built on such easily exploded historical fantasies, it nevertheless worked to an extraordinary degree through commerce, military prowess and expansionism, and through the institutions of a constitutional monarchy, established Churches and parliamentary democracy. As a consequence, it is impossible to talk about 'British identity' without regard to all these factors – a common standing army, economic success and necessity, religious tradition and heritage – alongside British institutions. Yet the fact is that much of the contemporary debate concerns only those elusive 'values' of 'fair play', tolerance, rights and responsibilities, respect for law, and so on, which are hardly the unique properties of Britain and which ultimately cannot be uprooted from the laws, institutions and traditions that guarantee them.

RELIGIOUS IDENTITY

What, then, about the vexed and difficult question of religious identity? It is all too common these days to dismiss this as being of no consequence, that Protestantism no longer matters, along with its mirror image, Catholicism. At first sight, this seems to be true. When religion gets the headlines, it is usually to do with Islam and is not always painted in positive colours. Andrew Marr comments in *The Day Britain Died* that 'the idea that the Christian religion can be a unifying force for Britain in the future looks forlorn'. However, this dismissive remark is made without any evidence and with the briefest of consideration. It flies in the face of facts. The Union Jack, for a start, must make the objector pause. Three overlapping flags, three crosses that express our allegiance to the Christian faith, the flags of St George, St Andrew and St David.

Ian Bradley, in his important book *Believing in Britain*, challenges those who dismiss religion as an identifying factor. He rightly refers to the 2001 census, where 72 per cent of the population described themselves as Christians, with 15 per cent stating no faith, 8 per cent ignoring the question and 5 per cent identifying themselves as adhering to non-Christian religions. He comments:

These figures suggest that we need to be careful about talking of Britain as a multi-faith society. A very small minority belong to non-Christian faiths and a rather smaller minority claim to have no faith at all, but the great majority of the British population regard themselves as Christian, a fact confirmed by other poll findings, which consistently show around 70 per cent saying that they believe in the central tenets of Christian religion.

The hard question, it has to be said, is what is the relevance of this, if the vast majority of those who claim to be Christian do not value it enough to attend church? I have only to think of my working-class parents, who started going to church in their 50s. They would have been astonished by the inference that churchgoing is the only measurement of being Christian. For them, there was always a residual commitment to the Christian faith in terms of their respect for the Church and the fact that they said their prayers in their own way.

The 2001 census revealed that 42 per cent of Scots still describe themselves as 'Church of Scotland', and 40 per cent of the English describe themselves as 'Church of England', despite fewer than 5 per cent attending its services. Bradley argues that the continuing relatively high level of identification with the two established national Churches suggests that these institutions may still play a significant part in defining national identity. This raises interesting questions about the actual and potential role of established Churches in the changing construction of Britishness.

When it comes to expressing the deepest moments of the nation's grief or celebration, there is no uncertainty about the place where this should be focused – on one of our national cathedrals. The churches also mark those moments of family celebration and tragedy through baptisms, weddings and funerals. At Christmas and Easter, increasing numbers have come to Anglican services, to bring an element of spiritual solidity to festivals that have become increasingly associated with bingeing and extravagance.

Disestablishment, should it ever come, will over time change all that, opening up a gulf between Church and community to the poverty of both. The signs are around us of an increasingly intolerant secularism that desires the disenfranchisement of religious leaders and the marginalisation of any faith voice from the public square.

And it is in this area of religious identity where some of the clearest dangers lie in the debate over British identity and the actions of the government to undermine it. Despite the fact that Gordon Brown has spoken at such length and with such persuasiveness on the importance of British identity, he has acted casually, to say the least, with regard to the royal prerogative on Crown appointments. Shortly after becoming prime minister he waived his right to choose bishops, the right by which two names are presented to him by the Crown Appointments Commission, and he, representing the monarch, is able to choose either name or request others to be submitted to him.

It is strange that neither the House of Bishops nor the Synod saw that, at a stroke, a step had been taken by this son of the Kirk to loosen the ties of the Establishment. When in the late 1970s, his predecessor James Callaghan undertook a lengthy exercise of consultation with Crown and Church to establish a partnership between Church and state in choosing diocesan bishops, he was rightly concerned to retain the prerogative because of the role of bishops in the House of Lords. It is a partnership that has worked well and in practice was one of the greatest guarantees of the reality of the Church's relationship both to the Crown and to Parliament.

Thirty years later, Gordon Brown's somewhat cavalier step in removing this link represents an example of New Labour's predilection for entering into issues of constitutional reform without any joined-up thinking. After all, slashing the hereditary peerage was clearly only one step, but the government has been unable during a decade in power to come up with any formula for the House of Lords beyond that one act of constitutional surgery. Furthermore, other constitutional reforms have been at best piecemeal. The Privy Council has been all but abolished, as has the office of Lord Chancellor in the House of Lords, one of the most ancient offices in the land. The danger of this scattergun approach to constitutional reform lies in the area of unintended consequences. Some, if not most, of these acts have been undertaken by prime ministerial 'fiat' rather than a wide-ranging public debate. This harms the constitutional balance that has taken centuries to develop. It undermines respect for the institutions themselves on which Britishness is founded. The prime minister's decision to give up his role in the royal prerogative to make Crown appointments in respect of diocesan bishops raises some important questions. Was the Archbishop of Canterbury's opinion and advice sought? We don't know. Was the prime minister aware that the prerogative was not his in the first place? (It was the Queen's.) We don't know. Did the decision get her willing consent? We have no idea. Possibly we shall never know the answer to these questions. However well intended the prime minister's decision – and I am sure it was – to take such a step with the minimum of consultation both with the Crown and the Church results in the unbalancing of constitutional rights and duties. In the light of devolution, Lords reform and the threat to the Church of England's Establishment, a strong case can now be made for a Royal Commission on constitutional reform. Such a Commission, with cross-party support, could ensure that future reform is congruent with the development of British identity.

GREAT BRITAIN

Benedict Anderson's definition of a nation as 'an imagined political community' is, perhaps, as close as one can get to a definition of the United Kingdom. The history of this colourful island owes as much to myth as it does to the history of conflict, both secular and religious. Britain has been forged into Great Britain not merely by its being home to so many tribes and peoples but also as much by its self-conscious understanding as being chosen by God and as a place where Christian values are cherished and upheld. Regrettably, that self-understanding is under attack and in danger of erosion from lack of historical appreciation as well as deliberate intentions on the part of some to blur the distinctiveness of Britain.

Ultimately, all attempts to capture the genius of Great Britain fail. We may find it in our democratic values, but these are shared by many other nations. To find one particularly and distinctive national characteristic is impossible. But deep down we know what it is about and why most of us want to hold on to it. Perhaps sport is one special place where Britishness is found and celebrated. At the 2008 Beijing Olympics, where our national team did so well, we cheered as Nicole Cooke, from Wales, claimed Britain's first gold, as Scotsman Chris Hoy won three gold medals, and as Englishwoman Rebecca Adlington collected two gold medals. At Beijing, sportspeople from the three kingdoms competed together for Great Britain. Proud though I am sure they were of their identity as English, Scots and Welsh, they were united in striving for Britain. In my view, the breakdown of the UK into its constituent parts would leave each part the poorer and more impoverished (not only in sport but also culturally and politically), with much less of a voice in the wider world.

I began this chapter with the story of Dietrich Bonhoeffer trying to find his identity. He found it in a transcendent relationship with the Almighty. It may be the case that a significant number of British people today, unlike an individual such as Dietrich Bonhoeffer or the country of Great Britain in 1707, have greater difficulty in reconciling this nation's identity with a

Christian identity, but to abandon the spiritual and religious heritage of this land is to succumb to amnesia. The deepest marks on this nation's landscape, architecture, literature, art and traditions have been left by the Church and the Christian faith. The vast majority of ordinary Britons continue to value this heritage. Without careful attention to the role of all faiths, particularly Christianity, in our history, culture and life, one important element of our identity will be lost. Should our three nations drift apart, we shall all be the poorer.

28

IN HEAVEN, THE POLICE
ARE BRITISH

SIR IAN BLAIR

I IMAGINE THAT MOST OF US KNOW A RATHER TIRED OLD JOKE, which draws on and contrasts stereotypes of European nations to populate heaven and hell. In heaven, the police are British, the cooks are French, the mechanics are German, the lovers are Italian and it is all organised and run by the Swiss. For the purpose of this piece, I don't need to go into what occupations in hell are provided by which nations.

There is something significant in the choice of it being policing that is the heavenly British occupation: my thesis, however, is slightly broader than the ideal of a celestial constabulary. It is that, in both a historic and contemporary sense, British policing is a quintessentially British institution and should be understood and, to a degree, celebrated as just that.

Its creation was deliberate and fundamentally different from anything that had gone before. How it has been seen as an institution mirrors some other major British institutions in that it has been held up, at various times, to unwarranted admiration and to probably unfair contempt and ridicule. Its characteristics of being unglamorous, dependable and quietly heroic, interested in practicalities rather than intellectual pursuits, as well as being definitively un-European, places it in the centre of what it is to be British, as do the issues of class that affect it. Lastly, like all great things in Britain, it matters, and its reputation abroad far exceeds its standing at home.

The Metropolitan Police was founded by Sir Robert Peel, then Home

Secretary, later to be prime minister, in 1829 (it actually began, rather oddly, at 6 p.m. on a Tuesday evening, 29 September of that year). The idea of a police force was not new: Glasgow had, in fact, the first city force in Britain; there was the Thames River Police to look after shipping; and the British had established police forces in a number of colonies, including the Royal Irish Constabulary. However, London was different and its police force was to be different. For nearly 40 years prior to the first Metropolitan Police Act, parliamentarians of all stripes had often debated policing. The previous system of night-watchmen was clearly inadequate, and the reliance on the quasi-privatised Bow Street Runners and occasional military support were unsatisfactory. It was not at all clear what was wanted.

What was clear, however, was what was not wanted, which was some form of 'continental' police service. Legislators looked across the Channel in horror at the police acting as agents of the state and, above all, as the employers of paid spies and informers. The bogey figure was Joseph Fouché, who, after having been a radical and brutal revolutionary figure, went on to serve as Chief of Police to Napoleon (twice: he carefully avoided working for Louis XVIII during the exile on Elba) and then finally for Louis XVIII. If anyone, during that tumultuous period, knew where the bodies were buried, it was him. Although actually uttered by Antoine de Sartin, Paris's Lieutenant General of Police from 1759 to 1774, the expression 'whenever three people talk together in Paris, one of them works for me' is often attributed to Fouché, and perfectly illustrates what was so abhorrent to those MPs who sought to preserve the rights of free-born Englishmen.

While not emulating France, the Tory government of the time could have chosen the military model they already used in Ireland, with barracks, sabres and guns. But they chose something very different, something that had not been tried before on any scale. This was an organisation low in numbers, low in powers and high in accountability. It was an organisation whose primary objects were neither the detection of crime nor the suppression of public disorder, but were based on the opposite approach: the prevention of crime and the maintenance of public tranquility. Its initial uniform of a tall black hat and swallow-tailed coat was far from military. Of its two first twin Commissioners, while one was a retired Peninsular War veteran, the other was a lawyer. The Commissioners and their force were independent of government ministers.

Peel wanted the police to be very close to the public. In fact, he actually remarked that 'the Police are the public and the public are the Police'. He described his new officers as 'only members of the public that are paid to give full-time attention to the duties which are incumbent on every citizen'.

The model that Peel created in London spread across Britain, first in towns and cities and later across more rural areas. It also spread rapidly across the common-law world, with the New York Police Department being founded in 1845 and numerous city forces across the British Empire being founded in emulation of the Met. In terms of its preventative role, its low powers and its separation from the state, what Peel created was, as I shall emphasise at the end of this article, a gift not just to Britain but also to the world.

It was designed to be a confident, modern institution. Peel was clear that this was 'not to be an occupation for gentlemen'. As recently as 2005, when I gave the Dimbleby Lecture, I misunderstood this remark (as I had done for 30 years). What Peel meant, I have since learned from the biography of Peel recently published by Douglas Hurd, was that the police were to be selected differently from what he saw as the archaic and ineffective selection processes of the army, navy and civil service. It would be many years before those great institutions would end the practice of purchasing commissions and appointments: the police were to be a meritocracy from the start.

Nevertheless, I know that the side effect of that decision has been to separate the police from the Establishment, and it is typically British that issues about the police and class – in recruitment and in service delivery – are quite obvious but never mentioned. I can remember many heads jerking backwards in the audience at that Dimbleby Lecture when I raised the subject directly.

One further development was crucial. In 1842, the Commissioner received permission from the Home Secretary to create a small detective branch, out of uniform. As so strikingly recounted in Kate Summerscale's recently published book *The Suspicions of Mr Whicher*, the detectives from what had now become known as Scotland Yard (the name of the street in which the Met's first headquarters stood) were, at first, the darlings of the mid-Victorian era. Those early detectives began to make the name of Scotland Yard synonymous with detection, a situation that continues even today, with a case in point being the request, in 2008, by the Pakistan government for Scotland Yard to investigate the circumstances of the death of Benazir Bhutto. Wherever the officers of the Metropolitan Police go in the world, the words 'Scotland Yard' open almost every door.

I do not intend now to launch into a history of British policing, and I would certainly not pretend that everything was benign. In Victorian times, the police were very much the protectors of the middle class against the dangerous poor. There were scandals of corruption, with the famous 'Trial of the Detectives' taking place in 1877. There was bitter politics, between Whig and Tory, over the very existence, let alone the role, of the police (the government that created the Met fell from office very shortly afterwards). There were long and acrimonious disputes between the Commissioners and the Home Secretary over both operations and money. A jury found the first police officer killed in a riot to have been lawfully killed. Irish and Russian revolutionary terror led to the creation of the Special Branch, getting a bit close to Fouché.

Nevertheless, and quite remarkably, despite scandals and challenges, a rather benign and, particularly in rural areas, somewhat bucolic model of policing developed and worked well, perhaps especially in the first half of the twentieth century. By then, it is probably fair to say that the 'bobby' had become an icon of Britishness, an image of a golden age of social cohesion with which more dangerous modern times can now be compared. The 'country house murder' was a staple of drama, while one character became the image of a sturdy, steady society: PC Dixon of Dock Green. Just like Dr Findlay and general medical practice, of course, George Dixon had the twin advantages of perfectly representing an ideal and of being completely fictional. Generations of children also grew up thinking that PC Plod was really rather nice.

From the 1960s onwards, this compact between police and public began to fail. The emergence of a substantial black and minority population in London proved to be an immense challenge for the Met. The relationship of the police with government and the people was thrown into sharp relief by protest movements, by the miners' strike and the long years of combating Irish Republican terrorism. Old methods of detection, *in extremis* based on hunch, prejudice and judicial complicity in downright lying, failed. Miscarriages of justice stained the reputation of the service. As society changed, the police service found itself a reluctant moral guardian, not sure whether to be soft cop or hard cop in relation to pornography, drugs and drink-driving, the last two of which brought the police firmly into conflict with the wider public and, indeed, the chattering classes. The word 'bobby' began to disappear; the filth, the fuzz, the cops, the pigs became the epithets.

The police service struggled. It lost confidence in the way forward. It began to abandon the primacy of crime prevention above detection. It withdrew into cars. It fiddled with how its uniform looked, and it agonised over whether it should have some form of officer class.

I believe it is now finding its feet. The relatively new re-emphasis on neighbourhood policing is the bedrock of the police contract with the public, while the increasing recruitment of women and ethnic minority staff throughout the service, the ability to work with other partners, ranging from local government to the Security Service, are indications of confidence, as is the falling crime rate.

That, however, is not the point of this argument. This policing journey reflects the way the British treat their major institutions, as well as how those institutions react to the changing mores of society. The Church of England, the BBC and even Parliament itself can sometimes be regarded as having lost touch with the public mood and to first abandon and then struggle to regain the core values that they represent, sometimes appearing to doubt whether they should keep or change their image, having at the same time to be constantly in the public eye, constantly open to criticism and yet having to remain independent and a force for public good.

In that sense, therefore, the history of British policing is the history of the interaction of the citizenry with one of the great institutions of the British state. Furthermore, like the Church of England, like the BBC, and like Parliament, British policing is not only uniquely national but has also served to shape, in part, our national character and consciousness: equally, like those other great institutions, it has been a gift to the world.

David Triesman was at one time a Minister of State at the Foreign Office. He once told me that on a visit to Darfur, hundreds of miles into Africa, he met with a group of women in a refugee camp. When they found out he was from Britain, they did not ask him specifically for aid in terms of shelter, water or education for their children; what they asked him for were British bobbies.

Not only in heaven, perhaps . . .

29

MORE HUMILITY, LESS HUBRIS

JOHN KAMPFNER

WHAT DOES BRITAIN STAND FOR AROUND THE WORLD? What influence does it have in these confusing and challenging times, a period that began with George W. Bush and the terrorist attacks on 9/11 and most recently witnessed a global economic crash and the election of Barack Obama? The post-war, post-colonial times are a distant memory; the Thatcher–Reagan hegemony is almost as remote. But after more than a decade of New Labour, it is still hard to discern what exactly underlies the UK's foreign policy and approach to the world.

One theme has been consistent. Only we, surely, could have come up with the phrase 'punching above our weight'. It evokes everything that this country should not aspire to be – belligerent, arrogant and clunky. It suggests militarism rather than the power of example. And yet for a medium-sized power off the north-west coast of a declining continent, we do still enjoy a surprisingly loud voice. Thanks to the English language, the BBC, the royal family, Premiership football and pop music, the British are recognisable and identifiable wherever they go. Our presence evokes strong emotions.

Each of our past four prime ministers has struggled to identify, let alone sell, a notion of Britishness abroad. For Margaret Thatcher it was waving the Union flag (for example, by covering the tail fin of a model British Airways jet for sporting an unpatriotic design); for John Major it was drinking warm beer while watching cricket; for Tony Blair it was Cool Britannia, Britpop, BritArt and a sidelining of fusty tradition; for Gordon Brown it is old-fashioned Presbyterian notions of hard work – an unglamorous, almost Victorian, Britain.

With the exception of Blair, each has championed the idea of the hardy Brits duffing up the recalcitrant foreigners whenever the need arises. Without exception, each of these leaders, and the political class they represented, has spoken repeatedly and passionately of British 'values'. The problem is that few are prepared to listen any more. I have lost count of the number of Indians or Chinese or Russians or Jordanians who simply laugh when we talk of the enduring strength of our democracy or adherence to human rights. Every time they were preached to about democracy or human rights, they would respond with any or several of the following questions: Is this not the country that supported an illegal war in Iraq and presided over 'rendition', the illegal secret transport of terrorist suspects? Is this not a country that – to use David Cameron's phrase – has a propensity to 'drop democracy from 10,000 feet'? Is this not a country where leaders regularly enjoy untrammelled power on the back of a 30 per cent share of the total popular vote? Is this not a country that is the world's second-largest arms seller?

Blair stands accused of the most pronounced Manichean lapses, but prime ministers past and present have all, at different points, portrayed themselves as leading the way in one crusade or another. Humility has so far not been our strongest suit in our global dealings.

Once in a generation the opportunity arises for a fresh start. The year 1997 presented one of those moments. The phrase 'new politics' was proclaimed as extending to Britain's role in the world. Was it only a decade ago when Robin Cook, New Labour's first and most accomplished Foreign Secretary, declared an ethical dimension to British external policy, and Blair cycled to the front of Europe's leaders during his first summit in Amsterdam? (Well, actually, they acceded to a request from Alastair Campbell to allow him to speed to the front for the cameras.)

For his first two years, the young and charismatic Blair drew crowds wherever he travelled. The high point was probably May 1999, when, in the ancient university town of Aachen, he was awarded the Charlemagne Prize for his services to European peace. By this point Blair was deeply embroiled in the Kosovo conflict. This was the second of the five military campaigns that I chronicled in *Blair's Wars*. I had supported Operation Desert Fox against Saddam Hussein and would support the deployment of forces in Sierra Leone and, with a heavy heart, the military action against the Taliban and

Al-Qaeda in Afghanistan. Iraq, before, during and after, was an altogether different proposition.

For all his moralising, Blair was deeply sceptical about the 'softer' aspects of Cook's foreign policy. He saw no reasons why arms sales should be cut or that the UK should be held accountable to those same civil-liberties rules that it lectured others about. But the damage wrought by Blair's approach was far deeper than that. In truth, it was not his approach but an approach handed down by Whitehall that he then took to its logical conclusion. Blair held the view that Britain could achieve next to nothing without being the prop of the US. His decision to commit to war in Iraq with President Bush was born as much of fatalism about Britain's role as it was by the more visible hubris.

Ever since, Britain has struggled to regain credibility and influence. The UK derives what strength it does enjoy from the post-Second World War settlement, from its roles at the top table of the world's international institutions – the United Nations Security Council, NATO, the European Union and the Commonwealth. Since Iraq, Britain has struggled to secure any success at the UN. Diplomats concede that the most effective tactic is to ask other members of the Security Council to table resolutions on its behalf. That particular institution is in crying need of reform. It has been for years, and it is other countries, not Britain, that are standing in the way. Eventually, however, logic will dictate that countries such as India, Brazil, South Africa, Japan and Germany will become permanent members.

Brown privately acknowledges that Britain long ago lost its clout as a lone performer. Instead of relying on the US, he set about a sensible recalibration. His first meeting as prime minister with Bush in the summer of 2007 suggested he might be less eager to please Washington. Brown's first Mansion House speech did not refer to a 'special relationship' (a phrase used by Americans to humour the British). Then it all started to be unpicked, and the UK approach reverted to type. No, the troops were not coming home early from Iraq. Our commitment to Afghanistan was not open to debate. Our relationship with Washington was as rhetorically 'special' as ever.

So does 2009 represent a second coming for an ethical dimension to foreign policy? The resounding victory of Obama in the US presidential elections has given rise to huge hopes. Part of this is the fact that he is African American and therefore the personification of the American Dream that most people believed was rhetorical rather than real. Part of this is the sense that anyone after Bush would constitute an improvement. Wherever he has gone around the US and in his brief forays during the election campaign around the world, people have lined the streets to see Obama. From pollsters to TV executives, everyone has noted that public interest in the election campaign reached new records. Obamania took root just about everywhere. People have placed on him the mantle of a Gandhi or Mandela.

Such expectations are unhealthy and unrealistic. Immediately on taking office, Obama sent signals that he would shift in some areas and not in others. Guantanamo Bay would eventually be closed, but the extra-territorial detention of terrorist suspects would continue. He would remain pragmatic with China, try cautiously to rebuild bridges with Russia, and shift attention from Iraq to Afghanistan. The big question remained: would he break the mould and start to put pressure on Israel? The signs were not immediately encouraging.

The Obama era holds the key for so much of Britain's sense of place in the world. Paradoxically, this is not because he wants to vest in the UK special status – as Brown saw as he was welcomed courteously but briefly into the White House in March 2009. Obama's predecessors at the White House began their tenures pledging to spread their friendships more broadly. In Bush's case, attention was first focused on Mexico. Clinton promised stronger links with Germany and France, as the leaders on Europe. Although events led them both to fall back on the default relationship with the UK in times of crisis, America's focus is now shifting towards the new powers of Asia.

Britain, therefore, is presented with two fresh challenges. One – the effect of a progressive at the helm of what is still the world's most powerful country – is welcomed on the centre-left. The other, the more gradual, shift away from the US–UK axis, raises fear among some in Whitehall. It need not. It is just what is needed, enabling this country to develop a more variegated approach.

The specific tasks for British foreign policy are these: any prime minister with any courage (and Blair came closest on this score) should proselytise about the specific benefits the European Union has brought, from the cleaning up of our beaches to the driving down of mobile-phone roaming tariffs. But they should do more than that. While criticising some of the more bizarre federalising tendencies, they should embrace the remarkable example that Europe has set. Where else has a structure been put in place that provides benefits for countries to embrace democracy and human rights? Would Poland or Latvia be as they are, were it not for the EU? Would Serbia not be on its way in that direction? So seldom is any of this ever proclaimed with conviction by British politicians. The EU's various joint foreign-policy initiatives, from Iran to Congo, are often useful exercises. Almost invariably, the policies of go-it-alone or tie-yourself-to-America-whatever-the-cost end up being the least effective. The more astute US politicians and diplomats acknowledge this. That is why, for some time now, they have turned to the likes of Nicolas Sarkozy in Paris and Angela Merkel in Berlin.

Underlying the need for a cleverer strategy abroad is the need for policymakers to think more intelligently about the kind of Britishness they wish to present. The bottom – so obvious, yet so frequently missed – is that if we are to preach, we should also practise. The last ten years have often worked against that. Curtailment of civil liberties in our country, and abuse of them by us in others, at a stroke disqualifies our credibility. The same goes for social and economic policy. Governments that speak the language of social justice and narrowing the wealth gap but struggle to make meaningful progress are given less of a hearing in the developing world.

Britain could, just could, be a beacon, if only it exercised its 'soft power' more effectively. Using its geographical position and language, it could, during times of plenty, have done more than present London as a centre for financial greed. If the lessons of the current financial crisis have taught us anything, it is that there must be better ways of attracting people over here than as an offshore, low-tax haven. We should be more than a home for oligarchs and other assorted spivs and crooks.

The big clash of the next generation will be between authoritarian capitalism and the post-1945 settlement of liberal democracy. It is already taking place, and, out of the global recession, the balance of power will be recalibrated. We have yet to get to grips with its implications. Why is it that increasing numbers of people around the world, albeit in different circumstances, appear willing to trade certain freedoms in return for either security or prosperity? We are not talking here about North Korea or Zimbabwe: this is not about thugs in pick-up trucks or men in dark glasses on street corners. This is about intelligent and well-travelled people who are aware of alternatives on offer elsewhere but are ready to enter into a pact with their own governments. That pact allows people to do pretty much what they want as long as they don't 'cause trouble', as long as they do not publicly criticise or challenge the state. Singapore provides the original model, but it is now being exported, not just to other city states like Dubai and Abu Dhabi but also across Asia and beyond.

China is the great test-bed. Such an arrangement requires strict parameters. The rule of law is essential. Arbitrary exercise of power encourages corruption and brute force. Russia provides the antithesis, a country where physical intimidation of critics is all too prevalent and where the law is interpreted by the powerful as the means of exercising political and economic influence. From Blair's early overtures to Vladimir Putin around 2000 to the bilateral hostilities around the time of the murder of Alexander Litvinenko, Britain has struggled to know what to do with the resurgent and unprepossessing modern Russia. To its credit, it has refused to succumb to energy blackmail, in contrast to the Italians and Germans, whose fawning has been demeaning. But, once again, a reasonable case that the British have tried to make to the Russians about international law and human rights has foundered on words such as 'Iraq' and 'rendition'. It is so frustrating to hear the case for democracy undermined by counter-accusations of hypocrisy and double standards.

Russia has the potential to be an irritant, but while the Kremlin has defined its foreign policy in hostility to the West, China just gets on with it, gliding over the criticisms of others. Think ahead, say, ten years, and imagine the consequences for future generations here if the Chinese experiment succeeds. What if the combination of high growth rates, hugely improved living standards and circumscribed liberties catches on? The so-called Beijing Consensus is already making inroads in much of Africa, which is tired of developmental assistance being tied to lectures about governance and democracy. Even more alarming was a sense I had in India where a number of young entrepreneurs talked about representative democracy as an impediment to national success and economic growth. They look increasingly to China.

This is where the self-proclaimed democracies of the West will have, genuinely, to win the argument. The very fact of Obama's election – a black man who campaigned with discipline, courage and passion – goes some way to that. As if his task wasn't hard enough, he will play a major part in determining the fate of Western democracy itself.

On this side of the ocean, our political class appears to have little understanding of the challenges facing our system. Our political argument is lamentably insular, operating within parameters that are far too narrow. We have failed to grasp the reasons behind the attractiveness of the alternative propositions.

The terrorist attacks of 9/11 in New York and 7/7 in London wreaked havoc. They led to a fierce debate about extremism, about community cohesion, multiculturalism and policy towards the Islamic world. But this was an asymmetric threat. No matter how much Bush and, to a degree, Blair whipped up fear, these were angry young men on a dangerous mission – a mission that can be repeated any time, but does not go to the heart of our political system.

The challenges now facing the West are more incremental but also more fundamental.

This is where Obama's performance in government will be so crucial. The American election of 2008 produced a remarkable resurgence in the faith of democracy. How else could one describe the long queues outside polling stations? Millions voted who had never bothered, or never been allowed, before. Obama demonstrated a quiet authority, sturdy intelligence and a refusal to succumb to populism.

Americans, with their affection for the flag and for other symbols of national pride, tend to find it easier to encapsulate the values for which they stand. Obama is setting about refashioning those for a new era after the disasters of the Bush years. But what about Britishness? Gordon Brown was right to open the debate. We seem to find it easier to define what we are not than what we are. We do not rule the waves; we have long given up any imperial or global pretensions (at least serious people have). We have, in spite of the abuses and excesses of the past decade, a good story to tell in terms of our entrepreneurship and individualism, and also our often untapped community spirit.

As others assert alternative models, we should have confidence in our own. Confidence is best manifested not through hubris but through humility. If we stopped trying to punch above our weight, we might actually carry more weight around the world.

30

A TALE OF ONE CITY

TIM HAMES

'Every city is a living body.'
St Augustine

'The people are the city.'
William Shakespeare, *Coriolanus*

ANY SERIOUS DISCUSSION ABOUT THE CHARACTER OF BRITAIN
and Britishness should surely have some reference to where most of
the British people live and how they live those lives. Yet Britishness is too
often either an abstraction that lacks such pertinent roots or, in so far as it
is considered at all, engages in a misplaced mythicism in which village life is
offered, as John Major once memorably did (old maids on bicycles, warm beer
and so on), as the essence of what Englishness or Britishness is, when the bulk
of the British population do not reside in such small locations and have not
done so for an extremely long time. Despite this, some of the most passionate
arguments about the nature of our national well-being remain focused on the
countryside, whether the matter be the vexed question of fox hunting, the decline
of rural bus provision or post office closures. Supporters of the countryside
camp demand to know why their preferred part of Britain does not enjoy the
same exalted (and, rather more relevantly, subsidised) status as their equivalents
in France, Spain or Italy. There is a very simple answer to this, namely that
the demography of the United Kingdom is fundamentally different to that of
those nations. The tiny settlement might have some claim to represent *la France*

profonde, although there is a very strong element of false romanticism to this notion. In this country, the city is the true Britain. It is very hard to envisage how some more robust sense of Britishness can be created without a similar rise in civic pride about urban Britain and hence in cities as well as in an individual city. What matters, therefore, is fostering that sense of the city and relating it to a narrative about what Britishness is, and its lasting value.

THE NATURE OF BRITISH CITIES

The British do not think about cities enough, and when they do, they fail to appreciate what it is that is special about them. Comparisons with our continental neighbours are rarely sought. They should be. Doing so assists the process of reaching three truly seminal observations.

The first is that Britain is a very urban nation. Its population is approximately equal to that of France, despite being notably smaller in land mass area. It is around three-quarters of that of Germany, even though it occupies a much more modest proportion of the European continent. It is larger than that of the substantial states of Italy, Spain and Poland. Not only is Britain heavily populated but its population is also skewed towards major urban areas much more dramatically than its European equivalents. No other major European state has such a bias, and only a few of the smaller ones such as the Netherlands and Denmark exhibit the same tendency.

Some comparative figures illustrate this forensically. Comparisons across local government divisions are difficult because not every nation defines cities in the same fashion. Despite this, a crude conclusion can be drawn. About half of the UK population lives in cities that have more than 150,000 citizens to them. In Germany and Spain, that figure is just above a quarter. In Poland it is a shade below a quarter. In Italy it is a touch above one-fifth. In France it is scarcely one-tenth. The only large countries in Europe (if they are to be accepted as purely European) that are remotely as based on cities as is the case for the United Kingdom are those of Russia, Belarus and the Ukraine (all hovering at a roughly 40 per cent urban ratio).

Cities are also responsible for the vast bulk of the ethnic and religious diversity of the United Kingdom (and probably the bulk of the same in sexual orientation as well). The term 'multicultural Britain' (whether deemed benign or not) is actually inaccurate. Britain is not multicultural, its cities are. Smaller towns and villages most certainly are not. Cities should, therefore, logically dominate the language and substance of our politics. This rarely happens. If there is a 'cities lobby', then it is not very effective.

240

That it is not is related to the second crucial element. Britain is dominated by a single city – London – to an extraordinary and exceptional extent. The population of London was, at the 2001 census, some 7.17 million. The second most populous was Birmingham at 971,000. This is a seismic disparity. London was slightly more than seven times the size of its closest rival. Indeed, interim population estimates are such that this lead was believed to have been stretched to 7.5 times as big by 2006 and could well hit an astounding 8 times by 2011. The population of London is about the same as that of the next 17 largest cities (Birmingham, Leeds, Glasgow, Sheffield, Bradford, Edinburgh, Liverpool, Manchester, Bristol, Cardiff, Coventry, Leicester, Belfast, Nottingham, Newcastle, Hull and Plymouth) combined. While London has had a massive edge on other cities in Britain for a long time – it was, for instance, many times larger than the next most sizeable place (Norwich) in the mid-seventeenth century – its dominance diminished somewhat during the Industrial Revolution and in Victorian Britain (which saw an immense amount of urban innovation outside the capital). Yet its perhaps almost suffocating sway over all other cities has reasserted itself awesomely over the last 100 years or so.

London is now the largest city in the European Union. It is topped only by Istanbul in the continent of Europe (and that solely if both of what some would forcefully deem to be the 'European' and 'Asian' sections of that city are put together) and, on most estimates, also by Moscow (although Russia, like Turkey, has to endure endless musing about whether or not it is properly part of the continent of Europe). This is, of course, partly because Greater London has been allowed to expand its empire over the decades, but this does not render the outcome a statistical illusion. Although it occupies vastly more square mileage than any comparable EU city, London still ranks fourth in population density after Copenhagen, Brussels and Paris. London is huge, and Londoners live very close to one another.

It is virtually never asserted in Britain how stark this division between London and all other British cities is. A few European comparisons would, again, be instructive. Paris is only 2.5 times larger than the next French city, Marseilles. Berlin is but twice as huge as Hamburg. Rome is about double the size of Milan in numbers. Madrid has slightly less than that margin over Barcelona. Warsaw has a similar edge over Łódź. London dominates city life in Britain to an extent that is unknown among the major nations of the EU and only matched by certain of those with far smaller populations, such as Vienna in Austria and Budapest in Hungary. So Britain is not merely a very urban nation by relative standards but a mono-city nation as well. Britain's population distribution is more like Africa's, Latin America's or even Asia's in many respects than the norm in Europe – the only three heavily populated nations on the planet (those with 50 million residents plus) with a city more dominant than London are Ethiopia, the Philippines and Thailand.

This produces the third distinctive feature of British cities – their administrative arrangements. London dominates all other cities culturally, economically and politically. Yet it is the single one that is permitted substantial institutional devolution. London is the only one of the twenty biggest cities in the United Kingdom to have a directly elected mayor (as the current incumbent of that office is a Classicist by background, it is interesting to recall that Aristotle once contended that 'a very populous city can rarely, if ever, be well governed'). It is a reflection on the size and complexity of public life in the capital that the legislation that brought about the shift to a directly elected mayor and Greater London Authority was the longest such parliamentary measure since the Government of India Act 1935. The next largest conurbation to have an elected mayor is currently Stoke-on-Trent (about 30 times smaller in population terms than London), but the burghers there voted in a referendum held in October 2008 to abolish the position shortly. This means that the next largest places other than London to have directly elected mayors are in fact three London boroughs (Lewisham, Newham and Hackney). Disregarding them, then the second largest city other than London to enjoy a directly elected chief executive is Middlesbrough, where Ray Mallon, or 'RoboCop', serves at the helm of the conurbation (which has a population about 50 times smaller than Greater London). This is, to put it mildly, a very strange outcome. It leaves the United Kingdom with a surreal form of quasi-federalism in which Scotland, Wales and Northern Ireland are allowed formal (and different) models of devolution, and in which London accepts independence for its own internal dealings but denies that right to the rest of England. There would seem to be no other equivalent in the democratic world that matches it.

THE BRITISHNESS DEBATE AND CITIES

What should all of this mean for the debate about Britishness? Before venturing some thoughts in that regard, it would be useful to observe how much urban renewal has occurred in Britain over the past 20 years and especially since New Labour came to office in 1997. There has been a very substantial overhaul of city centres in places such as Manchester (courtesy of the IRA blowing up a chunk of the old metropolis), Glasgow,

Liverpool, Leeds, Newcastle and Gateshead. Devolution has been a boon for Edinburgh and Cardiff (where the impact has been compounded by the bizarre combination of the Millennium Stadium, *Doctor Who* and a small industry around Charlotte Church), and the peace process alongside an on–off devolution process has worked miracles in Belfast (the hum of the immediate vicinity of the Europa Hotel near Belfast City Hall, once Europe's most bombed building, has to be experienced today to be believed). This is all to be cheered, but the brutal reality is that urban development outside London is inconsistent and hardly the consequence of a deliberate national strategy. What has been valid for Leeds does not necessarily apply to Bradford. Much of it has been the secondary result of something else; for example, a massive expansion of higher education in the past two decades has had the effect of placing much larger numbers of young people into these decaying city centres, breathing new life into them. And where positive developments have occurred, they have often been ignored by a so-called 'national' media that is incredibly and myopically London-centred in its thinking. Urban renewal outside the capital has often only been 'discovered' by the press and TV news when it is symbolised by an event such as the opening of a Harvey Nichols in Leeds, the awarding of the right to host the Labour Party conference to Manchester in 2006 (and, to a lesser extent, the choice of Birmingham as the venue for the 2008 Conservative Party conference) or the selection of Liverpool to act as the European Capital of Culture in 2008. By and of itself, this welcome progress will not correct the fact that cities are underestimated in British public discourse, the capital retains an unhealthy command over all other British cities, and the political arrangements that have evolved within the United Kingdom are close to irrational.

What, then, should be done? A shift in official thinking away from 'the regions' towards the cities would be a helpful first step indeed. With a few exceptions, the extent of regional consciousness in England is very weak, while there is a much stronger sense of an identity with the cities in which people live and work (and in some instances in England, the counties). Regionalism has failed in significant measure because of this failure to place weight on cities. Liverpool and Manchester are rivals, not allies or partners, so it is fruitless to attempt to create an essentially fictional 'North West England', while concern over the relative standing of Newcastle, Sunderland and Middlesbrough was one of the factors that led the north-east of England to reject the idea of an elected assembly there when a referendum was taken. Britishness is not to be advanced by seeking to merge cities into theoretical units to which virtually nobody has an instinctive loyalty. The focus has to be on encouraging and enabling cities to undertake their own reconstruction, not on bypassing them in favour of regionalism.

It is extremely difficult to correct the imbalance that has led London to hold the whip hand over all other conurbations in this country. Forced redistribution of populations is not really a viable option in a democracy. An element of correction might, though, occur naturally. The anticipated contraction in financial services in London after the banking debacle of 2008 might have an impact on one of the forces that has been potent of late, but it is not destined to reverse the staggering multiple that London holds over Birmingham and all other cities.

Where the public sector can assist a rebalancing, nonetheless, it should strive to do so. It should also be capable of securing significant cost savings in the enterprise. While the cores of departments do need to remain in Whitehall, it is far from clear that the number of civil service posts presently located in the capital must be quite as high as it is. This in turn demands a cultural recognition that the Britain beyond London is not the Siberia that it is sometimes portrayed as, not least by a media that, when it is not ignoring or patronising the Britain that lies beyond the M25, will howl in protest at the idea of senior employees being asked or informed of their need to relocate there (some of the noise that has occurred as a result of the BBC's effort to move a part of its operations to Salford Quay has been comical).

The more fundamental political requirement, however, is allowing cities outside London the freedom to improve themselves. The mayoral election in the capital in 2008 was the moment when that position finally came of age. It takes time for a public to come to understand what it is that a comparatively new political position is supposed to do, and through that come to regard the aspirants to serve as mayor as something more than anonymous figures wearing rosettes of familiar colours. It would take a similar gestation period before mayors in Birmingham, Leeds or Sheffield acquire such a standing, too.

Yet it must start swiftly. This demands serious institutional innovation. It means that directly elected mayors should become the norm and not the exception. It is absolutely ludicrous that London alone of the largest 25 cities in the UK should have such a champion. When Tony Blair pioneered that change in London he thought – in truth, assumed – that it would be the catalyst for others to swiftly emulate the capital for fear of being left behind if they did not. His ambition was thwarted in the legislation that his own government drew up, which in theory offered cities the right to travel down this route, but in practice restricted reform. A directly elected mayor could only be introduced if the sitting council decided it wanted to make way for it or if the public managed to produce a petition with enough signatures to insist on a ballot over the proposition. In the real world, few councillors would willingly devise a new office that would inevitably marginalise their own berths, and many individual Members of Parliament sensed that their status might be eroded by the arrival of an elected mayor, whose claim to a personal mandate would be arguably more convincing than their own. It might be paradoxical to call for decentralisation to be imposed almost by diktat by central authority, but it is a necessity all the same. Radical measures at a city level in this country will never emerge otherwise.

A change of this sort could only assist the broader cause of Britishness, because it would help to resolve the English dilemma. Devolution in Scotland, Wales and Northern Ireland has served to soothe popular sentiment there, but it has led to an imbalance elsewhere (except, as indicated before, and ironically, in London). As there is no direct retort to the West Lothian Question that is compatible with the constitutional integrity of the United Kingdom, a specifically English solution has to be devised to deal with the void that manifestly exists. Regions plainly are not the silver bullet, and despite its fashionable aura at the moment, 'localism' remains an extremely vague concept whose relationship with councils as they are currently constructed is yet more ambiguous. The best means of dealing with the problem that has become a running sore for Britishness is by ensuring that the London model of direct election is adopted first by the largest cities and then by all conurbations of any notable size at all (indeed, in principle, there is no reason why very small towns should not vote for a mayor). Civic pride relies on meaningful symbols and the genuine opportunity to take a city in a new and exciting direction. Too many British cities seem to be institutionally sterile locations.

The British are a city people, but do not fully appreciate this. This is mainly explained by the domination of a single city over the rest and a constitutional framework that stopped contemplating where cities should stand in its order of things at about the time that Joseph Chamberlain left his office as Mayor of Birmingham to become a Westminster figure. The revival of British cities would not simply have a welcome economic effect (such as the reduction of poverty) but would also ensure a stronger bond between citizens and country. Britishness has been attacked as an amorphous, even alien, ideal, but it is one that is essential to social cohesion. It has to be relevant to where the British work, rest and play. If Britishness is not about a stronger sense of the British city, then it is not about much at all.

31

FAIR PLAY: IT'S WHAT WE'RE ABOUT

TREVOR PHILLIPS

TAKE A LOOK AT TWENTY-FIRST-CENTURY BRITAIN. OVER THE past decade, record levels of immigration have changed the accent and complexion of our society. Our diversity is proliferating. The 17 ethnic categories of the last census now look ridiculously crude. More of us are disabled, and this increase is particularly marked in people under 16. Gay couples have legal rights that would have looked utopian a generation ago. We are living longer and starting families later. Around a quarter of households are now headed by a lone parent. New identities are emerging. Old certainties are dying. Now, economic systems that we thought we could rely on are crumbling. And it's all happening faster than ever before.

Constant change brings with it great stress. And societies under stress, no matter how progressive, are always in danger of one of two extreme reactions. One is fragmentation and collapse. The other is forced unity, where stability is achieved by coercion rather than voluntary assent.

Our challenge is to find an answer that is better than either of these two options; to find a way to live together so that we have enough in common to share experiences, ambitions and to work together communally, but also preserve the things which are essential to us as individuals.

That better answer lies in a single, albeit clunky, noun: Britishness.

We would be forgiven for thinking that sometimes the debate about Britishness serves no deeper purpose than to provide an opportunity for politicians and academics to flex their learned muscles in the public square.

There is value in this process of discussion; a national conversation about national identity is necessary, and it reflects a singularly British preference for evolution over revolution. But we mustn't forget that our discussions work towards an important end.

At the Equality and Human Rights Commission we argue that there are two important reasons why we need to articulate what it means to be British today. The first is adhesive; it offers us an overarching common identity, available to anyone who chooses to live here. Second, in and of itself it can provide a framework by which we negotiate our diversity and accommodate it. This is not easy. It takes tolerance, humility, ingenuity and patience. In practice it is assisted by large amounts of humour – our national propensity not to take ourselves too seriously is a vital lubricant in the often scratchy process of living together.

So where do we start from when we attempt to define our Britishness?

We could start from our symbols and traditions, the daft eccentricities of British life: Marmite and morris dancing, fish and chips washed down with a mug of milky tea, the spinsters on bicycles that John Major recalled, Betjeman's long shadows on county grounds, or T.S. Eliot's dog races, Ascot and Elgar. Emblematic as many of these symbols are, however, each will exclude some of the British public; many will leave us cold; others are downright elitist; all are akin to a private joke that wafts over the heads of newcomers.

We could start instead from certain foundational values. We could point to the rule of law, freedom of expression, the right to equality and the respect for privacy. But here we encounter the opposite problem. These values are Olympian and universal; they are values to which any liberal democratic society would subscribe. They do nothing to point out our distinctly British character, much less guide us through the changes we face today.

A more practical place to start might be our behaviour. In truth, our British identity lives and breathes in how we act, how we treat each other, and what we do: that is the beating heart of our Britishness. Our behaviour is the outward manifestation of our values. And while the values themselves have no national character, they do have national expressions that are unique to us.

These are encoded in our institutions and illustrated by our history; they are evident in our daily lives and in our unspoken, often unconscious habits. They are expressions for which we would fight and struggle; history shows that we would probably rather die than relinquish them.

Here are a couple of examples of how the same universal right can have a distinctive national spirit and expression. In France, the right to equality is embodied in a staunch republicanism that denies significance to individual identity. That is part of the reason why the French do not collect ethnic monitoring data as we do – for the French, equality is colour-blind. In Britain, by contrast, that same right to equality encourages us to collect monitoring information – for the British, equality means being alive to our differences.

Both we and the Americans believe strongly in liberty. However, because of America's history and, arguably, partly because of its geography, the American expression of liberty is very different to ours. In the United States, liberty is bound up with the frontier myth: you can race across the plains and drive your stake into the ground, and there you can be exactly who and what you want to be. But this idea of freedom also underpins America's persistent and ingrained racial segregation: people have the right to choose to live with their own.

In Britain, though, we interpret our liberty in quite a different and much more communal way. This was apparent in the first Queen Elizabeth's assertion that she had no desire to open a window into men's souls. For us, freedom means a distinction between our private sphere, in which we can believe, think and do as we like, and our public sphere, where we are required to show tolerance and willingness to compromise with people who are very different from us. In practice, this means that a critical part of the idea of Britishness is the manner in which we negotiate our difference.

Not all our behaviour is laudable. It would be instructive to examine what underlies our native tendency towards hooliganism, political apathy and haughtiness abroad, which rarely get a mention in our discussions of our national character. Often we have failed to live up to our values at great human cost. But there is no deception in the optimistic flavour of our attempts to define Britishness, because primarily it is an answer to a problem: it asserts who we would like to be, it articulates our distinctly British aspirations to deal with the changes we face and it calls us to higher standards of behaviour.

And central to this is fairness. Beloved across the political spectrum, espoused from Left to Right, exalted by Orwell and Churchill, fair play animates us as a nation. We are never more united than in our moral outrage at injustice. Observe the chorus of tutting when someone jumps the queue; it is not a trivial example – it points to a society where we hate the gall of someone who dares to gain unfair advantage over others. Fair play is more than just cricket.

When the Equality and Human Rights Commission opened for business in 2007, one of our first pieces of work was a public-attitudes survey asking what the general public most wanted the Commission to promote and protect. Fractionally behind a concern with being safe, the most important thing for people was fairness. Overwhelmingly respondents were more receptive to the idea of fair play than they were to the language of 'rights'. If you think that's uncontroversial, think for a minute how a French or American group might answer. Rights would be right up there, the rights secured by their revolutions and laid down in their constitutions. But we do things differently here.

Fairness sums up our belief in cooperation for the common good. It is made possible by a robust rule of law and stable institutions. It inhibits our naked self-interest while also giving us the space to be unique, different and as odd as we like. And that, in today's age of diversity, is crucial.

Our diversity is as subjective as it is objective – it is as much about who we think we are as who we really are – and this gives rise to an increasingly vibrant identity politics. The key is that we can have many different kinds of identity. We are many things; the bonds of trust that define us can be geographical, tribal, familial and ethnic. But they can also be about our gender, our sexuality or our age. We can have fierce loyalty to our football team alongside affiliations that are philosophical or political. And we can have all of these, be all of these things, all at the same time. In the best possible world, each of us moves easily and effortlessly between our identities, and adjusts the significance of what we are to the circumstances. Our protean human ability to hold several identities together in a single frame is exercised every day as people see us through the prism of their own experience. So a man may be a fellow football fan to the season-ticket holder who stands beside him every Saturday, but to the other parents at school he is his child's father, and to those at work he is the union representative with a predilection for loud ties. It's the mix of these identities, like an individual handprint, that so powerfully defines our individuality.

The fear that one of our many identities will single us out for hostile treatment can prompt different reactions in us. Mostly, the reaction is to fight, to defend that identity to the extent that we submerge every other aspect of who we are to force others to respect it. But sometimes the reaction is flight, to abandon it altogether or to sink into the warm certainties of others like us in that respect. For example, many ethnic minority people who can afford to live in the affluent end of town where there are fewer of their own kind won't take the risk for fear of harassment and abuse in areas where they feel isolated. White families, on the other hand, when faced with the prospect of there being a white minority in their children's school, will withdraw their children and even as they express their sincere regret for doing so, will scramble vigorously to find their offspring a place in a largely white school. As Robert Putnam said, 'Diversity, at least in the short run, seems to bring out the turtle in all of us.'

A stronger sense of Britishness could draw us out of our shells a little more. At its best, Britishness is easily adopted by people of all backgrounds; it is malleable and modern, it is capacious and inclusive. But it is not formless – its form is in our principled behaviour towards one another and the values that this behaviour represents.

And here is the paradox: Britishness, to be successful, needs to be both be predicated on, and characterised by, fairness. We will never feel the patriotic pull of a shared identity for as long as we see that some are unjustly blessed in the distribution of resources and opportunity. Take, for example, the fact that a boy born in Manchester is likely to die ten years younger than a boy born in Kensington or Chelsea, the fact that an Afro-Caribbean man is twice as likely to end up in jail than university, the fact that 85 per cent of poor white boys do not get five decent GCSEs, or the 45 per cent employment penalty facing women with children. Look at the hate crime that poisons our society, which sees 3 million women in Britain today suffer domestic violence, which sees the brutal murders of people with learning disabilities, which sees a wave of homophobic bullying sweep across our schools and workplaces. These stark injustices chip away at our bonds of trust and solidarity.

Resentments will simmer for as long as some feel that one aspect of their identity – their Muslim faith, for example – or the particular combination of who they are – a young single mum on a low income, say – singles them out for ill-treatment or disadvantage. Gaps in educational achievement and employment prospects, differentials in health, security and well-being all widen the chasm between those who feel they belong and those who don't. And poverty provides its own familiar trap, limiting by sheer necessity the very freedom people need to express their differences, no matter how open society may nominally be to them.

So any moves towards understanding and celebrating our national identity, whether citizenship classes or a Britishness Day, need to be supported by concerted efforts to tackle the entrenched inequalities in Britain today. Otherwise, they will ring hollow. The new Equality Act, which we hope will enter the statute books next year, could be an historic landmark in our country's journey towards equality. But not everything can be solved by legislation. That is why at the Commission, as the national advocate and champion of equality and human rights across the spectrum, we have set out to stimulate a deep culture change that locks equality into the core of our polity, practice and behaviour.

On those foundations, a British identity can not only offer us a common identity, it can also provide an effective framework for dealing with our differences, whether those are ethnic or religious, based on gender or sexual orientation, whether they are inter-generational or class based. It can give us codes of conduct, dignity and respect, to resolve – and, crucially, to avoid – disputes.

To try to make this clear, let me use a common metaphor. There are millions of cars on British roads. Not only does the vast range of vehicles reflect our human diversity; what we do with them mirrors the myriad tasks we have to perform in the narrow strips of highway that we share. Given all this, and the fact that each of us really wants to do our own thing in our cars and get where we are going in the shortest time possible, it is quite extraordinary that we manage this diversity of type and purpose so amiably and with relatively little conflict. That's because we have rules, encompassed in our Highway Code. We all learn it, and though few of us could recite it after passing our tests, we intuitively know what it demands of us in situations where we interact with other road users – at junctions, roundabouts and so on.

In the old days, when cars were fewer and pretty much identical, none of this mattered. But numbers and diversity bring special challenges. They demand ways of managing our interactions, most of which are voluntary and consensual. We drive on one side of the road; we stop at lights; we give priority to emergency vehicles.

But the Code is not simply a neutral document, with no intrinsic values. It has one basic underlying proposition – that all road users have equal entitlement to their place, and irrespective of how small or mundane your vehicle might be, it has the same right to respect as any other vehicle. We only make exceptions for vehicles that are serving the community's interest rather than their driver's – police cars, ambulances and the like. We take this for granted today, but it is not obvious that it has to be this way.

We do not have to imagine what it would be like to have a code based on other values. During the Soviet era, some cities reserved lanes for the ZiL automobiles of party officials. As they swished by, I don't suppose that the citizens of Moscow, in their Ladas, reflected that the special lane represented the correctness of democratic centralism and the leading role of the party, but they would know for certain that liberal democracies wouldn't do things that way.

The rules of our community are no different in principle, except that in this country they are not generally written down, nor are they made explicit.

It hasn't happened yet, but I predict that the test of our mettle as a Commission will be in a case of a certain type of conflict or dispute of values, where we will have to stand up and say, for example, that you cannot both uphold your desire to force your daughter to marry a man against her will and still claim allegiance to a British identity. One thing – and it will be pretty clear which – will have to give.

Finally, we need to challenge one traditional aspect of the way we do Britishness. We need to learn to be more explicit about the way we interact, bottom-shufflingly uncomfortable as that may make us. It calls to mind John Cleese's statement that the goal of every Englishman is to get to the grave unembarrassed. Setting aside the unforgivable conflation of Englishmen and Britons, that is one aspiration I think we will have to put aside – because the time has come for a written constitution which might define more closely what we aspire to in British citizenship.

It is also why at the Equality and Human Rights Commission we have been arguing for a constitutional guarantee of equality, which we would like to be located in the new Equality Act. This guarantee would be a powerful public declaration of what people can expect from public authorities and the state. It would be another step towards institutions being compelled to comply with basic principles of fairness. And it would be a promise that we make to ourselves as a society. We can no longer, in this changing world, take our inheritance of parliamentary democracy, the rule of law, freedom of expression and protection from tyranny for granted.

In times of great change, we need some constants. A simple, constitutional commitment to the fairness that should run through our behaviour – a fairness that embraces all of us and that guides our actions in times of change – would place the most noble feature of our national identity at Britain's institutional heart, to endure long after all of us, these discussions, this government and our Commission have been forgotten.

BRITISHNESS AND THE
IRISH QUESTION

PAUL BEW

THERE IS A FORMULA TO DEAL WITH THESE MATTERS. IT OPERATED under both the Major and Blair governments. In Dublin in May 1994, Sir Patrick Mayhew argued that Unionism was an authentic Irish political tradition: sometimes it was sectarian and embattled, but it should not be characterised as a purely negative movement:

> At the heart of Irish unionism lay a positive vision, a belief that all the people of these islands – English, Welsh, Scots and Irish too – share far more than divides them; a belief that there is as much value in their confirmed and various diversity as there is in their actual conformity; a belief that in a democratically established union there is more strength to be found than in the sum of its constituent parts; a belief, therefore, that it will gain from being freely associated together with a union that is a union.[1]

Shortly after his general election victory of May 1997, Tony Blair made a major speech at the Balmoral Hotel in Belfast. He said: 'The union binds the four parts of the United Kingdom together. I believe in the United Kingdom. I value the union.' In early 2008, the Foreign Secretary, David Miliband, echoed these words precisely.

But then in late March there came a surprise and, for some, a nasty shock. The prime minister, Gordon Brown, in an article entitled 'We Must Defend the Union' in the *Daily Telegraph* of 25 March 2008, opened with a loud call to arms to the British people, warning that the benefits conferred by the Union were in danger of being lost unless the British people defended it against seccessionist forces. But it turned out that in the rest of the article, the Union that was to be defended was only a mainland phenomenon – English, Scottish and Welsh, but decidedly not Irish. It was the mutually beneficial economic, cultural and political interactions of the larger island that were hailed as positive – no contribution apparently could be listed on behalf of the Northern Irish. It would have been easy to fix this. The prime minister hails the Scottish educational system, which in the end produced the Scottish Enlightenment and his personal hero Adam Smith – but Adam Smith's mentor was Francis Hutcheson from Drumalig, Co. Down, the inspiration for the ethical system of both Smith and David Hume. In the short term, this new definition of Britishness was politically maladroit – it is, after all, supposed to be one great selling point of the Good Friday Agreement to the Unionist community that it guarantees on the basis of consent their position within the United Kingdom. Anything that contributes to nervousness about the United Kingdom at this stage tends to undermine the stability and necessary flexibility of the Belfast settlement.

Some might be driven to reflect on the fact that Gordon Brown is the first prime minister for some time to have no known Irish family connections. Tony Blair was the son of an Ulster Protestant; John Major's grandmother was Catholic Irish; Mrs Thatcher famously told Sir David Goodall that she was 'completely English', but on reflection had to acknowledge her great-grandmother Sullivan. James Callaghan was anxious to convey to the Irish government that he had 'Irish blood'. But the problem is more serious than this mere accident of history.

One of the problems for New Labour in its efforts to face up to these difficulties has been its characteristic historical inheritance. On the Left in the 1970s, Gordon Brown's formative intellectual years, the key debate on Britishness was that promoted by Perry Anderson and Tom Nairn. (Nairn, of course, is now celebrated as one of the gurus of Scottish nationalism.) E.P. Thompson famously accused Anderson and Nairn of an 'inverted Podsnappery' in which local experiences were always contrasted negatively with progressive continental traditions. At the time Thompson was considered to have won the argument, though Anderson has recently claimed that his views have been vindicated by subsequent developments and historiography. More recently, it has become fashionable to stress the ways in which in the eighteenth and early nineteenth centuries Britishness was formed as a self-consciously Protestant ethos defined against continental absolutism and the Catholic 'Other'. This view implies that, from its inception, Britishness was driven not so much by Protestantism per se, or by any substantive loyalties, as by negative reaction against hostile overseas enemies. The xenophobic British developed a militarily driven aristocratic imperialism that collapsed after 1945, leaving behind a defensive Eurosceptic culture of narrow insularity. Some of the prime minister's sharpest Scottish nationalist critics, such as Professor Christopher Harvie, have noted New Labour's dependence on this historiography. However, the most striking feature of all is that both tendencies seriously neglect the Irish dimension of the British experience.

In the original conception of the Union in 1800, Prime Minister William Pitt drew heavily on the pro-Irish Catholic thinking of Edmund Burke: the idea was to create the emotional unity of one people across the United Kingdom by integrating Irish Catholics via the mechanism of an immediate Catholic Emancipation – a measure that was in the end to be delayed by the forces of British Protestant integralism until 1829, with tragic consequences. In large measure for this reason, the Union failed as far as Catholic Ireland was concerned. On the other hand, it worked as far as the previously alienated north-east was concerned.

Ironically, a prime minister confronted by the strength of a radical separatist republicanism in Scotland might learn something from the history of Northern Ireland. In the late eighteenth century, feeling alienated from all the available symbols of Britishness, a significant part of the north's Presbyterian community moved on from providing decisive support for the American Revolution to advocating an alliance between Ireland as a whole and republican France. Yet by the end of the following century, the same group, attracted by economic growth and liberal political reform, fully participated in the imagined community of Britishness. The classic articulation is the speech by the Belfast MP Sir James Emerson Tennent when debating the issue of the Union with Daniel O'Connell in 1834:

> I shall never fail to regard it as a proud distinction that I have myself been enabled, during the course of the last twelve months, to contribute my own humble vote, to extend the blessings of freedom from the confines of India to the

257

remotest shores of the Atlantic; to liberate the Hindoo, and to strike off the fetters of the African . . . How immensely, then, has this field of senatorial ambition been expanded and increased to every Irish Representative . . . by the Act of Union, he has been enabled to become the advocate of the rights of the whole human race, and to co-operate in extending the reign of liberty from hemisphere to hemisphere . . . These are the triumphs beyond the reach of a 'Local Legislature' . . . toward which the highest ambition of an Irish Parliament could never soar; these are the honours which enable us, whilst we pride ourselves upon our birth-place as Irishmen, to add to our distinctions, the glory of being Britons.[2]

It was a long historical labour, but these things can be turned around. The double irony, of course, is that in the 1880s a British Liberal prime minister (of Scots parentage), in effect, unavailingly tried to redirect this community back towards its original separatist republican roots.

Even many of those who responded to Gladstone's appeal continued to believe that the British connection should not simply be rejected and had produced something of value. When the southern Irish government introduced legislation in December 1948 declaring the state a republic, the only parliamentary opposition came from Senator J.M. Biggar, a member of a well-known Ulster Presbyterian dynasty, who warned that this move would prolong Ireland's own division, that Ulster Unionists' sense of Britishness could not simply be dismissed as illusory, nor the Irish experience of Britishness dismissed as an unmitigated evil:

My family ever stood for freedom. On my father's side it was represented in the Ulster land war of 1770, the Volunteers and the United Irishmen. In 1798 at the Battle of Antrim my great-grandfather stood beside Jemmy Hope. One at least of my mother's family, the Reverend David Warwick, gave his life for Ireland, and was hanged in 1798 in front of his manse. My great-uncle Joseph Gillis Biggar [a prominent Home Rule MP] and my uncle Francis Joseph Biggar [antiquarian and Gaelic revivalist] will be remembered for what they did for Ireland. I do not think I could be accurately termed an ex-Unionist. From my earliest days I have favoured in every

way self-government for the country. I was born a British
subject and served in the British army. If that entitles me to
be called, or if anyone calls me British, I cannot complain. I
have ceased to regard the term British as a term of contempt.
I remember when Britain stood alone, when free France was
only a name, when Russia had not made up her mind on
which side to fight, and when America stood aloof.[3]

But the circumstances under which this descendant of Ulster Presbyterian
rebels proclaimed that for Irishmen to see themselves as British was not
merely contemptible highlights the extent to which the original integrationist
project had been defeated. There is no doubt that by far the most striking
failure of the project of Britishness in the modern era is the departure of
what is now the Republic of Ireland from the United Kingdom – a failure
made even more poignant by the visible success in the political and economic
life of the United Kingdom of so many of Irish background, due in part,
it should be said, to the institutions of the labour movement. Anyone who
wanders around the Palace of Westminster can see many poignant signs
of the presence of the Irish within the system – the harps on the throne,
the Irish-language inscriptions in the main hall, and not least the paintings
by the Cork artist Daniel Maclise in the Royal Gallery and the House of
Lords, with their obvious Irish elements and imagery. It should serve as a
reminder to anyone who believes that Scotland cannot go along the same
path – despite the difficulties that the current economic crisis has created for
Scottish nationalism.

But this is not just the problem of Ireland, it is also the problem of the
Gladstonian inheritance, particularly insofar as it affects the concept of
devolution within the language of British progressive politics now that this
has lost any distinctive class dimension. Devolution as a concept is bathed
in the eternal sunshine of the progressive mind. For what might be called
the 'Roy Jenkins tradition' in both politics and history writing, Gladstone
provided the only viable answer to the Irish question, namely devolved Home
Rule. In this view, Conservative opposition both in the 1890s and 1912–14
was selfish, reactionary, opportunistic and illegal. Lord Donoughue's diaries
tell us that in a cabinet meeting on 4 December 1974 (unconsciously repeating
an argument that had as much influence as Gladstone's high-mindedness
amongst those Liberals who supported Home Rule), Jenkins said that:

everything he heard made him realise that Northern Ireland had nothing to do with the rest of the UK. He said that although the whole discussion was about how to impose the civilised standards of Britain on Northern Ireland, the real prospect and danger was of the barbaric standards of Northern Ireland spreading to us.[4]

Nor is this simply a liberal-leftist view. Many Conservative historians and politicians from Robert Blake to Chris Patten are embarrassed by this period in their party's history. Mrs Thatcher's former advisor, Ferdinand Mount, who can hardly be considered a conventional *bien-pensant* intellectual, denounces the leading Unionist jurist A.V. Dicey – inaccurately – as crudely authoritarian, 'egging on' the conflict 'from the safe distance of his All Souls study'. In fact, Dicey was ultra-cautious and scrupulous in his language (see, for example, his *Times* letter of 27 January 1912) while retaining the view that the Westminster Parliament did not have the right to expel the Ulster Unionist community from the United Kingdom. This is of course today what we fashionably call the principle of consent, which has come to govern not only Northern Ireland's but Scotland's relationship with the United Kingdom.

In this interpretation, the failure to implement Gladstonian Home Rule was responsible for subsequent Irish violence and the break-up of the United Kingdom. There can in fact be no certainty about this. Given the depth of Irish poverty (especially in the urban slums and among the smallholders of the south and west) and the weight of expectation that Home Rule would bring economic prosperity, considerable potential existed in the medium to long term for a new wave of populist protest politics against a Home Rule government blaming Ireland's continued problems on the persistence of the British connection. (The pro-Treaty government of the 1920s, though possessing more radical nationalist credentials than John Redmond's allies, was brought down by Eamon de Valera's claim that its free-trade policies were the result of subservience to Britain, and that a more independent Ireland would be able to raise living standards through economic protectionism – a claim which was favoured by most nationalist leaders in the nineteenth and early to mid-twentieth centuries and was only abandoned from the late 1950s after de Valera's own party had tested it to destruction.) More importantly, the post-Gladstonian tradition has ignored the crucial admission, made by Gladstone himself, that it would be right to exempt on the basis of the consent principle north-east Ulster from the operation of a Dublin Parliament. Gladstone's words were significant:

> It singularly happens that in the year 1886, in proposing the Irish Government Bill, we did face this very question, and we did state that if the inhabitants of the north-eastern corner of Ireland, forming a very small and limited proportion indeed of the general community, were absolutely desirous of being exempted from the operation of that Act, we should be prepared to entertain a proposal to that effect. Nor have we ever withdrawn that declaration.[5]

This was typical Gladstone. There is no clear evidence that he did make such a declaration at the time of the first Home Rule Bill, still less that Parnell accepted it. But it is instructive nonetheless.

Thomas MacKnight, Gladstone's long-standing Belfast journalistic advocate, who broke with him over Home Rule, recorded in his 1896 memoir *Ulster As It Is* that in 1886 proposals for some form of partition circulated in Liberal political circles,[6] and that Gladstone himself gave them some countenance:

> Though he brought forward no plans to effect the object, he was willing, he said, to consider one to constitute a separate Ulster or part of Ulster. His language was not free from ambiguity on this point or on several others; but this was the meaning drawn from it, and not denied by himself.[7]

What we see here is the rough formulation of the consent principle, which passes untheorised from Lloyd George to Churchill through to Major and Blair in the modern era. The consent principle is the love that dare not speak its name in British constitutional thought, with the consequence that somehow its implications have always been glossed over. Quite simply, if the Good Friday Agreement is the acme of civilised constitutional settlements, then the historic Tory/Unionist opposition to Home Rule cannot be portrayed as pure black reaction, however nasty some of its features.

This lacuna in our thinking has been linked to an uncritical assumption that devolution means stability. It is one thing to say that, for example, in the case of Northern Ireland it is essential to the achievement of a necessary historic compromise of the Good Friday Agreement sort. It is one thing to say that after the Thatcher and Major years some form of devolution was necessary to settle Scotland. Nonetheless, devolution is merely another site for an unpredictable political struggle. Only now is the gloss beginning to wear off. Remarkably, for example, a recent Dods poll showed that 75 per cent of Labour peers now considered that devolution had weakened rather than strengthened the Union.[8] It is sobering indeed to set this figure alongside the optimism that accompanied the Labour government's original devolution package. The prime minister's recent call to arms in the *Daily Telegraph* is yet another proof that the anticipated stable constitutional settlement was in fact a mirage.

This is not to say that the United Kingdom is finished. The truth is – as Professor Arthur Aughey has pointed out – that while theorists spill a lot of ink trying to define civic nationality, the United Kingdom has shown a capacity to maintain it in practice.[9] As far as the constituent nations – the national communities – of the United Kingdom are concerned, it is based above all on a sophisticated modern doctrine of consent. But the United Kingdom has been weakened by a profoundly sentimental and uncritical attitude towards the concept of devolution. Only the reversal of such an attitude can provide the context in which the broader civic nationality of the society and the devolution settlement itself can be preserved.

1   Quoted in Paul Bew, *Ireland: the Politics of Enmity 1789–2006* (Oxford: OUP, 2007) 574.

2   Quoted in J.P.A. Bew, *The Glory of Being Britons* (Dublin: Irish Academic Press, 2008) 136.

3   Seanad Debates, vol. 36, col. 82–104 (9 December 1948). (I owe this reference to Patrick Maume.)

4   Bernard Donoughue, *Downing Street Diary: with Harold Wilson in No. 10* (London: Jonathan Cape, 2004) 254.

5   Parl. Debs. (series 4) vol. 11, col. 1863 (13 May 1893).

6   Thomas MacKnight, *Ulster As It Is, or Twenty-eight Years' Experience as an Irish Editor*, vol. 2 (London: Macmillan, 1896) 123–4.

7   *Ibid.* 129.

8   Hansard, HL, vol. 702, no. 111, col. 1167 (29 June 2008).

9   Arthur Aughey, *The Politics of Englishness* (Manchester: Manchester University Press, 2007).

33

CAN NATIONAL IDENTITY SURVIVE THE WEB?

CHARLES LEADBEATER

TECHNOLOGY AND INNOVATION HAVE BECOME MORE CENTRAL than they have been in the past to the stories that nations tell about themselves. Take Finland, possibly Europe's most technologically adept society, where innovation has been central to a sense of national identity, embodied in Helsinki's modernist architecture, for example, for more than a century. In Finland, the embrace of modern ideas and technologies, often borrowed from abroad, has been vital to a sense of national purpose in the face of the looming power of Russia. Finns seem to see learning and innovating as almost a national duty, the only way tiny Finland could ensure its survival. A similar story is being played out in different ways in other small countries with larger neighbours, such as Singapore, Ireland, Israel and Taiwan.

The best example of a union between national identity and innovation and technology is the US, where a rhapsodic embrace of new technology has been essential to the American Dream of a society constantly finding new frontiers, from the nineteenth-century railroads out West to the aeroplane, the skyscraper and the Apollo moonshots. All these stories drink from the same deep well of US inventiveness, a society that was constantly seeking new frontiers and growth as it exploded upwards and outwards. Barack Obama's 'Change We Can Believe In' campaign for the presidency drew from the same well of innovation-based optimism.

By way of contrast, another highly technologically adept nation, the Netherlands, tells itself a much more modest story of national innovation, one that focuses on everyday, evolutionary tools: dams, dykes, locks, bridges and simple modular buildings that serve a utilitarian purpose. The Netherlands exists through a combined, cumulative act of communal innovation, to build a country out of swamp and sea. It tends not to laud individual superstar designers or aggressively expansionist technology. Instead it encourages a constant, adaptive, incremental and functional approach to innovation. Given the likely rise in sea levels in the years to come, the Dutch model of innovation – cumulative and collective innovation focused on management of the shared environment – will become more important for more countries.

The connections between technology, innovation and national identity are even more important for emerging powers in Asia. Japan leads the way, challenging US dominance in many industries through the capacity of its leading firms for continual learning, guided by the magical hand of MITI, the Ministry of International Trade and Industry. South Korea emerged from civil war with no natural resources, and only the support of the US and the work ethic and brainpower of its small population to survive on. South Korea is a society built on its capacity to learn and innovate. It had nothing else.

The upstart technonationalism one sees in Singapore, Taiwan and South Korea is being played out on a much grander scale in China, which is projecting itself internationally through its domestic technology champions such as Lenovo and heavy state investment in research and development. Scientific and technological prowess is a mark of China's power and potential. India, meanwhile, has risen to prominence as a global economic player largely through its role in information technology industries: the outsourced software and call centres of Bangalore, and the diaspora of engineers and entrepreneurs who ply their way between India and their second home in Silicon Valley.

These stories of national identity and innovation readied each society for the arrival of the Web. Finland's story of citizen-led innovation played straight into the emergence of the mobile phone and the Internet in the 1990s. That is one reason why Finland has produced both Nokia and the kernel for Linux, the open-source software program, two of the most significant European technology innovations of the last twenty years. In the US, the emergence of cyberspace played into the national story of technology opening up new frontiers; instead of sitting on rockets to explore space, Americans could explore cyberspace through their computers. The Dutch model of collaborative capitalism helps explain why the Netherlands has become one of the most sophisticated Web societies in Europe, embracing the idea of the collaborative, social web to spawn a mass of public and private initiatives on the Web, such as Amsterdam's ambitious 'digital harbour' to connect all households to broadband. The government recently embarked on an ambitious programme, the Dutch Model 2.0, to map out what the Web will mean for Dutch society. Ubiquitous broadband technology is central to the story South Korea tells of itself as a dynamic and innovative nation, feeding the rise of Korean mobile-phone companies, mass multi-player gaming and many of the largest Web businesses outside the US and China.

In China, the world's largest Web society, it is being used by people to route around censorship and state control. But it is also being used to rally people to the nation's cause, for example, in response to Western criticism of Chinese policy in Tibet. The Web is helping to integrate a country of many dialects, cultures and ethnicities. China has many spoken languages but a common written language. Thus the Web, a medium based largely on written communication rather than verbal, may prove to be a unifying force. India, meanwhile, has risen to command wider attention as an emerging economic power thanks to a generation who emerged from the prestigious Indian Institutes of Technology, and whose brains and money have helped to fuel the rise of many Internet start-ups in the US. Much of the engineering brainpower behind the Web comes from India.

In each of these countries, a more or less well-developed story linking national identity, purpose and innovation readied them to make sense of the Web in national terms. Britain, in contrast, does not have a story that binds all of society around either innovation or the Web.

The UK's dominant story about innovation is still a melancholy lament about opportunities lost, brains drained away and inventions commercialised elsewhere. The Blair government made efforts to develop an alternative narrative of a young, dynamic and creative country, echoing Harold Wilson's 'white heat of technology'. But the early rhetoric about the knowledge economy was sometimes confusing and ill understood by those telling the story as much as those listening to it. David Cameron's Conservatives are playing from the Blair playbook, positioning themselves as the Google generation, making their appeals on Webcameron and YouTube. What is striking about these attempts to create a British narrative of modernity, innovation and technology is how recent and flimsy they are compared to the more consensual, widely shared and rooted stories of Finland, Holland, the US, South Korea, Japan and India.

Working out what the Web means for Britishness is part of a much larger undertaking: studying the way it is remaking the relationship between the public, large-scale collective identities we inherited from the nineteenth century – such as class – and our private, micro-identities formed in much more intimate families and social networks. The Web is just one factor that is shifting the relationship between these different sources of identity. One way to make sense of how the relationship between these kinds of identities is shifting is to think of a world divided into boulders and pebbles.

BOULDERS AND PEBBLES

The media and cultural industries in the mid-1980s, the industries that provide most of our information and entertainment and so filter our access to the world around us and shape how we make sense of it, resembled a large, barren beach, strewn with a few very large boulders. These boulders were the big media organisations.

There were only boulders on the beach because media had high fixed costs – print plants for newspapers and studios for television, for instance. They were closely regulated, and resources, such as broadcast spectra, were scarce. All that created high barriers to entry. Anyone trying to set up a significant new media business could be seen coming from a long way off. Rolling a new boulder onto the beach took lots of people, money and machinery. In the mid-1980s, an entrepreneur called Eddie Shah tried to roll a boulder onto the British beach by setting up a national newspaper based in northern England. That provoked a protracted national strike. Rupert Murdoch caused controversy by moving his boulder – production of his News Corporation newspapers – from one part of London to another. Boulders were the only business in town.

Now imagine the scene on this beach in five years' time. A few very big boulders are still showing. But many have been drowned by a rising tide of pebbles. Every minute, thousands of people are coming to the beach to drop pebbles. Some of the pebbles are very small: a blog post. Others are larger: a video on YouTube or a piece of code for a complex open-source software program like Linux. A bewildering array of pebbles in different sizes, shapes and colours are being laid down the whole time.

Pebbles are the raw material for the new media businesses and much else. The new kinds of organisations being bred by the Web are all in the pebble business. Google and other even more intelligent search engines offer to help you find just the pebble you are looking for. Wikipedia, the free online user-generated encyclopedia is a vast collection of factual pebbles. YouTube is a collection of video pebbles, Flickr of photographic pebbles. Social networking sites such as Facebook, MySpace and LinkedIn allow you to connect with pebbles who are friends, people with shared interests. Some of the pebbles seem even more powerful than the biggest of boulders. In the week that Gordon Brown, Britain's prime minister, created his YouTube channel, a young videoblogger set up his own channel, 'charlieissocoollike', to post his views on the world. A year later, the prime minister's channel had about 6,000 subscribers, while Charlie had 85,000 subscribers.

There is still a lot of business in serving the boulders that remain, providing them with content, finance, advice and ideas. The boulders still employ a lot of people. But the dynamic, growing activity is in the pebbles. All around us in myriad ways, many of them very small scale and local, some global in reach, people are pooling their pebbles to have an impact, share ideas, get things done, entertain one another, gossip, flirt, bet, buy and sell. These collections of pebbles thrive on the Web's culture of lateral, semi-structured free association. It is not that the boulders have all disappeared, but they now operate in an environment that is quite different, where they have to compete for resources, attention and loyalty with the millions of pebbles that are filling up the beach.

National identity – Britishness – is another boulder, created along with many other big boulders, between the mid-nineteenth and mid-twentieth centuries. Like all boulders, Britishness is going to have a much harder time making itself seen and heard amid the rising tide of pebbles. The very attempt to define Britishness, to lock it in, is a signal of how fragile it has become. Britishness has always been remade bottom-up, bought into in ways that differ even between the same class – it could mean different things to working classes in Surrey than it would in Yorkshire. In future, even when people call up a sense of nationhood to give meaning to their lives, it will take a greater diversity of forms. There will be many more ways for us to be British and so many more hyphenated identities – Black-British, British-Muslim, British-Asian, British-Chinese. Britishness is likely to make a less compelling claim on future generations, and even when it does it will come in many shapes, sizes, colours and flavours.

We shape our identities in large part by how we draw on a shared culture to tell stories about ourselves. The Web is allowing more people than ever to tell their stories in the way they want, sharing and learning from others, forming communities and collaborating. The boulders of what it means to be British are being broken down into pebbles.

Take, for example, mapping the physical space we inhabit, our country. The emergence of modern mapping in the nineteenth century was wrapped up with everything that seemed to make Britain great: industrialisation, urbanisation and empire. The Ordnance Survey was created to map the sprawling industrial cities and the territories conquered during imperial expansion. Maps brought order to unruly environments. Before city maps, people used to navigate their way around by word of mouth. Maps instead created a shared, systematic public sense of where we all lived delivered top-down. Mapping Britain in this objective, standardised way was one of the chief achievements of the industrial-era information economy. We all knew where we stood.

Mapping is now a central activity on the Web, of course. Often Web-based maps still draw on Ordnance Survey data. But now, thanks to Google maps and other tools, we can annotate maps with our own information. Cities and groups have created their own WikiMaps of their cities, marking in information central to their interest group. Maps can be mashed up with other applications and information to create new hybrids. The Ordnance Survey once gave us a single unified account of the physical space of the nation. Soon we will be living with a multitude of maps providing myriad accounts of that shared space.

The postal system was another nineteenth-century communications innovation that helped to unify the nation. Prior to the creation of a cheap postal system – an act of radical social and business innovation – it was rare for people to write letters and to be in constant contact with people who lived far away. By the end of the nineteenth century such contact was commonplace: people could move from their rural home to a city and still be in touch with their family, part of the same nation. To this day the Post Office is a potent symbol of national connection, a shared public world in which fellow citizens can reach one another for the price of a stamp. Yet, of course, now we communicate in a plurality of ways, through email, social networks like Facebook and microblogging services such as Twitter. If we were to ask teenagers what they could not do without – the post, email or their social-networking site – the answer would probably be the last of these.

Another set of boulders, some created in the nineteenth century, others dating from much earlier, are national institutions of knowledge that embodied the union of the nation and the public: the public library system, the British Library, the British Museum and other national galleries and archives. Many of these are still thriving. Yet increasingly these centres of national knowledge, research and cultural, are being challenged and outmoded. Once the British Library was the embodiment of the nation's knowledge. Now scientific research is becoming ever more a question of organising a vast number of loosely connected pebbles. Young scientists, especially in emerging fields like bioinformatics, draw on hundreds of databanks; use electronic lab notebooks to record and then share their results daily, often through blogs and wikis; work in multi-disciplinary teams threaded around the world organised by social networks; and publish their results, including open-source versions of the software they used in their experiments and their raw data, in open-access online journals. What they do not do, at least not much of the time, is visit the British Library to do their research. The notion of a single, comprehensive, national knowledge base is a thing of the past.

Something similar is happening to the way we receive and then talk about news. News in the twentieth century had a distinctly national air to it. A posse of newspapers are distinguished by being 'nationals'. Our leading public media organisation is the British Broadcasting Corporation. These 'nationals' relayed news that mattered to the nation, creating a national news culture. The Web is eating into both. In the US, newspapers are in savage decline, their advertising market overtaken by the likes of Craigslist and eBay, their news and comment functions challenged by blogs. The UK is a long way behind. Yet the same trends are in play in news and broadcasting. Each of the words 'British', 'public', 'news' and 'broadcaster' is unlikely to be understood by a young person in ten years' time in the way their parents understand it now. The broadcast news, pushing stories at people, makes little sense in the world of unscheduled, permissive, free-associating information sources on the Web. The BBC, ITV, the national newspapers: all are boulders competing in a world of pebbles. As the pebbles rise so news organised around communities of interest, communicated through peer networks and informally disseminated will become more important. How we talk about what matters to us is changing.

National political parties are other boulders. In the nineteenth century the disenfranchised majority clamoured to be given access to the formal public political sphere to debate the issues that mattered. Now they are leaving in droves. In the 2001 and 2005 British general elections, four out of ten people chose not to vote, rising to six out of ten among 18–25 year olds. The 1997 election recorded the lowest post-war turnout. By 2007, membership of the main political parties was less than a quarter of its level in 1964, and members of political parties make up less than 2 per cent of the voting population. Less than 1 per cent of the electorate say they campaign for a political party. A more individualistic, consumerist culture has eroded the collective identities that mass political parties were based upon. Politics has become less ideological and more personality driven. The institutions of government seem more distant from and insensitive to the intimacy of people's lives and yet less able to protect people from impersonal global forces. People talk of their political representatives as invisible, distant, alien, partisan, arrogant, untrustworthy, irrelevant and disconnected. They want a politics that is both more conversational and honest, and that engages with their interests; thus the growth of single-issue campaigning.

It is ironic that the political party that has gained most from the Web puts Britishness at the heart of its politics. The British National Party website is dramatically more popular than any other British political party site and even makes it quite far up the list of the most popular UK sites. On 26 October 2008, the BNP site was ranked by Alexa's website rankings at 2,415 among UK websites. The Tories stood at 132,014, Labour at 213,815 and the Liberal Democrats at 290,294. Most significantly for the long-term future of the UK, perhaps, would be whether the Scottish National Party – a Web laggard – could ever match Obama's appeal to raise money and mobilise support on the Web to continue to fund its push for independence.

The Web is also changing how immigrants negotiate their relationship with Britishness. The stereotype immigrant is a low-skilled and able-bodied labourer emigrating from a less developed country in the hope of making a better living while sending money back home. After arriving in a poor neighbourhood, probably inhabited by waves of previous immigrants, the aspirant immigrant moves upwards economically and slowly assimilates into British society.

Whether this story of aspiration and assimilation was ever true, it is clear that modern immigration is less a transfer from one country to another and more an experience of living in two worlds at the same time. One measure of this is the trend to offer immigrants dual citizenship. In the 1970s, only 10 per cent of states offered forms of dual citizenship; now more than 50 per cent do. More people have complex affiliations and multiple allegiances to people, places, religions and traditions that lie beyond the boundaries of the nation state. The experience of being 'transnational', living as part of a diaspora detached from a homeland, used to be confined to communities fleeing persecution. Now it is much more commonplace. These diasporas are very diverse, embracing corporate executives, engineers and technicians, academics, entrepreneurs, unskilled labourers, students and refugees. They often have their own social structure and organisation. The media often provides a focal point for these diasporas to consolidate their identities through social rituals. That is as true for British expat communities in Spain as it is for young British Asians who supplement British television soaps with programmes that are specially made for the Indian diaspora. The modern media supports these hybrid identities.

The Web will increasingly facilitate these diasporas. The recent wave of Polish immigration has spawned sites such as PolishForums.com and AniasPoland.com, which are lively forums where Poles and UK contributors debate what they like and dislike about England, look for jobs and find places to live. GumTree is a kind of British Craigslist that allows travellers to sell their stuff, find jobs and connect to other travellers, and is heavily used by Australians, Poles and South Africans. About 300 million people of Chinese origin live outside mainland China. A 2007 study by the Pew Internet and American Life Project concluded that China's common written language would allow speakers of different dialects to come together via the Internet into a new, virtual community. The Web may make it easier for people to live with a foot in two worlds at the same time.

There is mounting evidence that the boulder of national identity is likely to be diminished by the rising tide of pebbles around it, reflecting the competing sources of identity and loyalty people will enjoy, be they cosmopolitan, transnational, diasporic, localised, issue-, interest- or values-based. The national identity boulder will fracture into more pebbles. But does that mean the coherence provided by a notion of Britishness is falling apart?

Probably not, for at least three reasons.

First, the rise of digital culture and more networked forms of work mean a new value is being invested in real-world, collective experiences that bring people together, albeit if briefly. We have become a society of festivals, carnivals, raves and live gatherings that generate the special, rare experience of really being there, with other people, bearing witness. Live, authentic experiences with thousands of other people give us a fleeting sense of what it is like to be caught up in something bigger than ourselves. In these moments we find ourselves together, often impassioned, shouting, clapping, swaying, enjoying being caught up in the action whether it's a rock concert or a football match: a kind of festive transcendence. These are like religious experiences, but tailored to the open egalitarian communities of the direct access, structured free-association society being created by the Web.

Usually in these moments we have no programme other than to be together, en masse, for not too long. They do not sustain common actions. They are more like spaces for mutual display, so we can show one another we are together. In the past, thousands of people might have gathered together to worship, march, protest or fight. These festive experiences are compelling, confusing and provisional. National symbols, moments, from culture and football to the Proms and royal weddings provide one source for these moments. This kind of celebration of national identity will be powerful but fleeting, an identity we can come back to, but not something we carry around with us the whole time.

Second, the Web is encouraging a kind of a micro-, everyday Britishness as people explore what it means for them to be British, bottom-up. This is especially evident in the way the Web has allowed people to trace their roots, reconstructing in great detail their story of who they are. The Family Records Centre estimates about 400,000 people are members of family history societies around the UK. The Web may encourage a flowering of bottom-up, Pro Am, vernacular nationalism, which might prove more enduring and adaptive than a story handed down from on high. Indeed, as Tim Edensor points out in *National Identity, Popular Culture and Everyday Life* (2002), national identity is not just embedded in national symbols, celebrations and events but also in the rituals of everyday life – how we eat, greet, queue, work, resolve disputes, complain and treat authority. This kind of peer-to-peer sense of national identity, based on how we behave with one another, is far better adapted to the world of the Web.

Third, it is just possible, perhaps, that the Web, in time, may allow a collective reinvention of national identity on a much larger scale. National identity has always been invented, drawing on myths of origins and hopes for the future, creating and embedding traditions. The Web, meanwhile, has already created some largely self-governing, recursive publics – the community around Wikipedia, for example, or the millions who play the World of Warcraft game together. These often idealised liberal communities, provide, in the words of the Canadian philosopher Charles Taylor in *Modern Social Imaginaries* (2004), new social 'imaginaries': ways in which 'people imagine their social existence, how they fit together with others, how things go on between them and their fellows, the expectations that are normally met and the deeper normative notions and images that underlie these expectations'. Hopes that the Web might provide the basis for the creation of large-scale shared identities of this kind might seem far-fetched. But consider: Dell has managed to attract more than 66,000 contributions and 10,000 ideas to its IdeaStorm website. Imagine we did something similar with, say, the Department for International Development budget, allowing spending to be shaped by an open dialogue with British citizens through a collective, facilitated discussion online? Or imagine an online space in which every child going through the British education system could have a voice in shaping the kind of education they get. If politicians are serious about trying to regenerate a sense of national purpose and belonging in the age of the Web, it is this kind of initiative that they will have to consider.

CONCLUSION

What kind of Britishness might make sense for the Google generation, which all political leaders are now desperately courting?

It would have to be built bottom-up from a vast collection of pebbles, drawn together by the promise of common values and aspirations, but made most evident in everyday ways of life and behaviour towards one another.

It would have to be:

- Highly permissive; it would be open to people to make their own highly individual interpretations and contributions, making individual meaning out of shared cultural resources and symbols

- Unfinished and generative, capable of growing and evolving

- Not planned out in advance, but emergent, more like a process of loosely structured free association

- A shared endeavour with a lot of decentralised initiative, with peer-to-peer communication rather than top-down

- Above all, it would have to be an identity created with and by people together rather than something delivered to, for or at them from on high.

The Web is a 'with' technology: it allows us to imagine new ways to work, govern and argue with one another to achieve things, including shaping our identities.

NOTE ADDED BY AUTHOR
I am grateful to Jen Lexmond for her research support in compiling this article.

34

ME, YOU, US: BRITISHNESS
IN A CONNECTED AGE

MARK EARLS

EACH DECEMBER, *TIME* MAGAZINE ANNOUNCES ITS PERSON OF the Year award. The event is managed as slickly as the launch of a new Bond movie – cover story, editorial, press releases, video clips and interviews all roll effortlessly out across the media in that bold and unquestioning Hollywood manner, leaving a trail of end-of-year glamour, glitz and dollar bills in its wake.

However, what happened in December 2006 marked a significant change in direction: rather than the award celebrating one of the Big Men Making Modern History (as Thomas Carlyle might put it) – the financiers, statesmen or women, the celebrities and the high-profile campaigners who normally take turns to be applauded by the mid-December issue of the magazine – the award went to us ordinary citizens, or 'You' as the cover line had it. This was not a sudden outburst of some populist, neo-democratic sentiment but simply a recognition of the wave of change that we – the ordinary folk – are creating through our adoption of the new Internet- and mobile-based technologies. We, not the Big Men or the Experts, are creating what the techies love to call 'the Social Web'.

Some dismissed this choice as a faddish move, a piece of adolescent nose-thumbing at the mainstream media's continuing obsession with celebrity gossip, diet tips and heroic struggles against heartbreak. Others, particularly those who might in other years have expected to be nominated – the would-be Big Men – were more likely to turn away in disdain: this 'Web' thing is the twenty-first-century equivalent of the hula hoop. It is for games and chat and is not at all *serious*. Nothing based on it can be taken seriously; it will not change anything significant about our world.

Which is to miss the point entirely: the award was not about the technology but rather what its adoption has enabled. And how this is dismantling the Big Man's world – the world of experts and authorities, of leaders and the led – in front of our eyes.

And this is my central point for our debate about Britain and Britishness: these new technologies create a *hyper*connectedness, and that, in turn, brings many unforeseen and unintended but fundamentally disruptive changes to our world – to our lives, our institutions and our ideas of identity, nationhood and leadership. Because of hyperconnectedness, everything is going to be different from here on in. Nothing – not our ideas about Britain and our British identity, our ways of talking about it or our tools for shaping it – is going to be the same again.

GET THE WAGONS IN A CIRCLE

Most behavioural scientists now agree that we humans are a social species, first, foremost and last: that is, our primary evolutionary strategies are based on our ability to live happily in large groups of our peers. We seem particularly well suited to the life of a social animal: as Professor Robin Dunbar has shown, for example in his *Grooming, Gossip and the Evolution of Language* (1998), there is a direct correlation between the relative size of primate brains and the size and complexity of the groups they live in: ours is the biggest by some margin. Together we can perform extraordinary feats: from the much touted 'Wisdom of Crowds' (whereby under certain conditions groups are smarter than the smartest individual member) to the corresponding amazing collective feat that every family and social group demonstrates every time they meet and retell family stories, so-called 'distributed' or 'social' memory. Equally, our ability to negotiate city life (coming into daily contact with hundreds of other individuals from other family groups) and doing so peacefully is unique in the primate world. Of the 100,000 people who walk up and down London's Oxford Street every day, how many collide? And how many of these incidents end in the violence our genetic cousins would quickly resort to?

Indeed, our social skills (particularly our ability to learn from each other) are seen by many behavioural scientists to be much more important than our 'cleverness': without these abilities, even the best ideas of the smartest human would not have much value; they would not spread very far. As one recent letter to the *New Scientist* magazine put it, the incredible and, frankly, *unlikely* success of our curious species seems more down to us being '*Homo mimicus*' than '*Homo sapiens*'.

So when trouble seems to threaten our little group – when individuals sense danger and/or pick up on others' fears – we do what any self-respecting social animal does: *we get the wagons in a circle and hunker down together*. Unlike our ape cousins, we have the gift of language, so we are able to talk together to renew and reinforce the mutual bonds that hold the group together. 'Who are we?', 'what do we share?' and 'what is our purpose or mission as a community?': all of these are good and sensible questions to consider when a community is faced with enormous challenges – asking and debating them fuels our ability to do what is necessary, together.

This is what is happening now. The debate about Britishness is really one of those 'hunker-down' moments in the shared history of the people of these isles – when we get the wagons in the circle and tell stories of our shared origins, our previous shared successes, of our values and what we believe in. The challenges are enormous – from those we face on our own doorsteps, such as child poverty, our seemingly unstoppable appetite for alcohol and drug abuse, our flair for petty gangsterhood, to those we share with our neighbours – economic devastation, climate change, global health issues and so on. Many other nations are also *getting the wagons in a circle* –the US presidential election of 2008 is in many ways best understood in terms of how Americans saw their shared identity. ('It's about you, not about me,' noted Senator Obama early on in the campaign. Rightly so.)

OUTSIDE IN

That said, it is worth remembering that the rest of the world – even our closest neighbours – aren't really having a debate about what it is to be British. The letters pages of Dutch, French, German and Irish newspapers are not full of correspondence about what might constitute core British values or what traditions and behaviours have shaped our national identity; our American counterparts are not agonising over what it is to be British over their 'damn fine coffee'.

Each nation makes do with a fairly simplistic, even stereotyped, working view of the members of other national groups. We Brits probably know enough about the Finns to get by with – and vice versa; both nations find their own national identity of much greater import than that of their neighbours.

277

Likewise, British expats have a simpler and more rigid view of Britain and Britishness than the people who still live here. Indeed, it seems an important part of being a member of a national group to contribute to the debate, to participate. Each wave of immigrants that has arrived here over the centuries has brought new things to add to our culture and thus helped shape our sense of who we are.

HYPERCONNECTED

Wherever we have looked to furnish this conversation in the past – to our traditions, our institutions, our habits or our values – we have been able to assume a certain shared history, a continuity of shared experience (even if borrowed), a shared understanding of where expertise and authority lie. But this is precisely what the adoption of the technology described by *Time* magazine is changing. Things are fundamentally different now.

We are now connected to each other to a degree that no previous generation of Britons has been: my father spent a year in Vienna after the war and wrote a handful of letters to those back home; as a student, I rarely wrote to my parents but I did call them from a college phone box once or twice a term; by contrast, most teenagers today dangle from what sociologist Frank Furedi in his book *Paranoid Parenting* (2002) calls a 'digital leash' – many are in contact with parents and peers on a near continuous basis.

The connecting technology is everywhere: in the UK we have more active mobile-phone handsets than people, we send more than five billion text messages to each other every month and it is eighteen months since the so-called social media (Facebook, YouTube, Flickr etc.) overtook pornography as the number one use of the Internet here (the US, you will be glad to hear, lagged behind us by three months in this act of collective morality!).

No matter that much of the communication enabled by these connections is 'phatic' (that is, it is less about whatever is being discussed and better understood as being about the relationship between the communicating parties), the important thing is that connection with other people is something that we humans – even we notoriously shy Brits – seemed programmed to seek. We will indulge this human need as much as the technology enables.

It seems that the ability to connect with our peers touches something fundamental inside us. Freud suggested elsewhere that we can never escape the 'Other'; every social commentator bemoans the fragmentation of modern life, yet, if the speed of our uptake of these new technologies is indicative of anything, it is that we Brits are as social as the next. We will climb tall buildings to interact with each other – more so, certainly, than our rather cold and stiff stereotype elsewhere would suggest. (Similarly, the company that effectively invented the mobile phone is the product of another famously taciturn nation: the Finns.) Even if the interactions we share seem inarticulate, we like the sense of 'ambient intimacy' (as social media expert Leisa Reichelt calls it) that connectedness brings.

So, forget the explosion in the number of channels your TV set can bring you, the really important technological advance of today is that contemporary Britons are connected horizontally to each other and to others around the world in all kinds of ways that our grandparents could not possibly have considered.

HORIZONTALLY 'US'

But the degree to which we are connected with each other, and the frequency with which we use those connections, is not really the point: the big deal is that this connectedness – hyperconnectedness, even – is actually changing us, our thinking styles and how we relate to each other.

Put simply, *connectedness makes us much more subject to the influence of our peers*: we know from behavioural economics that the more individuals see what their peers are doing and thinking, the more likely they are to follow suit – one recent experiment shows that music lovers' choices are very different when they are allowed to see what their peers buy as opposed to when they are forced to make independent decisions based only on the music. If you buy books from Amazon, you will know the truth of this. Amazon has 16 'social features' on every product page to help you see what others have thought or done with regard to the featured product (or to take your data and flip it over to other people).

We can gather together with the people we want to be with – people who share our interests and views rather than those we happen to share a workplace or a street with – and do so when and how we want to. Motorbike riders gather with each other online and share advice, information and general mutual support as well as suggesting 'ride-out events'; those with a particular medical condition can seek information and empathy from their peers; those interested in centre-right politics or Girls Aloud can find other people interacting around these things.

What this means is that the old power and *influence that experts or authorities used to wield over us has less and less traction*; we choose to follow our peers. GPs are the first to admit that the Internet makes their jobs that much harder because patients come with an opinion based on what they have read or heard others discussing, but the same thing is true in every aspect of our lives: the expert or authority is no more. Journalists have had to learn to live with the reality of blogging (both by journalists and 'civilians') and the fact that their audiences answer back (often in no uncertain terms). Sometimes this kind of mass collaboration is channelled into valuable knowledge-bearing structures like Wikipedia or into collaborative creative spheres such as the 'Million Penguins' wiki-novel project; more often the activity has no such tangible form or value but continues nonetheless.

Moreover, as we increasingly look to our peers for guidance as to what to do or think, *we are turning away from the traditional media as sources of authoritative guidance*: survey after survey reveals that we no longer trust what the traditional media tell us as we once did; the same is true of both politicians and company spokespeople (like CEOs). Instead, 'people like me' and 'friends, family and work colleagues' (even 'the Internet') are seen as the best information sources for a wide range of subjects and concerns. Of course this can – for already deprived groups – have the effect of increasing social dislocation further. Socially excluded youngsters can live much of their lives cocooned from interaction with the culture the rest of us share, in a world largely constructed of their peers and their peers' concerns.

Connectedness is even affecting our styles of thinking: British cultural traditions take great pride in independent thinking – the rationality argued for by the likes of Hume, Locke and Mill – but the truth is that connectedness actively encourages the opposite of independent rational thought. It effectively allows us to outsource thinking to our peers (and those whose blogs and so on we read). As the MMR scandal demonstrated, connectedness leads us to accept what other folk seem to believe over the hard evidence and what independent thinking about that evidence might lead us to conclude. Moreover, as Dr Alex Bentley of Durham University has shown in his wide-ranging studies of how cultural ideas and practices spread, if a population is so strongly exposed to the opinions and behaviours of its peers, then its behaviours and opinions can become volatile and unpredictable (this is a signature of a system based on copying agents interacting). This volatility looks very much like the kind of 'emotional' and 'irrational' behaviour that we Brits have been keen to attribute to other nations, *particularly those nearer the Mediterranean!*

A-NATIONALISM

Connectedness allows us access to a range of social groups and the ability to play with different social identities, and this can lead to what you might call *a-nationalism*: as our line of sight drops from vertical to horizontal, shared identities change and become much more fluid. British identity has to compete with a palette of other social identities: religious, neighbourhood, sports, hobbies and so on.

First, because each of us belongs to groups and networks that are not limited by geographical boundaries, we have begun to adopt a number of social identities, including some that are not in any obvious sense tied to our actual national identity or our national geography, but spread across them.

Second, when these groups or tribes are built around something we (and our peers) really believe in – be it a cause or a purpose – this binds us together into a community of purpose that is often much more important to us than our (comparatively distant) national identity. Many organisations around which we gather – the campaigning or commercially based ones – are a-national. No matter that Apple, Greenpeace and Nike all originated in North America, all of them cross national borders in their appeal; all of them have learned how to be part of our immediate social worlds.

Third, the sheer number of groups, communities and tribes that each of us can now have access to or participate in reduces the cognitive space for a particular national identity. While economic prosperity has allowed today's Britons to see more of the world than any of their predecessors (and in different ways), the new state of connectedness has done much to unpick our reliance on our national identity. And more of these other identities and issues appear more interesting than boring old Britain and Britishness.

Fourth, we have learned to treat social identity like dressing up: we pick and choose, chop and change depending on the context, our feelings and – of course – the behaviour of our peers! One day I can be part of the Welsh-Exile group, then the digerati, then of independent marketing consultants, then of European advisors to a particular US client, then of business writers and so on. And of my immediate family. All before lunch. *Why settle for just one social identity when you can have all the rest?*

Connectedness has had the same effect on the average citizen as extreme wealth has on the so-called 'non-doms' who haunt the higher reaches of the financial world: it loosens what previously might have been considered 'natural' national loyalties and encourages experimentation and play. What emerges from all this is a very different world: a shifting social soup of identities and values, with little to anchor things as tightly as was previously the case.

CONCLUSIONS AND IMPLICATIONS

To the Big Men of this world – those who see themselves as experts, authorities or leaders – then this view is no doubt worrying; indeed, it would not be surprising if such folk dismiss all I have described as a passing fad: technological hula hoops.

It *is* hard to see that the connectedness that these technologies bring can so fundamentally change the order of things. But the science of complexity tells us that change is what emerges from repeated interaction – new behaviours and patterns emerge, behavioural consequences that no one could foresee. Some of these changes are good, some less so. But whether or not you like it, they are *happening*.

Hyperconnectedness *is* reshaping who we Brits are – how we live our lives, how we think about ourselves, which social identities we assume, how many and in what way we assume and discard each in turn. No longer is our shared sense of national identity a given – we pick and choose identities as the mood takes us.

It is clear that our old conversations about our shared national identity are over, in particular the cluster of ideas that has it as something that is fixed, fixable or indeed something that can be imposed on any group is clearly gone for ever. And our way of talking about national identity must change: it is no longer something that can be crisply and clearly defined; no magic constellation of values, stories and information can capture it or its 'essence' (another attempt to fix it).

It is not even the case that anyone can even make us focus on the subject, or even prescribe the boundaries within which we do so. It's *our* – not your – decision whether we even talk about it or not (isn't it frustrating that the country talks about what it wants to talk about, not what you want to talk about?). Our shared sense of Britishness is no longer in the hands of the Big Men but properly in the hands of the huge, shifting web of interactions between the people of this island. And that makes things messy. And inherently uncontrollable.

There are many things that help create a greater sense of coherence among the people who inhabit these islands and the tools of hyperconnection can be of great use in getting us out of our silos, to do things together (and not just frivolous 'flashmobbing' at Liverpool Street station but also really valuable collaborative community challenges such as the StoppedClocks.com initiative, which turns the cataloguing and restarting of Britain's public clocks into a collective game of sorts). Perhaps out of these reconnections will come a new sense of us, of who we think we are. Not a fixed one, but a shifting and hard-to-define one. The simple fact remains that in a connected world, *Britishness ain't what it used to be.*

35

BRITAIN'S MOST DEFINITELY GOT TALENT

PIERS MORGAN

IF I COULD SPEAK LIKE CHURCHILL, BAT LIKE BOTHAM, COOK like Pierre White, kick a football like Best, joke like Cleese, write like Shakespeare, do battle like Nelson, build like Brunel, sing like McCartney, explore like Shackleton, lead like Thatcher, struggle like Pankhurst, row like Redgrave, run like Coe, broadcast like Humphrys, nurse like Nightingale, televise like Attenborough, inspire kids like Rowling, entrepreneur like Branson, earn respect like the Queen, invent like Berners-Lee, innovate like Fleming, amuse like Morecambe, box like Cooper, drive like Hunt, putt like Faldo, fly like Bader, shock like Lydon, command a stage like Olivier, drink like Burton, survive like Liz Taylor, popularise like Cowell, fascinate like Diana, calculate like Hawking, cycle like Hoy, evoke like Keats, kick like Wilkinson, serve the electorate like Bevan, fight like the Unknown Soldier, hector like Paxman, croon like Cliff, hack like Deedes, design like Paul Smith, sail like MacArthur, age like Mirren, chuck darts like Bristow, ride like Harvey Smith, read the news like Sir Trevor, sprint like Linford, be a champion like Daley, evolve like Darwin, scout like Baden-Powell, energise like Faraday, translate like Tyndale, print like Caxton, paint like Turner, pot balls like O'Sullivan, compose like Lloyd Webber and model like Twiggy, then I would consider myself to be truly, uniquely, greatly British.

BRITAIN'S EVERYDAY HEROES

GORDON BROWN WITH COMMUNITY LINKS

ISBN 9781845963071
Available now
£10.99 (paperback)

'This book is about people in all parts of Britain who have given me a fresh insight into the needs and aspirations of our country, what is great about it now and how it can become greater in the future. It is the story of Britain's everyday heroes: the kind of heroes who live next door, and in the next street, and throughout our neighbourhoods – the kind of heroes we might ourselves become.'

– Gordon Brown

In *Britain's Everyday Heroes*, Gordon Brown tells the stories of ordinary people whose willing commitment to a cause or a community has informed and inspired him. The stories tell of a real Britain, neither flawless nor broken down, but caring, innovative, passionate and determined.

He tells of the woman who has been the inspiration behind community reconciliation in Northern Ireland and the leader of a campaign tackling gang culture in Manchester. Of the innovator transforming the way we use the Internet as a tool of democracy and the campaigner who has established the world's first Fairtrade Town. Of councillors leading local regeneration efforts and public servants going far beyond the parameters of their job. Of a new generation of social entrepreneurs proving that successful business can benefit communities. Of the creative pioneers who brought the arts to a deprived housing estate, gardening to the refugees and opera to the homeless. And of the carers, mentors, coaches and volunteers he has met who give of themselves quietly, every day, never expecting praise or recognition.

'A remarkable new volume' – *Daily Mail*

'The imagination and fortitude shown by the actors in this book are undoubtedly immense' – *The Sunday Times*